INDIAN INDENTURE IN THE STRAITS SETTLEMENTS

Acknowledgements

Without generous financial assistance mainly from the Australian National University, as well as the University of Guyana and the Institute of Commonwealth Studies this study could not have been accomplished. For this reason, I wish to express my deep gratitude to these institutions. I would also like to thank the officers of the Menzies and Chifley Libraries of the Australian National University, especially Mr. George Miller; the Australian National Library, Canberra; the National Library, Singapore; the University of Singapore Library; the Institute of Southeast Asian Studies Library, Singapore; the University of Malaya Library; the National Archives of Malaysia; the Madras Record Office; the Public Record Office, London; the India Office Library; the Institute of Commonwealth Studies Library; the Royal Commonwealth Society Library; the British Museum; the British Newspaper Library, Colindale; the Rhodes Library, Oxford; the School of Oriental and African Studies Library; and the University of Guyana Library.

This study was initially supervised by the late Prof. C.M. (Mick) Williams, Dr. E.K. Fisk, and Dr. A.J.S. Reid for the Ph.D. degree at the Australian National University. I am most indebted and grateful to them for their wise guidance and constant encouragement.

In various ways I am also indebted to Prof. John Molony, Dr. A.C. Milner, Mrs. Barbara Hutchinson, Mrs. Shirley Bradley, Mrs. Paddy Maughan, Dr. Eric Fry, Miss Debbie Matthews, and Mr. Eric Broughton; to Prof. Mary Noel Menezes R.S.M., Mr. Mujtaba Nasir, and Mrs. Amna Mohamed; and to Prof. K.S. Sandhu, Mr. Stephen Wailoo, Mrs. Claris Allee, and the late Dr. Donald Wood.

The quality of Ms Roma Singh's typing is exceeded only by her charm, and I am grateful to her as well.

INDIAN INDENTURE IN THE STRAITS SETTLEMENTS

1872 – 1910

David Chanderbali

PEEPAL TREE

First published in 2008
Peepal Tree Press Ltd
17 King's Avenue
Leeds LS6 1QS
England

Copyright © 2008, David Chanderbali

ISBN 1 84523 036 1
ISBN13: 9781845230364

All rights reserved
No part of this publication may be
reproduced or transmitted in any form
without permission

Peepal Tree gratefully acknowledges Arts Council support

Dedicated in loving memory of
Professor Mick Williams
late of the Australian National University

TABLE OF CONTENTS

Preface		9
List of Abbreviations		10
List of Tables		11
List of Maps		12
Glossary		13
Introduction		15
I	Indian Indenture System: Evolution and Structure	20
II	Conflicting Interpretations of Indian Indenture	40
III	The Straits Demand for Indian Indentured Labour	56
IV	The Transition to Regulated Indenture	83
V	Recruitment	104
VI	The Emigration Process	127
VII	The Conditions of Labour	143
VIII	Wages	165
IX	Housing and Health	186
Conclusion		203
Appendices		206
Select Bibliography		217
Index		226

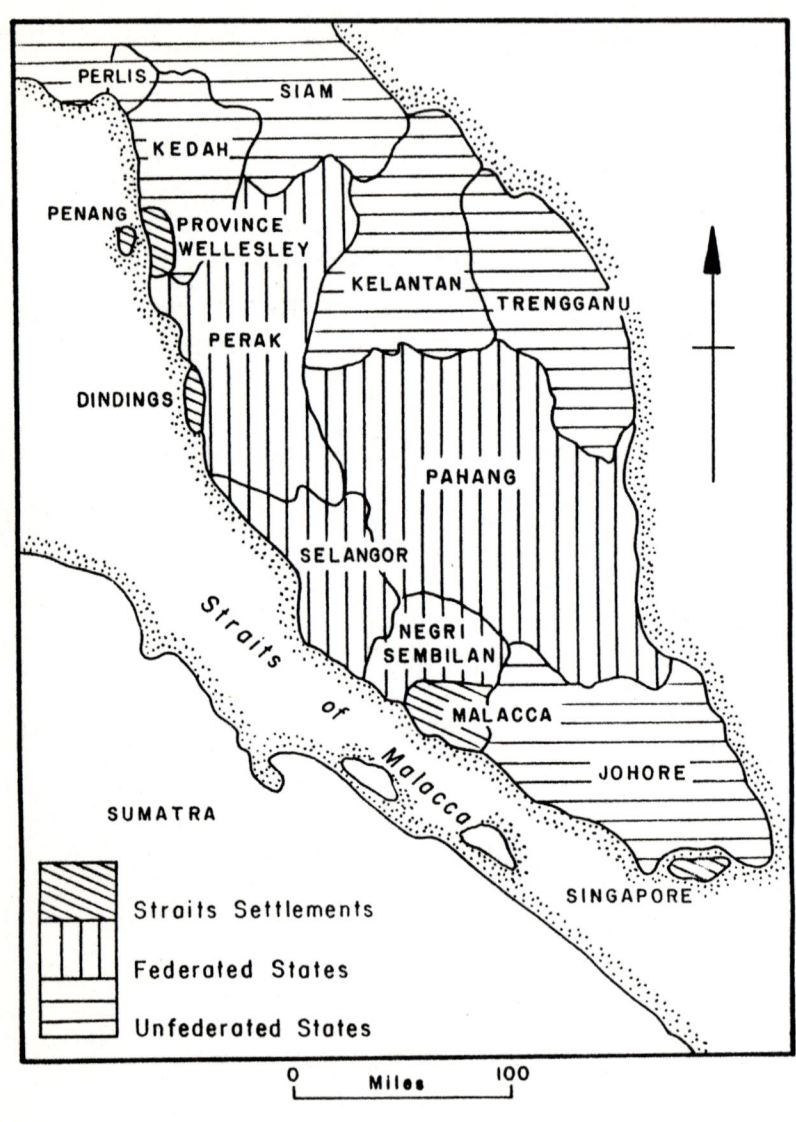

Fig.1 – THE STRAITS SETTLEMENTS AND THE NATIVE STATES OF MALAYA

PREFACE

Following K.L. Gillion's *Fiji' Indian Migrants*, published in 1962, a number of other rich and sophisticated studies of the Indian indenture system in the various sugar colonies began to emerge. But as far as has been ascertained, no full-scale study has been published on Indian indenture in the Straits Settlements. This is probably because the system there was of a comparatively small scale, and there would be a paucity of source material. To some extent this is true, due to several factors, a few of which should be mentioned. Although there was a sort of Indian indenture in the Straits Settlements from about the end of the eighteenth century, the traffic was not officially regulated, and besides, somewhat sparse documentation did not appear until 1872. Systematic documentation, however, commenced from 1879 when the first Annual Report on Indian (indentured) Immigration emerged. But with rapid changes of Protectors of Immigrants, who were the authors of these Reports, and the shortage of staff in the Immigration Department, the Reports were often incomplete, incomprehensive, and inconsistent in their presentation of data. Furthermore, Indian indenture in the Straits not having attracted independent external observers, such as C.F. Andrews and W.W. Pearson, as in the case of Fiji, this study could not benefit from their perceptions. Unless some sensational scandal occurred on the estates, even the Straits newspapers, located as they were some considerable distance away in Singapore, seldom disseminated any information on the system. These circumstances aside, in the C.O. 486 Register at the Public Record Office, London, against the title of literally hundreds of Straits Settlements emigration dispatches is stamped DESTROYED UNDER STATUTE. It is believed that copies of these dispatches may have been destroyed during the Japanese occupation of Malaya and Singapore during World War II.

Despite the lacunae in the availability of source material, if this study could generate further interest in the historiography of Indian indenture, it would have served its purpose.

I: Note on Currency

Unless otherwise stated, all dollar rates in the text are expressed in Straits currency. Throughout the period under review, the value of the Straits dollar varied, but its average equivalent may be taken as 2s 4d sterling, or US$0.33, or 1.55 Indian rupees.

II: Note on Spelling

The spelling in the source material has been retained. It will, however, be found that in some quotations there is a variation in the spelling of certain words such as "labour" and "labor", and "Penang" and "Pinang".

III: List of Abbreviations

ARII	Annual Report on Indian Immigration
ARSILFB	Annual Report of the South Indian Labour Fund Board
C	Command (Paper)
C.O.	Colonial Office
IEP	Government of India, Emigration Proceedings
IESHR	Indian Economic and Social History Review
JIA	Journal of the Indian Archipelago
JMBRAS	Journal of the Malayan Branch of the Royal Asiatic Society
JSBRAS	Journal of the Straits Branch of the Royal Asiatic Society
MHJ	Malayan Historical Journal
MJTG	Malayan Journal of Tropical Geography
MPP	Government of Madras, (Emigration) Proceedings in the Public Department
N.D.	No Date
n.p.	no page
P.C.M.O.	Principal Civil Medical Officer
PDARC	Government of Madras, (Emigration) Proceedings in the Department of Agriculture, Revenue and Commerce
PDCI	Government of Madras, (Emigration) Proceedings in the Department of Commerce and Industry
PHRAD	Government of Madras, (Emigration) Proceedings in the Home, Revenue and Agriculture Department
PP	Parliamentary Papers
PRAD	Government of Madras, (Emigration) Proceedings in the Revenue and Agriculture Department
PRCI	Proceedings of the Royal Commonwealth Institute
PSSLC	Proceedings of the Straits Settlements Legislative Council

RLC 1890   Report of the Labour Commission, 1890
RCII 1896   Report of the Commission on Indian Immigration, 1896
S.S.   Straits Settlements
SSAR   Straits Settlements Annual Report
SSGG   Straits Settlements Government Gazette

IV: LIST OF TABLES

I   Indian Immigration Into Selected Colonies, 1834-1916
II   Ethnic Composition of the Population of Province Wellesley for various years, 1844-60
III   Population of the Straits Settlements Showing Comparative Ethnic composition for Various Years between 1871-1911
IV   The Number of Indian Labourers Departing from Mauritius and Three British West Indian Colonies between 1842-70
V   Arrival and Departure of South Indians from Penang, 1867-69
VI   Indian Population of Penang and Province Wellesley for Various Years between 1812-71
VII   Sexual Proportion of all Indian Passengers Proceeding from South India to Penang, 1866-69
VIII   The Demand and Supply of Indian Indentured Labourers for Various Years
IX   Comparative Flow of Indian Labourers into Burma, Ceylon and the Straits Settlements, 1880/81-89
X   The Effect of the Stricter Selection of Emigrants on the Volume of Indentured Immigration into Province Wellesley, 1890-1900
XI   Comparative Flow of Indentured and *Kangany* Labourers, 1901-7
XII   Mean Density of Population Per Square Mile in India and Madras Presidency at Censuses between 1881 - 1911
XIII   Number of Tindals Prosecuted for Flogging Labourers, 1880-85
XIV   Number of Labourers Presented for and Absent from Inspections, 1884-85
XV   Recommended Diet for Adult Indentured Indians.
XVI   Details of Four Returned Immigrants who Died in Hospital in India in 1880
XVII   Statement showing the Physical Condition of Seven Immigrants that Returned from the Straits Settlements per *S.S.Elgin* on 21 April 1881
XVIII   Scale of Diet in the Criminal Prison, 1883
IXX   Daily Diet Served at the Butterworth Hospital
XX   The Effect of the Rise in Daily Wages in the Malay States on Desertion from Province Wellesley, 1879-84
XXI   Mortality Among Indentured Indians in Province Wellesley, 1901-10

V: LIST OF MAPS

1. The Straits Settlements and the Native States of Malaya
2. The West Indies
3. The Situation of India and Malaya
4. The South Indian Ports of Departure during Pre-regulated Indenture
5. The Main Districts of Origin of Indentured Recruits and their Population in 1871 – 1872
6. Penang and Province Wellesley during Indian Indenture

VI: GLOSSARY

adat: Malay, local custom; common or customary law.
arkati: Hindi, a recruiter of labourers in North India.
arrack: Armenian, spirits obtained by distilling a fermented mixture of rice and molasses: rice-wine.
attap: Malay, the dried branch of the neepa (nipah) palm used for thatching.
bringall: Hindi, purple fruit of egg-plant; boulanger; aubergine.
changkol: Malay, a large and heavy hoe in very general use in Malaya for purposes served by the English spade. Also called *mamotee* and *mumti* in Tamil.
chota-haziri: Hindi, literally, "little breakfast".
chulia: Tamil, Tamil Muslim resident in the Straits Settlements.
dal (*daal*): Hindi, split-peas; split-peas soup.
dhoby: Hindi, a washerman.
girmit: Hindi, the indenture agreement; the indenture system as termed by Indian indentured labourers in Fiji.
haji: Arabic, a Mohamedan or Muslim who has made *hadj*, the pilgrimage to Mecca.
izzat: Urdu and Punjabi, honour; self-respect.
kampong: Malay, an enclosure; a collection of houses; a village.
kangany: Tamil, an overseer or supervisor; in Ceylon and Malaya, the term was specifically used to designate a foreman (or headman) of a gang of labourers working together on a plantation or construction.
kanji: Tamil, the residual semi-liquid after rice has been boiled. (Also given as *congee*).
kerah: Malay, corvee.
kling: Malay, native of Madras Presidency; South Indian.
kongsi: Chinese, a society, gang, company; a term applied to a batch of Chinese hired labourers on the same estate or mine and living together.
kranny: Malay, clerk. Also given as *kerani*.
lallang: Malay, tall coarse grass.
maistry: Hindi, recruiting agent; recruiter of labourers in South India.
malim: Persian, ship's officer.
mirasi: Tamil, the Tamil districts of hereditary land tenure.
mirasidar: Tamil, holder of hereditary lands in South India.
nacoda: Persian, captain of a boat or vessel.
narak: Hindi, hell.
padi: Malay, growing rice; unhusked rice.
penghulu: Malay, headman or chief of a village.
pikul: Malay, a measure of weight approximately equal to 133.3 pounds.
rattan: Malay, the cane from the palm of this name.
rumah kechil: Malay, Chinese contract system operated on early Province Wellesley sugar estates.

sinkheh: Chinese, new comer; fresh arrival (from China); new hand. (Compare with *baba* – Chinese born in Malaya).
taluk: Hindi, a dependency or sub-district (held by a *talukdar*) in South India.
taluk peon: Hindi, an orderly of a *taluk*.
tindal: Malayalam, overseer or headman of a gang of hired labourers at work, usually on a sugar estate. Counterpart of *sirdar* (*sardar*) in Mauritius and the West Indies during Indian indenture and after.

INTRODUCTION

The now defunct Indian indentured labour system in the former British colonies involved a contract signed in India between the emigrant and the Emigration Agent of the colony that wished to employ him. In the case of some colonies, the contract (or indenture) bound the labourer to serve in the employ of his manager for three years as in the Straits Settlements (which was also referred to as British Malaya); elsewhere as in British Guiana (renamed Guyana on achieving independence on 26 May 1966), Mauritius, Trinidad, and Fiji, after experiments with three and five-year indentures, the period was finally fixed at the latter. In whatever colony the immigrant found himself, he was required by the terms of the agreement to work six days a week. If, at the end of the contracted period, a labourer fell short of this requirement for whatever reason, the period of deficit was added to his contract.

In the case of the Straits Settlements (which comprised Penang including Province Wellesley, Singapore, and Malacca) the recruiting agents in India provided each emigrant with a cash advance and, sometimes even clothes, and also defrayed the cost of the passage across the Bay of Bengal to the colony. The labourer was required by law to repay the total cost of these advances through weekly deductions from his wages. In the other colonies, such as British Guiana, the emigrant was not usually provided with a cash advance or clothes, but his passage was provided gratis. In all the colonies, the employers were required by law to provide free housing, a potable water supply, medical care, hospital accommodation, and regular work at the prescribed wage rates. It may be observed that by entering into a contract to labour for a given time, in this indirect but really practical way, the labourer actually defrayed the cost of his introduction and the amenities supplied to him.

On the expiration of the immigrant's contract he had three courses open to him: renewal of the contract; settlement in the colony with freedom to follow the vocation of his choice; or, except in the case of Mauritius after 1857 and of the Straits Settlements, repatriation at the expense of the colony that had imported him. In the case of the Straits Settlements, if after fulfilling his contractual obligations the labourer preferred to repatriate, neither his employer nor the colony was legally obligated to provide him with a return passage. In the other colonies, apart from Mauritius after 1857, it was different. The labourer was provided with either a free return passage or given a grant of land in lieu of the cost of the return passage but only if he had fulfilled the terms of his contract and had served an additional five-year "industrial residence", which was a euphemism for another indenture. If he had not commuted his entitlement to free repatriation in return for a grant of a parcel of land, he could still return to his native country at the expense of the colony whenever he chose to do so.

Indenture in the Straits Settlements: Genesis
The officially regulated Indian indenture system in the Straits Settlements was somewhat connected with its older and more elaborate counterparts in Mauritius

and the West Indies. In the early 1840s, two Mauritius sugar planters, Leopold Chasseriau and Joseph Donadieu, took up cane cultivation in Province Wellesley.[1] From the West Indies came Thomas Braddell in 1844,[2] and J.M. Vermont in 1854.[3] As they had done previously, these planters employed mainly Indian immigrant labourers.[4] Having been said that the indenture system in the Straits was mainly favoured by planters having West Indian experience or traditions,[5] it is not surprising that as Professor Kernial Singh Sandhu rightly asserted: "The system in Malaya differed from that in the sugar colonies but mainly in detail and less so in spirit".[6] Furthermore, the Report of the Committee on Emigration to the Crown Colonies and Protectorates observed that in the West Indies and Mauritius, the planters had been "long accustomed to a mentality of coercive control over slaves and tended to overlook the fundamental difference between … [the indentured Indians] and their former labourers."[7] With the adoption of such Mauritian and West Indian traditions, it was inevitable that certain characteristics of Indian indenture in these colonies would be adapted into the system in the Straits Settlements.

Also incorporated into Indian indenture in the Straits were certain features of the local Chinese *rumah kechil* system. One of these was to pay the immigrants' passage, in addition to making a cash advance. In return, the immigrants contracted to work for a specified length of time or until they liquidated their debts. The European planters of Province Wellesley in the Straits Settlements adopted parts of this system because they found them economically advantageous in terms of systematic cultivation of sugar.[8] Operated by the Chinese sugar planters during the first half of the nineteenth century, the *rumah kechil* system was generally viewed as being "exploitative in nature …. Ill-treatment, brutality and inhumanity were not uncommon. With low wage rates and wretched working and living conditions, many of the Chinese coolie-Sinkeh [i.e. Chinese immigrant labourers] were, from the start, condemned to a state of destitution."[9]

Until now, no full-scale study of the Indian indenture system in the Straits Settlements has been published. There are, however, two general works on Indians in Malaya covering the indenture period: Professor Sandhu's *Indians in Malaya: Some Aspects of their Immigration and Settlement* and Professor Sinnappah Arasaratnam's *Indians in Malaysia and Singapore*.[10] Neither of these studies is primarily concerned with indenture. Sandhu's scholarly work traces Indo-Malayan relationships from the start of the Christian era and examines the causes of modern Indian migration to Malaya, the system of recruitment and the various types of immigrants, and emigration policy and practice. He also describes the patterns of settlement and occupation and the position of Malayan Indians in the economic, political and administrative fields up to independence in 1957. Arasaratnam's outstanding book also briefly discusses the long historical association between India and Malaya. He examines the characteristics of Indian migration to Malaya, the nature and composition of the new immigrant community, and discusses inter-racial tensions and the Indians' religious, cultural, social, and educational progress up to the 1970s. There are other rich and sophisticated publications on the Indian diaspora such as those by R.B. Krishnan, N. Gangulee, S. Nanjundan, C. Kondapi, N.V. Rajkumar, I.M. Cumpston, J.N. Parmer, R.N. Jackson, Usha Mahajani, and Hugh Tinker. But these authors have either concentrated on Indo-Malayan issues other than indenture or have investigated Indian immigration on a broad spectrum, giving only glimpses of the indenture system.

FIG. 2   THE WEST INDIES

This study is confined to the system of Indian indenture as it was operated on the European-owned sugar estates in Province Wellesley, the territory opposite the island of Penang. Province Wellesley was some thirty miles long by about eleven to thirteen miles wide. It was acquired by the English East India Company from the Sultan of the Malay state of Kedah in 1800 to serve primarily as a staple food-producing area for Penang. The Province was named in honour of the Marquess of Wellesley, the Governor-General of India (1797-1806). Administratively, Province Wellesley was a part of the Settlement of Penang whose local government was itself subject to the central government of the Straits Settlements located at Singapore, the capital city situated just below the southernmost tip of Peninsular Malaya.

Malaya has been inhabited for at least 6000 years; and before the dawn of the Christian era, about the second century B.C., Indian adventurers, merchants, missionaries and others were known to have arrived and initiated over 1000 years of Indian influence. In 1819, the British administrator, Sir Thomas Stamford Raffles (1781-1826), founded a settlement on and secured the island of Singapore. By 1867, the British gained control of the Straits Settlements, the collective name for the former British colonies in Southeast Asia. The three British East India Company territories (of Penang, including Province Wellesley, Singapore and Malacca) were given a unified administration in 1826 and called the Straits Settlements. The Company was dissolved in 1858, and the territories were placed under the jurisdiction of the India Office. In 1867, the Straits Settlements became a crown colony and was administered by the Colonial Office. The colony was dissolved in 1946; Singapore with its dependencies became a separate crown colony, and Penang and Malacca were included in the Malayan Union, which became the Federation of Malaya in 1948, now Malaysia. The Sultan-ruled Malay States of Perak, Selangor, Negri Sembilan, and Pahang became known as the Federated Malay States of Malaya in 1896. At about the same time the Federated Malay States accepted British advisors under the Residency system. From the 1890s, the British invested heavily in Malaya, developing especially transportation and rubber plantations. After World War II the British were faced with anti-colonial opposition and the rise of Malay nationalism. They relinquished their powers, and in 1957 Malaya became independent. During the period of Indian indenture, 1872-1910, British Malaya's largest population groups were, in order of size, the indigenous Malays, immigrant Chinese, and Asian Indians mainly from Madras Presidency. It was from among these latter that the indentured labourers were drawn to work on the sugar estates of the Straits Settlements (referred interchangeably herein also as British Malaya and the Straits).

The Straits Settlements indenture system was regulated in the Indian sub-continent by an Emigration Act passed by the government of India. In this Act were embodied certain measures calculated to safeguard the recruits against fraud and misrepresentation and to secure their proper treatment at the emigration depot and during their transit to Penang. In the Straits Settlements, until 1876, there was no counterpart to the Indian Emigration Act just mentioned. But for the period between the beginning of indenture in 1872 and 1876 from when the system was officially regulated and supervised, the Governor promised the government of India that he would exercise a "watchful care" over the labourers until comprehensive protective measures could be enacted. These measures were embodied in a labour ordinance passed by the Straits government in 1876; and imposed upon the employers a wide variety of obligations towards the labourers. For its part, the Straits government established an Indian Immigration Protectorate in the colony and appointed a number of magistrates to adjudicate labour grievances. To superficial observation, it might seem that the immigrants, being so advantageously placed, could hardly have any just ground for dissatisfaction.

References

1 J.C. Jackson, *Planters and Speculators: Chinese and European Agricultural Enterprise in Malaya* (Kuala Lumpur, 1968), p. 143.
2 W. Makepeace, G.E. Brooke, and R. Braddell, eds., *One Hundred Years of Singapore,* Vol. I (London, 1921), pp. 423-24.
3 PRAD, no. 25, August 1884.
4 In the Straits Settlements, Indian immigrant labourers under indenture were variously referred to as "Statute Immigrants", "Protected Immigrants", and "Indentured Labourers".
5 *Report of the Committee on Emigration to the Crown Colonies and Protectorates*, Lord Sanderson, Chairman, Command Papers 5192-94 (London, 1910), p. 110.
6 K.S. Sandhu, *Indians in Malaya: Some Aspects of their Immigration and Settlement, 1786-1957* (Cambridge, 1969), p. 76.
7 I.M. Cumpston, *Indians Overseas in British Territories, 1834-1854* (London, 1953), p. 13.
8 *Singapore Free Press*, 5 October 1848.
9 Tan Kim Hong, "Chinese Sugar Planting and Social Mobility in Nineteenth Century Province Wellesley, "*Malaysia in History*," No. 24 (1981), 31.
10 S. Arasaratnam, *Indians In Malaysia and Singapore* (2nd ed., Kuala Lumpur, 1979).

I

INDIAN INDENTURE SYSTEM: EVOLUTION AND STRUCTURE

> To superficial observation it would seem, that persons who have been rescued from a state said to be bordering on destitution in their own country who are provided with free house room, regular work and wages, when they are in health, and in sickness have the advantages of a hospital, the attendance of a medical man, and medicines free of expense, who have moreover a magistrate always at hand to hear their complaints, and a department of officers with the especial duty of securing their good treatment, can have no just ground for dissatisfaction. A closer scrutiny, however, would detract much from the apparent value of these advantages, and would show that some of them at least are more nominal than real.
>
> George William Des Voeux[1]

The Indian indenture system was rooted in the consequences that followed the abolition of the slave trade by Great Britain in 1807. Ever since then, there had been a steady decline in the number of slaves, as those who had died were not replaced by new arrivals. In British Guiana, for instance, from a slave population of 101, 712 in 1807, only 89,786 remained in 1829.[2] In the British West Indies as a whole, between 1808 and 1830, the number of slaves fell from 800,000 to 650,000.[3] The perceived consequences of this state of affairs on the paramountcy of the commercial interests of the sugar planters in the colonies were of considerable concern to the Colonial Office. Yet, despite the British government's agreement to allow Africans captured on board slave ships by British cruisers to be sent to her colonies,[4] the addition being small, it had only an infinitesimal effect on improving the slave population and hence the labour supply.

What gave the Indian indenture migratory movement its start was the greater shortage of labour anticipated by the planters in the "King Sugar" colonies following the abolition of slavery in 1833-34 and the termination of the system of Apprenticeship in 1838-39 and full Emancipation. According to the Abolition of Slavery Act of 1833, the Apprenticeship system was to last until 1840, but mainly because of the ill-treatment meted out to the apprentices and the consequential protests[5] which combined with the British government's own humanitarian mood, this euphemism for actual slavery was brought to an end in 1838-39. Originally, the British government had intended the Apprenticeship period to be one of transition to give the planters an opportunity to adjust themselves to the new post-slavery conditions so as to reorganize the administration of their enterprises, in the light of the new economic and social realities. On the other hand, it was also aimed at enabling the apprentices to adapt to their new lifestyle when they would be fully emancipated.

For the planters' part, some of them had realized that Emancipation was inevitable, and had early reconciled themselves to its implications, and had been more prepared to deal with its consequences. A few shrewd planters began to treat their slaves kindly with the expectation of retaining their labour when they became free.[6] But generally, the planters apprehended the worst consequences from the termination of the Apprenticeship system. This feeling sprang from their fear that the disappearance of free labour would rob them of a labour supply so necessary for the maintenance of high-cost fixed capital and for the continuation of profitable production to recover those costs and to cover recurrent expenditure. They also harboured quite realistic fears that full freedom would bring about a radical change in the way in which plantations were financed. Before Emancipation, the planters had been able to operate with comparatively little working capital. They did not have to pay wages and had been able to reduce their expenditure on food supplies by encouraging the slaves to grow food on provision grounds. But Emancipation meant paid labour and this implied less profits. They also feared that with Emancipation their coercive and controlling power would vanish and the freedom to bargain, the prerogative of free labour, would actualize. It was mainly on these considerations that the planters began to look for a cheap and adequate supply of labour. After a number of failed experiments in some colonies with labourers from various sources, the planters in the sugar colonies eventually turned to the Indian subcontinent.

Labourers from India had been recruited to work in other lands long before the introduction of an organized system of Indian indenture in various colonies in the 1830s. One of the earliest positively traced schemes was in 1735 when forty French-Indians were recruited in Pondicherry to work in Mauritius.[7] This experiment was soon aborted. The planters criticized the immigrants as being "soft and lazy" and complained that on the slightest provocation they resorted to incendiarism by way of retaliation against their perceived mistreatment.[8] Another such experiment was tried by certain Mauritius planters in 1819,[9] but the circumstances surrounding this venture are obscure. In 1830, a French merchant, Joseph Argand, carried some 130 Indian labourers to Bourbon (now Reunion) with the permission of the government of India.[10] According to John Geoghegan, a government of India official and author of a comprehensive history of Indian emigration up to 1873, the labour contracts, which were for a term of five years, "looked liberal enough on paper, 8 rupees, in addition to an ample dietary, being fixed as the minimum monthly wage". But in 1832, Geoghegan added, two of the immigrants petitioned the government of India complaining of their wages being withheld. Enquiries having been made, the government did not consider the complaint serious, and furthermore, disclaimed any obligation to repatriate the labourers in consequence of their alleged disappointment.

Indian indentured emigration received its first great impetus from the abolition of slavery in the British colonies and the concomitant shortage of labour. Mauritius enjoyed moderate success with Indian labourers from 1834 when 36 men of the Dhangar caste were contracted to work there. The agreement required them to work for five years on a sugar estate, and both their outward and return passages would be provided free. They were to receive five rupees a month, with six months' pay given in advance.[11] This was all explained to the recruits by the Chief Magistrate of their district, and the agreement was thumb-printed in his presence. A comment here seems necessary. Legally speaking the recruits were bound by the terms of the contract. On the other hand, these contracts were intrinsically valueless as those simple and mainly ignorant, helpless rural folk could neither have had the capacity nor the sense of discrimination to grasp the significance of the agreements they had entered into. Nevertheless, since the emigrants seemed to have voluntarily accepted to go to Mauritius, the Bengal provincial government saw no objection in allowing them.

The success of this tentative venture encouraged the planters to put the experiment on a firmer footing. Consequently, by the end of 1839, over 25,000 indentured Indians were imported into Mauritius.[12] By the end of indentured emigration in 1910 there, nearly half a million emigrants were engaged, by far the largest number introduced into any of the colonies importing indentured labour.

Although the first importation had been sanctioned by the Colonial Office, the government of India was uneasy about any general scheme, and besides, it did not take the humanitarians in India long to recognize the continuum with slavery. In this, they were justified. The labourers had been smuggled away under the idea that Mauritius was a village in India. The voyage took two months instead of the labourers' expectation of between one to ten days, and having been accommodated on the open deck, the emigrants had to bear all the inclemencies of the weather including those of the monsoon. Upon arrival, they were made to live in huts which resembled very much the habitations of the ex-slaves. They were put to work two or three days after arrival. The recompense for the oppressively heavy tasks was disproportionate since they had to work from sunrise to sunset and were seldom free on Sundays. They encountered financial difficulties which placed them in a deplorable state of destitution. Access to the Protector of Immigrants was difficult and sometimes impossible. Charges of absenteeism and vagrancy were regular and pervasive; and no consideration was given for their religious sensibilities.[13]

In Calcutta, Thomas Boaz, a clergyman who interviewed some immigrants who had returned from Mauritius in 1836, publicly denounced the indenture system as merely an extension of slavery. Together with other sensitive and enlightened members of the Indian public, Boaz petitioned the President of the Council of India protesting the suffering of the immigrants and demanding an immediate suspension of what they hastened to call the "coolie trade" until reforms were introduced to purge the abuses in the system.[14] The efforts of all these reformists were ineffectual.

The sugar planters in British Guiana soon followed the Mauritius example of importing Indian labourers. In 1836, John Gladstone, father of the British Liberal Leader, W.E. Gladstone, together with three other planters, arranged with a Calcutta firm, Messrs. Gillanders, Arbuthnot and Company, for the introduction of a batch of Indian labourers. The planters promised to provide them with "good food, comfortable dwellings, clothing, schools, and religious instruction."[15] Two years later, on 5-6 May, 1838, the *Whitby* and the *Hesperus* landed 396 immigrants in the colony.[16]

Embargo on Emigration
The overlapping of neo-slavery in the form of the Apprenticeship system and Indian indenture in Mauritius and British Guiana witnessed the transfer of some of the worst characteristics of coerced labour. This was inevitable, since the engagements and obligations of slavery left strong traces in the habits and minds of the planters. In British Guiana, although initially some of the planters' promises had been fulfilled, within a few months of the immigrants' arrival in the colony, reports of neglect and ill-treatment were sent to England. On 9 January 1839, the *British Emancipator*, the official organ of the Anti-Slavery Society of Great Britain, reported thus: "The British Public has been deceived with the idea that the coolies are doing 'well'; such is not the fact; the poor friendless creatures are miserably treated". This charge is sustainable. Some of the labourers, including a number from Gladstone's estate, Vreedenhoop, had frequently been beaten, one former slave said, "as my matties were during apprenticeship".[17]

The Anti-Slavery Society's Secretary, John Scoble, having personally investigated wrote: "To detail the whole of the iniquities practised on the wretched Coolies on that [Gladstone's] estate would fill a volume".[18]

The condition and treatment of the Indians in the two colonies provoked loud protests among other humanitarians in England. Some of those who petitioned the Colonial Office in 1839 deprecated the "intention to revive slavery"; others indignantly characterized Indian indenture as "a revival of the Slave Traffic".[19] A journalist of *The Times* of London said the "whole scheme would degenerate to jew-jobbing and crimping, thus reviving most of the horrors of slavery."[20] Adding to these denouncements, was the distinguished British statesman and indefatigable reformer, Lord Henry Brougham, who delivered in the House of Commons "an able and eloquent speech in opposition to the ill-treatment of the labourers."[21] In his perception, there was such a strong nexus between slavery and indenture that he found it difficult to distinguish one from the other. In this frame of mind, he condemned the entire indenture system in unequivocal terms and concluded that he had no choice but to act as he had done through the whole of his life, maintaining to the end "the implacable enmity with which he had at all times pursued this infernal trade."[22]

These pressures persuaded the Council of India to prohibit any further emigration from India with effect from 1839 so that it could endeavour to devise adequate measures for the protection of emigrants. The humanitarians had won the first round!

The suspension of the supply of labourers from India put the planters' pecuniary interests in serious jeopardy. After the slaves were emancipated in 1838-39, the situation in the sugar industry in Mauritius and British Guiana became more despairing, for the ex-slaves inculcated a more acute aversion for employment on the plantations and expressed this by working desultorily. Even when necessity compelled them, they exercised their newly-given right to work on their own terms rather than on conditions dictated by their employers.

Not even inducements could entice the former slaves. In British Guiana, even though the planters had spent the sum of two and a half million dollars in purchasing new land, on improving those already occupied, and in constructing over 10,000 housing units between 1838 and 1848,[23] the labour given was still intermittent and unpredictable and was often arbitrarily withdrawn. The partial withdrawal of labour was increased by the freedmen's refusal to work overtime; by their choice to send their children to school rather than to work; and by the devotion of previously working women to household chores and to tending little garden plots and their livestock.

The attitude of some planters made labour scarce for others. With the planters' coercive and controlling power removed, they began to compete with one another to attract labour to their own plantations. Some offered higher wages; others sold plantations below the open market price, and with the money thus realized they erected new cottages in place of the old with the intention of inducing their labourers to remain.[24] Such competition eroded the planters' solidarity; and to their further detriment, created an artificial increase in the price of labour, which strengthened the freedmen's resolve not to be cajoled by the planters into working as if they were still slaves. Moreover, the planters' economic concepts were conditioned by unlimited free labour during slavery. They had not invested money realized from profits or money they had received as compensation for the loss of their slaves in machinery and other labour-saving devices, which would have softened the impact of the labour shortage.

Declining Production
The inevitable consequence of the decreasing labour supply was a diminution in the production of sugar in the colonies. In British Guiana, for instance, the average annual tonnage of 57, 197 produced in the last five years of slavery fell to an average of 31,865 tons between 1838-46.[25] From the British West Indies as a whole, whereas during the period 1829-33, the average annual amount of sugar exported into the United Kingdom was 195,893 tons, the average between 1842-45 was 129,115 tons.[26] In Mauritius, while a slave used to cut three cartloads of cane per day, the freedmen cut only two.[27]

Why the freedmen worked when necessity impelled them three or even less days per week was actuated by several considerations. Barton Premium, a contemporary writer in British Guiana, perceived that the slaves had been "accustomed to regard slavery as the natural distinction between man and man";[28] it would, therefore, have taken them some time to understand why a free man should indulge in manual labour. Furthermore, it would have been difficult for the freedmen to detach regular employment on the sugar estates from the stigma of slavery. Neither could they have been expected to return to the relentless pace of hard work under harsh discipline and in an enervating climate for which the planters were prepared to pay what the labourers considered a pittance. "Men lifted above their own former condition," the Colonial Office aptly observed, "despise that condition not less than men who have always been in a higher."[29] Moreover, among the freedmen there was little or no anxiety over procuring a basic sustenance. The plantains and yams they cultivated supplied their wants; fruit trees grew in profusion; and the trenches yielded an abundance of fish. Working casually on the estates, therefore, was only intended to complement their recourse to the resources in the environment and to enable them to purchase those commodities they could not otherwise acquire. Only those would work regularly who had developed a taste for "finery in dress, even to extravagance, and for good living." Secretary of State for the Colonies, Lord John Russell, emphasized certain basic human attitudes when he wrote that "it was not to be expected, that men who can subsist in comfort, without hard labour, will continue to devote themselves to it." He added that the state of planter and slave had left the West Indian colonies without a middle class but that the "more careful and intelligent of the emancipated negroes became petty traders."[30]

Those freedmen who earned high wages bought or hired plots of land and discontinued working for their former masters. This was not what the planters wanted; but was partially the fulfilment of the British government's plan. In the words of Lord Russell, it was "a blessed achievement which evidence has enabled us to accomplish." He saw no economic immorality in the freedmen's petty business ventures when he asserted: "There is nothing in this singular or culpable. No man in this country who has capital sufficient to keep a shop, or rent a farm, will follow the plough as a day labourer or work from morning till night as a hand loom weaver."[31] To the freedmen, Emancipation was a revolution of rising expectation. It widened the range of their expectations and these, in many cases, could not be satisfied in plantation labour and residence. They were given an occasion to move from a stage of geographical mobility conferred by freedom to social mobility bestowed by opportunity.

Summing up the ex-slaves' attitudes towards working on the sugar estates, an official of the Colonial Office wrote:

> For the greater part of the Negroes abandoned not only field labour, but service of every kind, almost as soon as they were at a liberty to do so. No present kindness, or memory of past benefits, no persuasion or pecuniary inducements could prevail upon them to remain; and it is to be feared that the time is yet distant when motives of interest, or the pressure of necessity, will bring them back to serve as agricultural labourers.[32]

Indeed, conscious of their new status and dignity as free men, and their access to the law, they refused to work as before. All of this, together with the increasing mobility of labourers and their preference for other kinds of work aggravated the labour shortage.

Alternative Sources

The decline in sugar production in the colonies might have been decelerated but certainly not averted had the planters been successful in their attempts to procure adequate and suitable labour from alternative sources. In British Guiana, the planters failed to attract the indigenous, hinterland-based Amerindians to work on the plantations, all of which were located along the fringe of the Atlantic coast. These inhabitants of the forest were generally a nomadic people who derived a livelihood as hunters, fishermen, and subsistence farmers.[33] Their temperament and attitude to work were inconsistent with the rigour of sugar cultivation. On their farms they worked desultorily[34] for they were not materially acquisitive. The main object of their existence was to pass through life with as little bother as possible.[35] Above all, the Amerindians [some of whom the sugar planters had retained to capture runaway slaves] equated plantation labour with slave labour.[36]

The planters' failure to attract indigenous labourers to their plantations made it obvious to them that a cheap and sustained supply of labour would have to be met from overseas. Initially, they looked to Europe and Africa. Between 1834-37, Jamaica planters imported some 3,000 English, 1,000 Scottish, 1000 German, and 100 Irish labourers.[37] A smaller number of Europeans were also imported into St. Lucia.[38] The importation of Europeans was apparently intended to create a white working class and hopefully for them to set an example of industry to the ex-slaves. But the whites were disappointing to the Jamaica planters. The experiment failed because of the lack of adequate sanitary precautions, general demoralization, and most importantly the "unsuitability of raw, unacclimatized Europeans for field work in the tropical sun, with the added temptation of unlimited drink".[39]

The importation by planters in British Guiana of immigrants from Madeira beginning May 3, 1835, enjoyed minimal success. Despite that the Governor, (later Sir) Henry Light, found the early batches to be "quiet, frugal and content with small gains", generally they failed as agricultural labourers, having been put to work before becoming acclimatized and having been provided with poor accommodation.[40] Consequently, a great deal of sickness and a high mortality rate ensued among them. Subsequent batches fared little better, and those who survived took to the retail trade. By the end of 1841, by which time the planters had imported 4,297 Madeirans,[41] the nature of the experiment remained the same. Much smaller experiments with Maltese, German, and Irish labourers also failed. Some of the immigrants suffered terribly from yellow fever and the lack of appropriate medical care. Others were described by the *Royal Gazette* thus: "The paleness of death sat on their countenances and their sunken eyes and emaciated frames proclaimed with silent eloquence that hunger was hard at work within them."[42]

The small number of immigrants imported by some West Indian colonies from the southern United States were no better in quality. Recruiting was successful mainly among mechanics, carpenters, and bricklayers, and people of similar occupations.[43] Thus unsuited to the rigour and regimentation of sugar estate employment, the seventy of them either sought other jobs or returned home.[44]

Planters in Trinidad had also made attempts to import labour from neighbouring Grenada, St. Christopher, and Nevis. Captains of small trading vessels were paid a bounty for every labourer landed. The planters, too, often dispatched their own vessels to engage labourers for the reaping season, with the promise of returning them at the end of the crop. But because there were no legal provisions specifying the terms of the engagement, or for making the agreement enforceable, corruption soon set in. The "ill-contrived and injudiciously managed" bounty system also ended in failure not long after its inception.[45]

Attempts by planters in British Guiana to import labourers from the small West Indian islands were disappointing. The Barbados planters opposed emigration of sizeable numbers of agricultural labourers on the economic ground that it would induce the rest of the labour force to demand higher wages. In the other small islands, many labourers wanting to try their fortune in British Guiana were prevented from leaving by the trumping up of false accounts made out against them.[46] The small number that did manage to emigrate soon followed the example of the local ex-slaves by drifting from the sugar estates to set themselves up independently.

Failure in these ventures generated an interest in West Africa as a source of cheap, abundant, and reliable labour. The black labourer was considered a better worker than any other immigrant. According to the Report of the 1871 Commission of Enquiry in British Guiana, "there is no other race who can earn as much in a given time as the negro. He works longer hours than the East Indian. He gets through his task at great speed." It was envisaged that African labourers would set an example of industry to the ex-slaves, and being black, they would inspire the locals to recognize that there was nothing odious about working on the estates. It was also expected that working and living with Africans would render the freedmen's erstwhile status less identifiable. These expectations failed to consider the new attitudes and frame of mind adopted by the ex-slaves towards plantation employment. Nevertheless, the attempts to import African labourers, especially from Sierra Leone and St. Helena, were not attended by great success. In Sierra Leone particularly, prevailing good economic conditions complemented by frustrations encountered in recruiting labourers caused by missionaries and commercial interests[47] generated inertia among the population. Some Africans were prevented from leaving by the imposition of false debts.[48] Others were told by employers in West Africa that they would be taken to be eaten and that their blood would be used to dye soldiers' coats.[49] Even if recruiting attempts had been more successful, it was unlikely that large-scale migration from Africa would have been sanctioned by Britain. I.M. Cumpston has rightly noted that: "Africa was the most sensitive spot on all of England's international commitments, and it is difficult to believe that a large scale programme for movement of African labourers would have received legislative sanction. Even the legitimate traffic from Sierra Leone soon came to an end."[50] Back in the sugar colonies, the African immigrants quickly realized their incompatibility with plantation labour and evinced a "general tendency to forsake the estates on which they were located to wander off either in search of work or into the villages."[51]

Labourers from China were also tried but not until emigration from India had been well established. The Colonial Office believed that "the Chinese labourers possessed greater intelligence than either the Negro or the Indian, and learnt to manage machinery quicker."[52] He was described as a careful and neat worker, and displayed a greater independence than the East Indian. It was not usual for this type of immigrant to make a frivolous complaint; and it was difficult to convict him of lying, because he displayed extreme ingenuity in the construction of his case, and in the instruction of his witnesses. He resented apparent injustice and loved the use of knives and pointed weapons. As a class, the Chinese were inveterate gamblers and confirmed smokers of opium. They were not as thrifty as the Indians, but they were more cosmopolitan in their habits.[53] Of greatest importance to the planters, the Chinese had built up a favourable reputation as hardworking labourers. An observer in the West Indies described them in 1844 as:

> Well made, robust, and active, inured to field labour, and able to work during the heat of the day, in fact, they are equal to our best Creole field labourers; they are eager for gain, and will do anything for money; they are quiet and very intelligent for their class, and not lazy. They value money, and are shrewd; and I do not think no class of men can be better adapted to our wants than they are.[54]

These very desirable qualities motivated the Chinese to aspire to higher economic pursuits. Being "further developed in civilization,"[55] as one official put it, the Chinese tended to move out of the plantations as soon as they were able to enter the retail trade. The failure of all these schemes impelled the planters to canvass more strenuously for a renewal of immigration from India.

The Need for Immigration
There were good economic reasons for this clamour. Most of the planters were heavily indebted and wanted to lower wages. It is true that they had received compensation for the loss of their slaves, but very little of this money remained in their pockets. Most of it was used to pay off mortgages and sub-mortgages.[56] Money for capital development was short; and some planters were sometimes even short of money to pay their labourers. Immigration from India was perceived as a means of suppressing wage rates. When the East Indians were contracted in India, the wage they were offered was below that demanded by the freedmen. Consequently, through unfettered importation of Indian labourers it was hoped that the supply of labour would exhaust the demand, thus creating competition amongst the labourers for available jobs – a situation which would likely result in a fall in the wage rates.

The planters' petitions to the Secretary of State for the Colonies, Lord John Russell, carried a common theme. They posited that the colonies were potentially rich, but that many freedmen were withholding their labour and thus, compared with the days of slavery there was an increasing labour shortage and that labour must be brought to the colonies. These petitioners did not accuse the freedmen of idleness, nor did they forecast their eventually taking to crime, but they stressed the importance of the labour problems. In one particular petition, it was emphasized that:

The falling off of output has not been caused by bad seasons or any want of liberality on the part of the proprietors, in regard to wages and allowances, they being in fact extravagantly high in proportion to the labour performed; but, entirely owing to a want of continuous and regular labour, many of the emancipated labourers having since the 1st of August 1838, betaken themselves to petty trading, and other employments in preference to the cultivation of the soil, most of the women having altogether withdrawn, and the children afforded scarcely any assistance.[57]

The planters' assertion that the freedmen earned "extravagantly high" wages on the plantations needs to be examined. The daily rate for the completion of one task, which normally takes about seven and a half hours, was one guilder or one shilling and six pence.

If a labourer was "industrious" and worked fifteen hours and completed two tasks, he could earn three shillings a day. At this latter rate he would earn £46 per annum if he worked a ninety-hour week. A comparison would reveal a sizeable disparity between this labourer's earnings and the cost of living. In 1838 when Governor Henry Light of British Guiana requested the Colonial Secretary, Lord Normanby, to raise his salary from £2,000 per annum to £6,000 he pointed out that he paid each of his domestic servants £60 per annum because the cost of living was high.[58]

The freedmen did not agree with the planters' view that they were being paid extravagantly. They displayed this difference of opinion in the most obvious way. Those who had saved money bought land communally, built houses, and by farming their own plots of land were able to establish themselves as petty traders. In British Guiana, a vast land settlement scheme was put into operation by labourers who acted very largely under their own leadership and by pooling their resources. This was the start of the so-called Negro Village Movement. Up to 1848, over 400 plots of land were bought and more than 10,000 houses were built and occupied by 44,443 persons.[59]

From these villages the freedmen went out to work on the neighbouring sugar estates under the direction of one of their own body, called the task-gang driver (or headman). The manager of the estate contracted with the driver to do work on his estate for a given rate. The driver then employed the men from his village, collected the money on completion of the job, and then paid the labourers, keeping a percentage for supervising them. Under this system, most of the trenching and cane-cutting was done by the freedmen but the supply of labour was capricious and whimsical and hence unreliable. The planters continued to see their salvation only in immigration.

Immigration was the planters' weapon to prove to the freedmen that they were not indispensable since large scale importations could be used to lower wages. According to Sir Charles Metcalfe, the Governor of Jamaica, in a dispatch to the Secretary of State in 1839, "wages were settled at the will of the labourer, rather than that of his employer, and could only be changed by a great increase of the labouring population, thus making labour cheaper."[60] To achieve this end the planters represented to the Colonial Office that in the larger territories there were immense tracts of land unsurpassed in fertility by any other in the world, while the population numbered to not more than one individual to the square mile. They also adverted to the great superiority that the colonies, forming an integral portion of the British Empire, possessed as a market for British manufactured goods, over any foreign state, and to the mutual intercourse between the parent state and its dependencies, which was not liable to be disturbed by capricious changes in a system of commercial policy. They argued that the operation of the Act of Abolition of Slavery and the Act for total Emancipation had so diminished the number of agricultural labourers that not only were vast tracts of fertile soil lying unproductive in the colonies, but also large areas of cultivated land in the estates were deeply affected by the partial withholding of labour causing a decrease in the production of the staple exportable commodities. Other estates would inevitably be abandoned, unless the supply of labour to the colonies was speedily and largely increased beyond the extent existing in 1838. Any greater deficiency of labour and industry, they further argued, not only would create "a state of things pregnant with ruin to the landed interest of the colonies but would also be prejudicial to the moral condition of the labourers themselves," since "idleness tends to increase and is almost universally the originator and companion of crime."

Immigration Renewed
The cause of the planters in the British colonies was taken up and zealously promoted by mercantile interests in Parliament. But the Secretary of State, Lord John Russell, firmly declared that he was "not prepared to encounter the responsibility of a measure which may lead to a dreadful loss of life on the one hand, or, on the other, to a new system of slavery."[61]

Russell, however, was not to have the last word. Investigations instituted by Mauritius and British Guiana after the suspension of emigration from India revealed that while there had indeed been some exaggerations and sensational reporting, there was unanimity in the portrayal of much material improvement in the condition of the immigrants.[62] Meanwhile, a House of Commons Committee appointed in 1841 confirmed the declining sugar production in Mauritius and the West Indies and attributed it squarely to the lack of adequate labour. The Committee declared: "The obvious and most desirable mode of endeavouring to compensate for this diminished supply of labour, is to promote the immigration of a fresh labouring population, to such an extent as to create competition for employment."[63] Consultation between the Board of Control and the Court of Directors of the East India Company on the one hand and the Colonial Office on the other coincided with the succession of Lord Russell by the immigrationist Lord Stanley as Secretary of State of the Colonies in 1841. In 1842, Lord Stanley announced that in so far as Mauritius was concerned, the embargo on emigration from India was lifted. It is significant to note that in none of the reports pertaining to Mauritius were grave charges preferred against the planters.

Mauritius thus opened the way, and it was not long after that the West Indian colonies renewed their requests for Indian labour. British Guiana recommenced receiving in 1845; and in the same year, Trinidad and Jamaica landed their first consignment. To the smaller islands such as Grenada, St. Lucia, and St. Vincent, emigration started in 1856, 1858, and 1861 respectively.

TABLE I

INDIAN IMMIGRATION INTO SELECTED COLONIES, 1834-1916

COLONY	PERIOD OF MIGRATION	NO. OF IMMIGRANTS
Mauritius	1834-1900	453,063
Br. Guiana	1838-1916	238,909
Trinidad	1845-1916	143,939
Jamaica	1845-1915	36,412
Natal	1860-1911	152,184
Fiji	1879-1916	60,965

Source: Compiled from Geoghegan, *Emigration from India*; Fred H. Hitchins, *The Colonial Land and Emigration Commission* (Philadelphia, 1931); PP, Vol. LVII (1900), pp. 467-68; Government of India: *Report on Emigration and Immigration,* 1900-20; G.W. Roberts and J. Byrne, "Summary Statistics on Indenture and Associated Migration Affecting the West Indies, 1834-1948," *Population Studies*, Vol. XX, Pt. 1 (July, 1966), 125-34; Hugh Tinker, "Indians Abroad: Emigration, Restriction and Rejection," in Michael Twaddle, ed., *Expulsion of a Minority: Essays on Ugandan Asians* (London, 1975), p. 15.

The number of Indian indentured labourers imported into the lesser islands was comparatively small, and they are mentioned merely to indicate the range of the demand. Natal began importing in 1860.

The last British colony to import Indian indentured labour was Fiji whose history did not feature African slavery. But as in the West Indian colonies, similarly cheap and abundant supply of labour became necessary in the 1860s when an increasing number of European settlers in the colony began cultivating cotton and coconut plantations.

Until 1879, labour for these enterprises was imported from the adjacent Polynesian island groups, especially the New Hebrides, and from the Solomon, Gilbert, Ellice, and Tokelau Islands.[64] The system by which the labourers had been obtained, referred to as blackbirding, earned a notorious reputation; and the stricter enforcement of new governmental regulations to eradicate the abuses and atrocities led to considerable difficulty in procuring the required number of recruits. The overtures made by the white settlers to the autochthonous Fijians to give their labour was met with minimal success for reasons to be given at a more appropriate point. By 1879, the labour shortage became greater for in that year Fiji was annexed by Britain, and the British government pledged in the Deed of Cession to preserve the native social structure and to prevent any disruption of the village economy.[65]

The shortage of both labour and capital in Fiji persuaded the (first substantive) Governor, Sir Arthur Hamilton Gordon, to attract off-shore entrepreneurs. The Colonial Sugar Refining Company, based in Sydney, Australia, accepted Gordon's invitation, and extended its operations in 1882.[66] The problem of securing a cheap and dependable supply of labour remained but not for long. As Governor of Mauritius and then Trinidad, Gordon had witnessed the successful operation of the Indian indenture system, and it seemed natural for him to turn to India. The arrival of the first batch of 498 immigrants on board the *Leonidas* on 14 May 1879 initiated a migratory movement that was to last until 1916 by when 60,969 men, women, and children were taken to the Fiji islands.[67]

From the resumption of Indian indenture in 1845 until the system was finally ended in 1920, the government of India subjected the entire process to official regulations and supervision. The importing colonies were required to appoint Emigration Agents and Protectors of Emigrants in India to interview intending emigrants to ensure that they understood the nature of their engagements and to ascertain that they were not being entrapped or deluded by false representations into unfair bargains. The colonies were also required to employ Surgeons-General and lesser officers on board emigrant ships to attend to the health and comfort of the emigrants and to safeguard them against neglect and malpractices. In each colony, the local government had to appoint various officers including Inspectors, Stipendiary Magistrates, Protectors of Immigrants, and Immigration Agents-General and others to take care that the freedom of the labourers was not hampered by unnecessary and vexatious restrictions; that they were not carelessly and oppressively dealt with; and that they were accorded such treatment and provided with such amenities that would tend to encourage them to settle permanently rather than repatriating to India.

Decision to Repatriate
It was mentioned earlier that with the exception of the indentured labourers in the Straits Settlements, those in the other British colonies who had completed their contract and had fulfilled the five-year "industrial residence" requirement were entitled to free repatriation. The advantage of the free return passage was not taken by a majority of immigrants in the more distant colonies. Between 1842 and 1870, for instance, 76 per cent of the immigrants in Mauritius, British Guiana, Trinidad, and Jamaica remained to settle.[68] By comparison, for the same years, of those who had sought employment in Ceylon, Burma, and Malaya, 80 per cent returned home, and at their own expense. Why the 24 per cent in the more distant colonies decided to repatriate is not easy to establish. The immigrants were not questioned before their departure from the colonies; and the Protector of Emigrants in India, although required by law to do so, seldom interviewed repatriating labourers. Even when they did, it was cursory and unsystematic. Nevertheless, the following brief explanations are ventured.

For many immigrants, their expectations based on the recruiters' promises had been too high, and a number of labourers would have been disappointed when they confronted reality. For some immigrants, the shortage of marriageable Indian women coupled with their apparent aversion to exogamous marriages would have been a source of great discontent. That more men retro-migrated did not alleviate the sexual imbalance since more males than females continued to arrive in the colonies. Other immigrants would have been overcome by the nostalgia of Mother India and the memory of a wife or an old parent whose funeral pyre his religion required him to light. Those immigrants who had arrived weak and sickly and were able to strengthen themselves by better food and medical care could not have been daunted by the perils and uncertainty of the long voyage home. The belief in the loss of caste was probably inconsequential to many who repatriated. With the money saved, they could establish themselves in another community and keep their transmarine experience a secret, or, as many had actually done, give caste-dinners at which they were re-initiated, often in a higher caste. A number of immigrants in the colonies would have been dissatisfied as a result of the treatment received from medical officers. It was common practice for medical men to discharge immigrants from hospital before they were completely cured, and to this may be attributed a large percentage of the so-called idleness charges which were brought before magistrates. By the strict letter of the law, an indentured immigrant was bound to do his daily task of work if he was not in hospital or in gaol, and although the magistrate had a discriminatory power of declining to convict, if he believed the accused was physically unable to work, it was difficult for him, on account of the alleged malingering propensity of the East Indians, to decide, other than in extreme cases, against the expressed opinion of the doctor.

The immigrants' perception of unfair dealing by the courts would also have encouraged repatriation. Of the majority of immigrants who were weekly committed to gaol for breaches of contract, a very considerable proportion was convicted of neglect to do what they were physically incapable of doing. Even pregnant women were liable to punishment for neglecting to perform the ordinary task of work despite that they pleaded their delicate condition in this respect, and were evidently, by their appearance, near their confinement. A sense of the injustice of such convictions was a very potent cause for the prevailing discontent amongst the immigrants.

Another cause for discontent was the fact that invidiously distinct positions in court were assigned to managers of estates. Some of them being Justices of the Peace were allowed to remain on the bench even during the trial of their own cases. It very often happened that a manager would in open court whisper to the presiding magistrate upon the subject of the case being tried and in which he was a complainant. Such behaviour would give the immigrants the impression of partiality even to a conscientious magistrate.

Finally, the East Indians experienced a social problem which would have persuaded a number of them to return to India. During the early days of immigration few of them were educated. The batches in which they came were described as "a leaderless mass which proved extremely difficult to absorb in the general life of the community."[69] They, however, were able to retain their religion, their social habits, and to some extent, their language. By comparison, the Negroes and their children who had experienced the barbarity of slavery had their culture and language destroyed and became "decivilized". The type of civilization to which their forefathers were accustomed in Africa was flogged out of them; therefore, they adopted the European civilization and language. On the other hand, the East Indians, with their mixture of castes and religions and their different languages and dialects, became narrow in outlook and less prone to become cosmopolitan. Moreover, their contractual terms created a mentality and an atmosphere amongst them of a mere temporary stay in the colonies. Consequently, the provision that colonial governments in the West Indies, for example, made for public education during the period of indenture tended to pass the Indian by. Of all the races in the various colonies, it was found that the East Indians experienced greatest difficulty in regarding themselves as West Indians; it is so even today, to a lesser extent.

Decision to Settle
Those who chose to settle in the colonies would have been motivated by one or more of the following factors. After ten years' residence among *jahaji bhais* (i.e. brothers of the boat, as indentured shipmates affectionately addressed one another) and sometimes among kith and kin, and new alliances, the nostalgia that would have afflicted the immigrants would have dissipated. In the early years of indenture, they would have experienced the trauma of a contraction in the field of social participation. But with every new wave of immigrants landed on the estates, that field would have expanded to encompass a growing social circle comprising little Indias. All of this would have eased the pressure of living in a foreign country.

At the end of the tenth year also, many labourers had acquired a family and built their own home and owned livestock and other property. Those who had renounced their right to repatriation through commutation of their entitlement to a free passage would have added to their material acquisitions the compensatory parcel of land. All of this would have placed them in a position of comparative wealth and comfort instead of the comparative uncertainty they would have had to face upon returning to India. Generally, living conditions in Indian villages from which most of the labourers had been recruited were not up to the standard of the conditions prevailing on the colonial estates, even as early as the 1840s. Wage rates, too, were far lower. In India, around the same time, the daily wage rate in terms of purchasing value was the equivalent of four cents; in the colonies, it ranged between the equivalent of thirty and forty cents. Furthermore, in India, the ryot had to contend with the vagaries of nature, often expressed in droughts and floods both of which often led to famine. There was also the rapacity of man – the moneylender or the landlord – both of whom utilized their cunning to bind their victims into a lifetime of debt.

Those labourers whose first indenture had expired had acquired five years' experience of their work; they would have become acquainted with their position in all its aspects; and would have been able to decide, according to their own practical knowledge, whether it would be advantageous for them to return to India or to remain in the colony.

For acclimatized and experienced labourers, there was competition among planters for their services. Many employers were not content with offering the usual fifty dollar bounty money to those who re-indentured, but also offered a bonus incentive of five and sometimes ten dollars. For the thrifty, this bounty money and the bonus, the equivalent of about a year's income, became the nucleus of a fortune. It was thus that a number of labourers were able to invest in cattle and become milk vendors,[70] and to open shops. To a number of labourers, re-indenturing would have been viewed as being better than the status of a free labourer as it was the only way to ensure free medical attention, free hospital accommodation, and free living quarters. The temptation for them to re-indenture over and over again must have proved irresistible.

Another possible motivation for settling concerned the implications accompanying the loss of caste. Before leaving India, the immigrants had been rigidly fixed in a stratified social system based on caste. But once they had crossed the *kala pani* (i.e. the black water) they lost all claim to their erstwhile caste, readmission to which was achievable either by travelling to the sacred Indian city of Benares to wash seven times in the holy water of the Ganges or by giving lavish caste dinners and elaborate gifts to often unscrupulous priests. Initially, the popular belief among the immigrants was that failure to thus cleanse themselves was to invite divine retribution. However, towards the end of the nineteenth century and afterwards, the injunction on travelling by sea was widely discredited, and it was not applicable to all strata of Hindu society.

The immigrants' ability to preserve their values and to practise their customs must be accorded considerable significance as a factor encouraging settlement in the colonies. Despite the pervasive and socially and culturally destructive influences of the plantations, the immigrants managed to keep intact the central tenets of their cultural values which in later years were given elaborate expression. This they achieved mainly through their strong desire to use their own languages and through their tenacity to resist imbibing Western civilization. The frequent visits by missionaries and other emissaries from India also tended to keep intact the umbilical cord that bound the immigrants to India. The practice of their culture, the availability of most of their native foodstuffs, the presence of a growing number of their compatriots, and the sight of masjids and mandirs on every estate must have made them feel, in a vicarious sort of way, that they were still in their homeland.

Of importance, too, was the British government's assurance to the immigrants and their descendants that an indispensable condition of a decision to settle in the colony was that "they would be in all respects free men, with privileges no whit inferior to those of any other class of British subjects resident in the colony."[71]

For a number of immigrants there was the fear of the long voyage to India occupying 100 days or more and often witnessing dozens of deaths. Chief among the causes for excessive mortality on board ship were the debilitated condition of some of the returnees; the deficiency of animal protein and fresh vegetables; and the damp condition between decks, which rendered the atmosphere unwholesome and conducive to disease.

Finally, there was widespread knowledge among the immigrants that suffering inevitably came to a sizeable proportion of those who repatriated, especially those who did not have or could not find relatives in their native villages. Often adding to this problem was the fear of ridicule and shame in India that usually accompanied an inability to demonstrate material progress.

Despite these restraining factors it must be observed that throughout the period of indenture, pressures had been brought to bear upon the British government, the government of India, and the colonial governments, most especially by the findings of various commissions of enquiry and by vociferous local and overseas critics, to enact protective legislation to safeguard the interest and welfare of the immigrants.[72] Legislative enactments did not, of course, completely eradicate all the evils in the system, but they did go a long way to alleviate some of the sufferings of the labourers, to make life in the colonies more tolerable, and consequentially encouraging a very large number of the immigrants to settle in the colonies.

* * * * *

The question that has often arisen is whether the indenture system in the sugar colonies had been necessary at all. The preference of the sugar planters for the system was rooted mainly in the nature of sugar cultivation. At a time when mechanical tillage, harvesting, and transporting were either non-existent or nascent, unless there was a labour force bound down to the plantations, especially at certain seasons, there was a risk of severe loss. For the larger colonies where sugar was "king", that is, where it was the dominant crop and the mainstay of the economy, the planter, banker, insurer, merchant, and shipowner were all concerned in the viability of the sugar estates; the professional man derived his maintenance from them; on them also, the labourer was dependent for his wages; and the petty shopkeeper or retail trader looked to the wage-earning class as a market for his goods. In short, while there were many divisions of labour, there was also a coincidence of interest. The maintenance of that interest after Emancipation became utterly dependent upon the Indian indentured labourers.

References

1. Des Voeux had been a Stipendiary Magistrate in British Guiana for five years before he was promoted Administrator of St. Lucia from where he wrote a long letter, from which this excerpt is taken, to the Secretary of State for the Colonies, Earl Granville. See *Report of the Commissioners Appointed to Enquire into the Treatment of Immigrants in British Guiana* (London, 1871), p. 2.
2. Robert M. Martin, *History of the Colonies of the British Empire* (London, reprinted ed., 1967), p. 124-26.
3. Hugh Tinker, *A New System of Slavery: The Export of Indian Labourers Overseas, 1830-1920* (London, 1974), p. 1.
4. Kenneth N. Bell and W.P. Morrell, eds., *Select Documents on British Colonial Policy, 1830-1860* (Oxford, 1928), p. 413.
5. Following a visit to the West Indies early in 1838 by Joseph Sturge, a Quaker philanthropist, and three of his colleagues to examine the Apprenticeship system, they edited and published *The Narrative of James Williams*. It was an account of the barbarous ill-treatment suffered by one apprentice, and they incorrectly concluded and alleged that this was typical of the punishment meted out to most offenders. Although Sturge's zeal outran his discretion, British public opinion was roused, and consequently, Parliament passed an Act to Amend the Abolition of Slavery Act, forbidding the punishment of female apprentices by flogging or on the treadmill. (The treadmill was a large hollow cylinder with a series of steps round the circumference. The person under punishment was required to tread on these steps, and as their weight caused the cylinder to revolve, they were compelled to hurry from step to step as the cylinder turned. As the cylinder turned rapidly, it became difficult to tread on the next step. Inevitably, the unfortunate person would fall. Both men and women who failed to catch the steps were often flogged).
6. Barton Premium, *Eight Years in British Guiana* (London, 1848), p. 17.
7. A. North-Coombes, *The Evolution of Sugar Cane Culture in Mauritius* (Port Louis, 1937), p. 11.
8. *Ibid.*
9. John Geoghegan, *Note on Emigration from India* (Calcutta, 1873), p. 2.
10. *Ibid.*
11. P.P., Vol. XVI, Session I (1841), p. 392.
12. G.W. Roberts and J. Byrne, "Summary Statistics on Indenture and Associated Migration Affecting the West Indies, 1834-1948," *Population Studies*, vol. XX, Pt. 1 (July, 1966), 125-34.
13. K. Hazareesingh, *A History of Indians in Mauritius* (Port Louis, 1950), pp. 28-40.
14. P.P., vol. XVI (1841), p. 149.
15. Edgar L. Erickson, "The Introduction of East Indian Coolies into the British West Indies," *The Journal of Modern History*, Vol. VI, No. 2 (June, 1934), 128.
16. C.O. 885/1. (Miscellaneous. No. XII). *Memorandum on the Hill Coolie Papers,*

1839; Dwarka Nath, *A History of Indians in British Guiana* (London, 1950), p. 21.
17 Nath, *Indians in British Guiana*, p. 16.
18 John Scoble, *Hill Coolies: A Brief Exposure of the Deplorable Conditions of the Hill Coolies in British Guiana and Mauritius* (London, 1839), p. 12.
19 See Erickson, "East Indian Coolies", pp. 12-33.
20 *The Times* (London), 29 July 1839.
21 See Great Britain, Parliament, *Parliamentary Debates* (House of Commons), 3rd ser., Vol. LX (3 February 1842 – 3 March 1842), p. 1322.
22 Hazareesingh, *Indians in Mauritius*, p. 35.
23 Allan Young, *Some Milestones in Village History, 1839-1956*. A series of six radio talks (Georgetown, 1957), p. 2.
24 James Rodway, "Labour and Colonization," *Timehri*, VI(1919), 27.
25 Alan H. Adamson, *Sugar Without Slaves: The Political Economy of British Guiana, 1838-1904* (New Haven, 1972), p. 163.
26 W.L. Burn, *The British West Indies* (London, 1951), p. 127.
27 Panchanan Saha, *Emigration of Indian Labour, 1834-1900* (Delhi, 1970), p. 9.
28 Premium, *British Guiana*, p. 30.
29 C.O. 884/1. (W.I. No. II). *Results of the Evidence as Exhibiting the Character of the Negro in Respect of Industry and the Conduct to be expected from him as a Free Agent*, n.d.
30 Parliamentary Accounts and Papers. XXXIV. 30 July 1838.
31 *Ibid*.
32 P.P. Vol. XXXVII (1840), p. 459. See also D.W.D. Comins, *Note on Emigration from India to British Guiana* (Calcutta, 1893), p. 5.
33 Everard F. Im Thurn, *Among the Indians of Guiana* (London, 1883), reprinted New York, 1967), pp. 227-54.
34 W.H. Brett, *Indian Missions in Guiana* (London, 1851), p. 230.
35 *Ibid*.
36 Mary Noel Menezes, *British Policy Towards the Amerindians in British Guiana, 1803-1873* (Oxford, 1977), p. 190.
37 Saha, *Emigration of Indian Labour*, p. 12.
38 D.W.D. Comins, *Note on Emigration from the East Indies to St. Lucia* (Calcutta, 1893), p. 3.
39 P.P., vol. XXXV (1844). p. 316; Comins, *St. Lucia*, p. 3.
40 David Chanderbali, "Sir Henry Light: A Study of Protection and Paternalism." (M.A. dissertation, University of Guyana, 1977), p. 212 ff.
41 Mary Noel Menezes, *Scenes from the History of the Portuguese in Guyana* (London, 1986), p. 9.
42 *The Royal Gazette*, Friday, 5 September 1839.
43 Donald Wood, *Trinidad in Transition: The Years after Slavery* (London, 1968), p. 68.
44 D.W.D. Comins, *Note on Emigration from India to Trinidad* (Calcutta, 1893), p. 3.

45 Papers Relative to the West Indies. *Report of the Agent General on the Prospects of Emigration from the Antilles to British Guiana,* 19 November 1841.
46 *Ibid.*
47 K.O. Laurence, *Immigration into the West Indies in the Nineteenth Century* (Kingston, 1971), p. 13. See also Fred H. Hitchins, *The Colonial Land and Emigration Commission* (Philadelphia, 1931), p. 245 ff.
48 George R. Mellor, *British Imperial Trusteeship, 1738-1850* (London, 1951), p. 193.
49 Graham Cruickshank, "African Immigrants after Freedom," *Timehri,* VI (1919), 84.
50 Cumpston, *Indians Overseas,* p. 55.
51 Laurence, *Immigration into the West Indies,* p. 15.
52 Parliamentary Accounts and Papers. 1871. Vol. XX, para. 325.
53 *Ibid.*
54 P.P. vol. XXXV (1844), p. 551.
55 See Saha, *Emigration of Indian Labour,* p. 16; Hitchins, *Emigration Commission,* p. 224 ff.
56 J.H. Parry and P.M. Sherlock, *A Short History of the West Indies* (London, 1965), p. 198.
57 Parliamentary Accounts and Papers. XXXIV, p. 169.
58 *Ibid.*
59 Parry and Sherlock, *History of West Indies,* pp. 195-96.
60 *Ibid.,* p. 193.
61 Bell and Morrell, *Select Documents,* p. 413.
62 Cumpston, *Indians Overseas,* p. 38.
63 P.P. Vol. XXXVII (1840), p. 459.
64 Brij V. Lal, "Fiji Girmitiyas: The Background to Banishment," in Vijay Mishra, ed., *Rama's Banishment: A Centenary Tribute to the Fiji Indians, 1879-1979* (Auckland, 1979), pp. 12-13.
65 Shiu Prasad, *Indian Indentured Workers in Fiji* (Suva, 1975), p. 1.
66 Lal, "Fiji Girmitiyas," p. 12.
67 Prasad, *Indian Workers in Fiji,* p. 2; Lal, "Fiji Girmitiyas," p. 13.
68 Geoghegan, *Emigration from India,* pp. 66-67.
69 Parry and Sherlock, *History of the West Indies,* p. 37.
70 *Appendices to the Report on the Treatment of Immigrants in British Guiana.* Part II (London, 1871), p. 68.
71 Parliamentary Accounts and Papers. 1871. Vol. XX, para. 537.
72 See, for example, Appendix I.

II

CONFLICTING INTERPRETATIONS OF INDIAN INDENTURE

> Slavery is a word which has been very loosely used in recent years, but the original definition included a complete surrender of personal liberty, the absence of right to a wage for labour given, and for generations in many parts of the world an unrestricted power over the person of the slave. The indenture system in the British Colonies cannot be said to impose these limitations; liberty is considerably restricted, it is true; the wages in several of the colonies are inadequate; punishments are administered with deplorable frequency; but granting there is a certain amount of deception, the coolie enters into the indenture with no more compulsion than unfortunate circumstances impose.
>
> John H. Harris[1]

Before Indian indenture was finally terminated in 1920 and afterwards, a wide variety of views were expressed on the system. For the sake of convenience, these views may be classified into two major divisions of interpretation. The first school of thought expresses an essentially favourable opinion of the indenture system. It emphasizes mainly the economic, moral and social progress made by the immigrants and their descendants, while underestimating the abuses and oppression perpetrated against them. The second grouping adopts quite the opposite opinion arguing that indenture was an inhumane and degrading system akin to slavery. A comprehensive review of indenture or of its historiography is not within the scope of this part of the work. The main aim here is to cite a number of views that exemplify each of the classifications, and at the same time, to provide some background information and the milieu in which the views were expressed.

Favourable Impressions
One of the earliest known favourable views was expressed by Dr. M.F. Mout, Inspector of Jails in Bengal, and formerly Professor of Medicine at the Calcutta Medical College. In 1852, he wrote:

> When carefully managed, as I know them from personal observation to be both in Bourbon now Reunion and Mauritius, they are far better off than in their own homes. They leave India full of prejudices, utterly ignorant, and as low in the scale of humanity as it is possible to imagine such beings to be. They acquire in their transmarine experience habits of thought and independence, a knowledge of im-

proved means of cultivation, a taste for a higher order of amusements, a greater pride of personal appearance, and an approach to manliness of character rarely if ever seen in the same class in their native villages.[2]

Of the indentured labourers in British Guiana, the Governor in 1864, Sir Francis Hincks, had this to say: "It must be borne in mind with regard ... to the Indian Coolies that the number of those who do very well and save considerable sums of money are only a small percentage of the aggregate body of immigrants. Their accumulations too are not always the result of steady industry."[3] Such accumulations were often derived with the assistance of proceeds accruing from self-employment of which, a contemporary writer in the colony said, cattle rearing and milk vending were the most commonly remunerative.[4] It should be noted that although Hincks' observation gives only tangential support to the sanguine view of indenture, at least, it suggests that some immigrants did derive some measure of benefit as a consequence of the indenture system.

Of the indentured Indians in Trinidad, an English priest, Canon Kingsley, is reported in 1871 to have said: "Their location in the West Indies presents favourable opportunities for aiding their advancement into civilization, bringing them under good influences, and breaking down superstition and caste."[5] Also on the Trinidad Indians, Surgeon-Major D.W.D. Comins, the Protector of Emigrants stationed at the port of Calcutta, who was commissioned to investigate the conditions of the immigrants in that colony in 1891, reported to the government of India thus:

> In this colony Indian coolies have already very exceptional advantages, and a still brighter future is before them. Of all the colonies of the West Indies Trinidad is the favoured home of the coolie settler, where he can easily and rapidly attain comfortable independence and even considerable wealth with corresponding social position.[6]

Comins was also commissioned to enquire into the conditions of Indian immigrants in British Guiana where after spending some time in the colony in 1891, he wrote:

> No one who knows the Indian coolie well can fail to be struck by the great difference between the coolie in India and his children born in the colony. Whatever be the cause, whether change of climate, better food, easy times, more responsible duties or position, the influence of travel, or freedom from the narrowness of caste prejudice, the result is very apparent. The children born in the colony of Indian parents revert to a higher type of civilization, and in appearance, manners and intelligence are so much superior to their parents that it is difficult to believe they belong to the same family. The boys and young men are stronger and better looking, and are able to turn their hand to anything at a moment's notice, with a smartness and knowledge of the world which would vastly astonish their grand parents in India; while the girls and young women have a beauty and refinement rarely seen in public in India, many having all the appearance of good birth and breeding usually associated only with families of the best blood.[7]

Despite the foregoing reports, around the turn of the century, public opinion both in India and Britain was becoming more aware of the conditions Indians suffered abroad. News of their oppression in South Africa solidified Indian opinion against indenture, and won greater support for Mahatma Gandhi's struggle. In Mauritius, Manilal Maganlall Doctor arrived in 1907 to practise at the bar and soon joined the struggle for Indian rights.

In the colonies where there was a substantial creole population, there was opposition to indenture mainly because the creoles considered it unfair to tax them to finance the importation of immigrants who would compete with them for employment, social services and so on. This attitude deserves some comment. The necessity for Indian immigration arose from the unwillingness of the ex-slaves to work regularly, and it seems only reasonable that they should be required to contribute towards the restoration of prosperity by means of labour other than their own. Further, the extension of sugar-cane cultivation resulting from increased Indian immigration created a demand for those desultory and well-paid services which many of them were unwilling to render. Admitting, therefore, that on the one hand, the creoles were taxed for the maintenance of immigration, it must also be conceded, on the other, that through Indian immigration, and that alone, they had become possessed of the means to pay such taxes. Black working men's associations, however, were formed in several of the larger West Indian colonies with the specific purpose of opposing Indian immigration. In British Guiana, a black people's association vehemently opposed the taxation levied to promote immigration.

In this atmosphere, the Sanderson Committee was appointed in 1909 by the Secretary of State for the Colonies, the Earl of Crewe, to enquire into (a) the general question of emigration from India to the Crown colonies; (b) the particular colonies in which Indian immigration may be most usefully encouraged; and (c) the general advantages to be reaped in each case – (i) by India itself; (ii) and by each particular colony.[8] The Sanderson Committee did not visit any of the colonies but sat in London and took evidence from eighty-three witnesses, the majority of whom, the British Anti-Slavery and Aborigines Society claimed, had "financial interests at stake".[9] The Committee published its report in 1910, a decade before indenture ended. A part of the report reads:

> It may be confidently stated that as a general rule the immigrants in all the colonies to which they go improve in health, strength and independence of character …. These results, even though they may affect only a fractional portion of the vast population of India, cannot be regarded otherwise than with satisfaction.[10]

The Committee did not intend these assertions to refer specifically to Indians still under indenture; they were principally applicable to those Indians who remained in the colonies after the expiration of their indentures, either as small proprietors or as free labourers, and also to the second and third generations.[11] The Committee added:

> The close of this portion of our Report offers the most suitable opportunity for some observations on the imputation which is still at times advanced, that the system of indentured labour, as established for Indian immigrants into the British Colonies,

partakes of the nature of slavery. Our unhesitating opinion, after examining the best and most authoritative evidence that we could obtain on the subject, is that, whatever abuses may have existed in the more remote past, no such charge can be substantiated against the system as it at present exists and has been in practice during the last 20 or 30 years.[12]

The Sanderson Committee's Report was read by Gopal Krishna Gokhale, the moderate Indian nationalist leader and newly appointed leader of the Imperial Legislative Council of India, who drew upon it to denounce the indenture system. The terms of reference directing the inquiry of the Committee, Gokhale contended, had invited its members to approach the question of Indian immigration from the standpoint of how the system should be maintained and extended. That being so, he asserted, whatever was against indenture was more or less lost sight of and whatever was in favour of the system was prominently brought forward. Other Indian politicians, moderate and extreme alike, openly disagreed with the conclusions contained in the Sanderson Committee's Report. They asserted that the indenture system, which they did not hesitate to call by the name of slavery, had branded their whole race in the eyes of the British colonial empire with the stigma of helotry.

Following the publication of the Sanderson Report, Gokhale and his fellow politicians made frequent and clamorous calls through numerous petitions and resolutions for the immediate abolition of the indenture system. Their exhortations went unheeded, though in 1913 the government of India commissioned James McNeill, a British Officer of the Indian Civil Service, and Chimman Lal, a young Indian businessman and honorary magistrate, to enquire into the conditions of Indian immigrants in Trinidad, British Guiana, Jamaica, and Fiji, and the Dutch colony of Surinam (Dutch Guiana).

Like the Sanderson Committee, the McNeill-Chimman Lal Commission did not advocate the abolition of the indenture system. But an inexplicable delay in the circulation of their report aroused suspicion in the minds of Indian politicians that the report contained material damaging to the system. This seems far from reality as the Commission's conclusive view of indenture illustrates.

> The great majority of emigrants exchanged grinding poverty with practically no hope of betterment for a condition varying from simple but secure comfort to solid prosperity. Emigrants live under very much better conditions than their relatives in India, and have had opportunities of prospering which exceeded their own wildest hopes. They became citizens of the colonies to which they emigrated and both they and their descendants have attained to positions commanding general respect and consideration.[13]

Around the same time the McNeill-Chimman Lal Report was published, Governor Henry May, of Fiji, asserted: "The introduction of Indian indentured labour into Fiji has been, and continues to be, an inestimable boon to this country, and a great benefit to a large number of the population of India".[14]

Finally, in 1919, one year before Indian indenture was finally terminated, the Indian Section of the Imperial Colonization Deputation of British Guiana[15] visited New Delhi to present to the government of India a scheme for the further colonization of the territory by Indian agricultural families[16]. In referring to the status and prospects of the indentured labourers already in the colony, the Deputation said:

> We must, however, mention that ... the treatment meted out to Indians was better in British Guiana than that given them any where else. They are better, safer, happier and more prosperous there than those residing in other parts of the world, and even we venture to say in India itself. It may well be to mention that in the social and religious aspects Indians enjoy perfect freedom. Their general ideas in these respects are somewhat more westernized than in India. All children in the Colony are entitled to receive free and compulsory education.
>
> No barrier of any kind is erected against Indians in British Guiana – as is the case in Natal, South Africa etc. Here they enjoy equal rights and privileges in the truest sense of the words.[17]

No one who is acquainted with the historiography of Indians overseas can deny that indentured migration had not been an attractive palliative for many poor, dispossessed, and uprooted Indians. But those commentators like Comins who propagated the sanguine view of indenture had only emphasized the humane, paternalistic, and advantageous dimensions of the system, and failed to recognize the degradation and privations the beneficiaries had to endure before they could attain a modicum of material prosperity. The comparison made between the economic and social progress achieved by the immigrants and their descendants in the colonies and the position of their kinsmen and compatriots in India must be viewed with considerable skepticism. In India, kinship support and material and intangible public charity were ready to cushion personal calamities; whereas in the colonies, the immigrants were thrown more or less on their own devices and resources; and in order to fulfil their objectives as immigrants they naturally became acquisitive. The absence of an established community and of kinsfolk, especially in the earlier years, would have emphasized their relative loneliness and aggravated their sense of alienation. These are only a few concomitant costs of Indian indenture. They must be weighed against the undeniable benefits derived from the system before an objective appraisal can be made.

Contemporary Unfavourable Views
The contemporary unfavourable opinions expressed on Indian indenture subscribed to the contrary interpretation that the system was simply just another version of slavery. A cautionary remark here is called for. The views expressed by critics such as certain Christian missionaries and members of reformist groups like the British Anti-Slavery Society must necessarily be taken with due reservation because their commitment and determination to agitate against the system would have naturally inclined them to highlight its darkest aspects. Let us now peruse the uncomplimentary views.

In Mauritius, despite evidence of some care for the welfare of the indentured labourers on the part of both the Governor of the colony and the government of India,[18] the private importation of Indians between 1834 and 1838 attracted trenchant denunciation from several quarters. Commenting on the charge that the immigrants were "objects of mercantile speculation and profit", the Acting Senior Magistrate of Police in Bombay wrote in 1837 thus:

> The deportation of Indian labourers is a measure open, I fear to great abuses, for I have been credibly informed, there are instances of coolies, who agreeing at Calcutta to proceed to Mauritius on Fixed engagements have nevertheless on their arrival there, been transferred to the higher bidders; that in short the practice has to a certain degree, been converted into profitable speculation.[19]

Of this early traffic, too, the *Bombay Gazette* of 15 June 1838 reported:

> These poor deluded men are seduced from their homes under the pretext of an engagement. They are shipped off to their destination, and from that moment they are more under the domination of the taskmaster than if they had been born in slavery. They are carried to a colony in which slavery has been abolished, and they become slaves.

Another newspaper, the *Bengal Hurkaru*, in its edition of 17 August 1838, quoted from a letter written by the captain of an emigrant ship, the *Earl Clare*, thus:

> Now come the misery of those creatures, they have no idea but that the voyage will be the same as sailing on the Ganges, and generally ships are crammed almost to suffocation, and many , I believe, have barely standing room below for them. The officer's receipt for the number is given, and then the commander of the vessel is called on to sign a bill of lading for so many heads running in the usual form, 'shipped in good order and well conditioned' etc. and to be delivered at the aforesaid port of Mauritius in like good manner. This, I think becomes something near akin to slavery.

Likewise, *The Times* of London branded the traffic to Mauritius and British Guiana a "novel abomination" and "a new slave trade."[20] Such reports having aroused the attention of the British Anti-Slavery Society who, suspicious of the character of this new movement of labour, delegated its secretary, John Scoble, to make enquiries in the two colonies. Having done so, Scoble concluded that "the whole business was nothing short of systematic kidnapping."[21]

In Mauritius itself, the government appointed a Commission, comprising four local British officials, ostensibly to enquire into these charges. But the actual terms of reference required them to ascertain whether the Indian labourers were satisfied with the manner in which their employers were complying with the terms of their indenture; whether they had any grievances over the quality and quantity of food provided; and if the payment of stipulated wages was regularly made.[22] The enquiry was, however, impeded. The magistrate of each district disregarded instructions to assist the commissioners in their enquiry. Furthermore, because of the language barrier, there was no effective communication between the commissioners and the immigrants. However, the Commission was able to admit unanimously that many immigrants had been deceived as to their terms of contract, some having been told they were going to do gardening. The Commission also agreed that "contracts generally speaking were not fulfilled by planters; they had been literally fulfilled in no instance, and no money wages at all seem to have been paid in the majority of instances."[23]

The majority of the commissioners, while pointing out some injustices, did not pass any severe strictures on the planters. But one of them, Mr. Special Justice Charles Anderson, made very unpleasant remarks at almost every point of the enquiry, which were not included in the report. Anderson, however, wrote separately to the Secretary of State for the Colonies, Lord Glenelg, in a letter dated 18 November 1838, charging:

> With a few exceptions, the immigrants were treated with great and unjust severity by overwork and by personal chastisement; their lodgings were either too confined and disgustingly filthy, or none were provided for them; and in case of sickness, the most culpable neglect was evinced in withholding the accommodation, advice and attendance which the utter helplessness of the sufferer so urgently required.[24]

Echoing some of these defective aspects of indenture, one member of the British House of Commons stated that the "emigrants were deceived and misled by the duffadars[25] and robbed of their advances in India; ... at the Mauritius they were prevented by fear from complaining of the bad usage they received; ... no attention was paid to their comforts, and no consideration shown for their prejudices".[26] Another member added: "No doubt, in some cases they had been treated as slaves".[27]

Finally, Lord Stanley, who but a year before in 1841 had succeeded Lord Russell as Secretary of State for the Colonies and who had favoured Indian immigration, made the following observation: "This agreement (i.e. the indenture) was made on the part of private individuals for their private interest, and the consequence of this unjust and fraudulent mode of proceeding was, that the labourer was often a virtual slave in the Mauritius during the five years for which he was contracted."[28]

It will be recalled that Indian indentured migration was suspended in Mauritius in 1839 and resumed there in 1842 and in the West Indies in 1845 under an officially regulated and supervised system. Of this new arrangement, Sir Lindsay Darcy[29] observed: "Despite the precautions abuses grew up".[30] This observation was amplified by the Under-Secretary to the government of India, John Geoghegan, who wrote as follows:

> Broadly it may be said to have proved that very grave abuses had prevailed in India, emigrants having been in too many cases, entrapped by force and fraud, and systematically plundered of nearly six months wages, nominally advanced to them, but really divided, on pretences more or less transparent, among the predacious crew engaged in the traffic ... some of the ship captains engaged in the traffic were, from brutality or apathy of character, little fitted for the charge of coolies.[31]

In the late 1860s, Edward Jenkins, an English barrister delegated by the British Anti-Slavery Society and the Aborigines Protection Society visited British Guiana. Afterwards, Jenkins wrote copiously filling two sizeable volumes entitled *The Coolie: His Rights and Wrongs* which was published in 1871. Even some of his bitter critics recognized that the author's intention was to convince his readers that many evils attended the indenture system in British Guiana, which he felt fully bound to examine and expose. Of the Indian labourers on the Guiana plantations Jenkins wrote: "Socially he is not only a labourer, he is a bondsman ... he is not free to come and go, to work and rest, as he pleases."[32] He added: "I should be sorry to see any people so successfully degraded as to sit down quietly under disadvantages so monstrous."[33]

In October of the same year the author of a pamphlet writing under the pseudonym "West Indian" believed that some of Jenkins' allegations against the indenture system had been grossly exaggerated, and that others, to which an invidious prominence had been given, could be reasonably explained. "West Indian" wished it to be distinctly understood that he was not writing as the representative of any body or any interest and that he was writing out of his own knowledge of indenture in the colony. In a vicious attack on Jenkins' book, "West Indian" contended it contained "much grotesque sensationalism and spurious sentiment, many baseless insinuations and misrepresented facts."[34] He further claimed that the philanthropy of the two Societies that Jenkins represented was based upon the assumption that whenever whites employed coloureds, the latter were necessarily treated with injustice and oppression, and made to suffer in proportion to the degree of their colour. Evidence has not been found of any rebuttals by Jenkins, but he had emphatically boasted his dispassionate approach during his enquiry and an impartial judgment in expressing his views on the system. Curiously, Jenkins' views coincided almost exactly with those of a colonial official who was employed in the colony at the time of his own visit – Chief Justice Beaumont.

One of the more telling critics of Indian indenture in British Guiana was Joseph Beaumont, the colony's Chief Justice from 1863 to 1868. He was popularly known for his impartiality in the administration of justice and he consistently maintained a fearless independence of the local plantocracy. What angered the ruling class most was Beaumont's disregard of what had apparently come to be accepted by the courts as a settled principle, viz. that when "the evidence of 'white' and 'coloured' was opposed, that of the 'white' must necessarily prevail."[35] Beaumont's refusal to be partisan to this principle resulted in his dismissal in August 1868 upon a recommendation by the Judicial Committee of the Privy Council. But in the opinion of the Secretary of State for the colonies, Lord Edward Cardwell, the allegations against Beaumont were insufficient to sustain such a proceeding as the suspension of a judge. Beaumont was reinstated, and because he continued his policy of impartiality he was removed from office towards the end of 1868. Upon his return to England, he wrote *The New Slavery: An Account of the Indian and Chinese Immigrants in British Guiana* in which he denounced the suffering and mortality among the Indian immigrants in what may be considered language of violent exaggeration. One of his famous views on Indian indenture reads:

> This is not a question of more or less, of this or that safeguard, of an occasional defect here, or excess there. But it is that of a monstrous, rotten system, rooted upon slavery, grown in its stale soil, emulating its worst abuses, and only the more dangerous because it presents itself under false colours, whereas slavery bore the brand of infamy upon its forehead.[36]

This view was based upon Beaumont's own observations some of which are as follows:

> Practically an Immigrant is in the hands of the employer to whom he is bound. He cannot leave him; he cannot live without work; he can only get such work and on

such terms as the employer chooses to set him; and all these necessities are enforced, not only by the inevitable influence of his isolated and dependent position but by the terrors of imprisonment and the prospect of losing both favour and wages.[37]

In Trinidad, the indentured Indians were tarred by the ex-slaves with the brush of slavery because of, *inter alia*, their subjection to the Vagrancy Laws. Author Bridget Brereton wrote that only the Indians were required to carry "passes" when off the estates. In 1873, this indignity provoked the common taunt: "Slave, where is your free paper?"[38] The author remarked: "To the African, indentureship was no different from slavery".[39]

Early in the twentieth century, criticism of indenture heightened, partly because of rising Indian nationalism following the founding of the Indian National Congress in 1885, and partly because of the availability of a larger number of first hand accounts of the condition and treatment of the immigrants in the various colonies through improved communication.

One of the more notable early twentieth century critics who monitored the indenture system with the utmost vigilance was Gopal Krishna Gokhale, the moderate Indian nationalist leader. In the Imperial Legislative Council of India in 1912, Gokhale often denounced indenture as being inherently wrong and objectionable, and asserted that because the safeguards were illusory and ineffective, there was appalling human misery and frightful immorality among indentured Indians in the various colonies. He once concluded thus:

> The contract is not a free contract. You have here the right of private arrest, just as they had in the case of slavery. Moreover, the labourer is bound to his employer for five years and he cannot withdraw from the contract during that period. And there are those harsh punishments for trivial faults. Therefore, though the system cannot be called actual slavery, it is really not far removed from it.[40]

In the South Pacific colony of Fiji, Walter Gill, an overseer who had once been employed by the Colonial Sugar Refining Company, an Australian enterprise, wrote thus: "The indenture they signed was for five years' slavery in the cane fields of his Britannic Majesty's Crown Colony of Fiji – to them it was a *girmit*, an agreement – and it contained some of the most pernicious clauses thought up by man."[41]

Similarly, in his slim monograph entitled *Indentured Labour: Is it Slavery?* H.E. Holland described the Indian indentured labourers in Fiji as "bond slaves, herded in compounds."[42] Likewise, the Rev. J.W. Burton, an Australian Methodist missionary who had spent several years in the colony, wrote in 1910:

> The life on the plantations to an ordinary indentured coolie is not of a very inviting character. The difference between the state he now finds himself in and absolute slavery is merely in the name and term of years. The chances are that as a slave he would be both better housed and better fed than he is to-day. The coolie themselves for the most part, frankly call it narak (hell). Not only are the wages low, the tasks hard, and the food scant, but it is an entirely different life from that to which they have been accustomed, and they chafe, especially at first, at the bondage.[43]

In K.L. Gillion's *Fiji's Indian Migrants*, which is generally regarded as one of the best balanced interpretations of Indian indenture, the author finds Burton's writing "highly emotive", but he himself admits: "Still, Burton's impressionistic picture was closer than the official portrait to the truth of life, if not to the statistics and the statutes."[44]

The Indian National Congress viewed with grave concern the degradation of the status and rights of indentured Indians in the colonies and the consequent smear on the *izzat* (i.e. honour and self respect) of all Indians. Congress began to oppose indenture by passing numerous resolutions. The first of these moved at Karachi in 1913 and again at Madras in 1914 reads: "That owing to the scarcity of labour in India and the grave results from the system of indentured labour, which reduces the labourers, during the period of indenture, practically to the position of slaves, this Congress strongly urges the total prohibition of recruitment of labour under indenture."[45] This resolution was re-affirmed at Bombay in 1915. In the same year, Lord Hardinge, then Viceroy of India, said: "For Indian politicians, moderate and extreme alike, consider that the existence of this system, which they do not hesitate to call by the name of slavery, brands their whole race in the eyes of the British Colonial Empire with the stigma of helotry."[46]

Around 1918, the Rev. C.F. Andrews joined other Christian missionaries and critics to register a scathing attack on the indenture system. In 1917, his deep sympathy for the degraded and oppressed labourers in Fiji had earned him the respectful and affectionate title of "Deenabandhu" – friend of the humble. Andrews became particularly critical of the moral aspects of indenture after witnessing the cramped conditions in the labourers' dwellings; of the moral degradation engendered by the paucity of marriageable females; and of the consequential fragile family life. His published findings on Fiji, Andrews contended, had not been controverted even by the most ardent advocate of the system. He wrote:

> The semi-servile existence of the indentured labourers on the plantations led to moral evils which were hardly less than those connected with the fraudulent means by which they often were recruited. Though admirable regulations were made to prevent abuses, the faults inherent in the system were so great that it could not be radically reformed. To give one glaring instance, the proportion of men to women was roughly three to one. As a result, sexual crimes were frequent, and murders, followed by suicide, were terribly common.[47]

For his enquiry into the recruiting system, Andrews collected evidence through interviews with indentured labourers and colonial government officials in Fiji and British Guiana. Consequently, he wrote: "Allowing for every exaggeration on the part of the illiterates there can be no doubt that the frauds practised by recruiting agents have been immense". The recruiter (or *arkati*), he asserted, "becoming a man of power carries the exercise of his authority far beyond the limits of recruiting. He becomes not seldom a blackmailer whom the villagers actually bribe to live in peace."

In 1918, Florence E. Garnham, of the London Missionary Society, Calcutta, was chosen by the Combined Women's Organization of Australasia to enquire into the moral conditions of the Indian community in Fiji. In her report Garnham wrote:

> This utter abandonment of morals is unfortunately not confined to the adult section of the community. I have heard little children speak of things which showed

an appalling knowledge of vice of the worst kind. Children over three years of age, whose mothers are working on the plantations are quite uncared for as a rule, while the parents are at work. This neglect of childhood is one of the gravest features of life in the lines.[48] It is scarcely to be wondered, in the circumstances, that Australian women in charge of the Methodist Mission Orphanage find that tiny children brought to them show a knowledge of evil that is exceedingly difficult to counteract.[49]

A sum total of the foregoing views leaves a distinct impression. By dwelling at length on the unusual hardships and deep humiliation the labourers endured on the plantations, there is a suggestion that the majority of labourers derived little, if any, economic and social benefits from their indenture. This interpretation is indefensible as any objective reading of the documentary evidence would show. It appears that deep sympathy for the immigrants had often combined with a ready acceptance of impressionistic evidence to give cogent exposition to the view that indenture was simply another version of slavery. This appraisal embraces a number of facile assumptions and fails to recognize the nature of the significant differences between the two systems.

The Views of Modern Analysts

The hostile opinions expressed by the contemporary observers have been more or less confirmed by a number of modern researchers. To pre-empt any criticism of the selection of the following views an explanation is offered. Individual historical studies on Indian indenture are available for most major overseas Indian communities. Some such, as those for British Guiana, Trinidad, Jamaica, and Fiji, are scholarly and sophisticated, while for others such as Mauritius and Natal surprisingly less so. For yet others such as Surinam, St. Lucia, Guadeloupe, and Martinique, serious historical research is still in its infancy. With this understanding, let us now turn to the views of modern analysts.

Under the pseudonym "Emigrant", a writer of unknown nationality and ethnic belonging, expressed his view on indenture in 1924 as follows:

> Its achievements in the Colonies varied, but nowhere gave complete satisfaction. It was handicapped by the desire of the employer to secure an adequate supply of labour at a minimum cost and for the maximum period that effort or ingenuity could secure, and the inadequacy of mere persuasion to change self-interest into humanitarian altruism.[50]

In British Guiana, Peter Ruhoman, a retired Indo-Guianese civil servant, believed that the moral blemish of indenture had not only denied the Indians "the opportunity of releasing the full stature of a decent and upright manhood, but which rather vitiated their minds and prevented the free development of their moral being".[51] This he attributed to the planters' almost total neglect of the moral welfare of the labourers because they were "generally regarded as a machine capable of exerting so much power for certain ends".[52]

N. Gangulee wrote in his historical survey of Indians in the British Empire, thus: "Since plantation economy could not function without some means of assuring the labour supply, the European planters ... adopted a 'semi-servile' system of indenture .... Thus a new 'species of colonial bondage' arose out of the abolition of slavery; and its yoke came to fall upon the neck of the Indian labourer."[53]

In his work published in 1960, *Involuntary Labour Since the Abolition of Slavery*, W. Kloosterboer makes this observation:

> The system of (Indian) contract labour, no matter how reasonable in theory ... led to most unfavourable results in practice. The many serious abuses connected with the recruiting, with the treatment in the colonies, and with the practices after the completion of the contract period made of the system a real plague for many years, and with penal sanctions gave it a marked aspect of compulsory labour.[54]

Ahmed Ali, an Indo-Fijian, agreed that although the comments above referred specifically to indenture in the West Indies and Mauritius, they were equally applicable to *girmit*, as the system in Fiji was termed. Ali's own evaluation reads: "The labourers' sojourn on the plantation was traumatic, destabilizing and disorienting .... *Girmit* for those who migrated was an inevitable purgatory towards an earthly paradise."[55] He added: "*Girmit* was part of the contradiction of human existence, where neither good nor evil is total, but where pain, suffering and joy engage in a contest out of which emerges profit and loss and the struggle for survival."[56]

In K. Hazareesingh's study of indenture in Mauritius, he confirmed reports presented earlier herein that despite the protective agencies in India, the immigrants had been "'entrapped' through fraudulent means".[57] Another writer on indenture in Mauritius, S.B. Mookherji, asserted with supporting evidence that it was an "iniquitous system". "To all intents and purposes," he added, indenture was "the old wine of slavery in a new bottle with a new label. [It was] slavery preserved in pickles."[58]

K.L. Chattopadhyay, an Indian professor who published a series of newspaper articles written by his compatriot, Dwarkanath Ganguli, in *The Bengalee* from September 1886 to April 1887, wrote in 1972 of the Indian indentured labourers in the plantations of Assam in the north-east of India thus:

> Though slavery as an institution was unknown to the laws in British India, it came into this country through the backdoor under the name of Contract-labour or the Indentured system. Slavery assumed a peculiar form when the indigo-planters began the practice of giving the people forced advances for production, thus virtually converting them into slaves.[59]

Ganguli himself wrote: "The position of the labourers in many tea-gardens [of Assam] is almost as bad, if it is not worse than the condition of the American Negro slaves before their emancipation."[60]

The slavery thesis finds the most cogent expression and comprehensive treatment in Hugh Tinker's *A New System of Slavery: The Export of Indian Labour Overseas, 1830-1920* published in 1974. Tinker reveals the deception practised by unscrupulous recruiters on the recruits; he exposes the perfunctory supervision of emigration procedures in the depots at Calcutta and Madras; he unveils distressing mortality rates on board the emigrant ships and on the colonial plantations; he elaborately illustrates the helplessness of the immigrants which he claims was compounded by their ignorance and timidity and reinforced by the distant and often rudimentary hand of justice; he lays bare the degradation and brutalization of the labourers; and he dwells at length on the scandalously common occurrences of sickness and mortality among them. Tinker has also produced a mass of documentary evidence to support his contention that although the governments of Britain, India, and the colonies had instituted a variety of protective measures, the indenture system was slavery in a new guise but for one basic difference: whereas slavery was a permanent institution bonding the slave for life, indenture was a transitory evil limited by the duration of the contract. Tinker concludes:

> The Blacks on the West Indian plantations were known as chattel slaves; the dictionary defines a chattel as a 'moveable possession', and such an ascription is also appropriate to the condition of the Indian coolies, the successors to the chattel slaves. With the legal termination of slavery, there came no end to bondage upon the tropical plantations.[61]

Maureen Tayal, a descendant of indentured Indians of South Africa, believed that the experience of the immigrants in Natal fitted the general pattern which emerged from Tinker's research. She added: "Dislocated from a familiar existence, and subjugated to a labour coercive system in which there was little room for even such basic human comforts as family life, the conditions for agricultural indentured labourers in Natal were generally harsh at best and inhumane at worst."[62]

George Lamming, the distinguished West Indian writer, summarized his impressions of the system as follows:

> Indentured labour was bound labour. It was deprived of all mobility and was therefore condemned to provide that reliability of service a crop like sugar demanded. The planter class, with the full permission of the metropolitan power, had given itself the legal right to deploy this labour as it pleased …. What the ruling class could not acquire by the normal play of market forces had now been appropriated through legal sanctions. Indentured Indian labour was enslaved by the tyranny of the law that decided their relations to the land where they walked, and worked and slept.[63]

Finally, in an address entitled *Roots and Reminders: Reflections on Slavery, Indenture, Apartheid – and Some Personal Conjunctures* delivered to the Commonwealth Society of India on 20 January 1986 at New Delhi's India International Centre, Sir Shridath Ramphal, once the Commonwealth Secretary General and himself a descendant of Guyanese indentured foreparents, described his findings on Indian indenture thus:

> For three-quarters of a century, in what amounted for the great majority to an 'exile in bondage', the plantations imposed their servitude on the Indian labourers, who were but mute pieces on the chequer-board of worldwide colonialism. Although nominally free, they were little more than slaves. Often their emigration was a result of fraud and outright force. They endured cruel and degrading conditions of work, frequently under the former slave masters or their descendants.[64]

In the foregoing interpretations of modern analysts, the equation of indenture with slavery on the presumed premise that the Indian immigrants had endured practically identical conditions from which the slaves had been liberated is facile, erroneous, and misleading. Indian indenture was not distinguished by an essentially unchanging character. The available evidence shows that widespread reformist pressures and ameliorative measures had frequently punctuated the indenture period right from the start, gradually purging the system of some of its worst evils. The principal difference with slavery was the duration of the bondage: whereas the slaves were bound for life or as long as slavery lasted, indenture presented the Indians with an opportunity to return to their homeland at the end of their contract. This entitlement was enshrined in the immigration Acts of the government of India, in the immigration ordinances of the colonial governments, and in the conventions between these two parties. There was also the difference in the legal definition of the slaves and the indentureds. Whereas the slaves were defined in terms of chattel, the Indian immigrants enjoyed legal rights of personality, infringement of which was liable to criminal punishment. Undeniably, transgressions of the rights of the Indian labourers did occur, sometimes with light punishment or entire impunity. These occurrences became less frequent as the system progressed and were, by comparison, not as serious as during slavery. The contention, therefore, that indenture was akin to slavery is tenuous. It may be valid for the early years in some colonies but it could not be accurately applied throughout its tenure in all the colonies.

References

1 John H. Harris, *Coolie Labour in the British Crown Colonies and Protectorates* (London, 1910), p. 9.
2 Cited in Herman Merivale, *Lectures on Colonization and Colonies* (London, 1928), p. 345.
3 Cited in Basdeo Mangru, "Imperial Trusteeship in British Guiana with Special Reference to the East Indian Indentured Immigrants, 1838-1882. Myth or Reality?" (Unpublished M.A. dissertation, University of Guyana, 1976), p. 85.
4 H.V.P. Bronkhurst, *The Colony of British Guiana and its Labouring Population* (London, 1883), pp. 320-21.
5 "West Indian", *The Coolie in Demerara* (London, 1871), p. 10.
6 Comins, *Emigration to Trinidad*, p. 50.
7 Comins, *Emigration to British Guiana*, p. 8.
8 Sanderson, *Report on Emigration*, p. ii.
9 Harris, *Coolie Labour*, p. 9.
10 Sanderson, *Report on Emigration*, C5192, p. 14.
11 *Ibid.*, p. 22.
12 *Ibid.*, p. 23.
13 James McNeill and Chimman Lal, *Report to the Government of India on the Conditions of Indian Immigrants in Four British Colonies and Surinam*, Pt. II (Lon-

don, 1915), p. 322. When the Viceroy of India, Lord Hardinge, read the Report, he said: "I confess I had hoped their investigations would prove a death blow to the system. In one sense it had done so, but not in the immediate and decisive manner which I had hoped and expected." See Nath, *History of Indians in British Guiana*, p. 121.
14 K.L. Gillion, *Fiji's Indian Migrants: A History to the End of Indenture in 1920* (Melbourne, 1962), p. 169.
15 This Section comprised W. Hewley Wharton, Chairman; Parbhu Sawh, Member; and Joseph A. Luckhoo, Secretary.
16 The proposed scheme did not materialize.
17 *British Guiana. An Indian Colony. Homes for Indians in South America.* (Allahabad, 1919), pp. 7-8.
18 See Geoghegan, *Emigration from India*, p. 2.
19 Cited in Saha, *Emigration of Indian Labour*, p. 104.
20 *The Times* (London), 12 July 1838.
21 Cumpston, *Indians Overseas*, p. 68.
22 Hazareesingh, *Indians in Mauritius*, p. 39.
23 Cumpston, *Indians Overseas*, p. 32.
24 Hazareesingh, *Indians in Mauritius*, pp. 38-39.
25 A variation of *arkatis*, the North Indian labour recruiters.
26 Great Britain, Parliament, *Parliamentary Debates* (House of Commons), 3rd ser., Vol. LXV (12 July – 12 August 1842), p. 655.
27 *Ibid.*, p. 663.
28 *Ibid.*, Vol. LX (3 February 1842 – 3 March 1842), p. 1333.
29 Sir Lindsay Darcy occupied for many years an important position in the business community of Calcutta and was described as an active member of the Indian Legislative Assembly from its commencement in 1921 till 1930. It was said that he had "always shown a keen interest in matters affecting the position of Indians overseas." See p. 247 of reference that follows.
30 Sir Lindsay Darcy, "Indians Overseas," in Sir John Comming, ed., *Political India, 1832- 1932: A Cooperative Survey of a Century* (Delhi, 1968), p. 249.
31 Geoghegan, *Emigration from India,* p. 6.
32 Edward John Jenkins, *The Coolie: His Rights and Wrongs*, Vol. I (London, 1871), p. 291.
33 *Ibid.*, p. 290.
34 "West Indian." *Coolie in Demerara*, p. 5.
35 William Des Voeux, *My Colonial Service*, Vol. I (London, 1903), p. 122.
36 Joseph Beaumont, *The New Slavery: An Account of the Indian and Chinese Immigrants in British Guiana* (London, 1871), p. 14.
37 *Ibid.*, p. 48.
38 Bridget Brereton, "The Experience of Indentureship, 1845-1917," in John Gaffar La Guerre, ed., *Calcutta to Caroni: The East Indians of Trinidad* (Port of Spain, 1974), p. 36.
39 *Ibid.*, p. 37.

40 R.P. Patwardhan and D.V. Ambedkar, eds., *Speeches and Writings of Gopal Krishna Gokhale,* Vol. I (London, 1962), pp. 367-68.
41 Cited in Ahmed Ali, *Girmit: The Indenture Experience in Fiji* (Suva, 1979), p. xxiv.
42 H.E. Holland, *Indentured Labour: Is it Slavery?* (London, n.d.), p. 7.
43 J.W. Burton, *The Fiji of To-day* (London, 1910), p. 271.
44 Gillion, *Fiji's Indian Migrants*, p. 167.
45 N.V. Rajkumar, *Indians Outside India* (New Delhi, 1951), p. 55.
46 Cited in Florence E. Garnham, *A Report on the Social and Moral Conditions of Indians in Fiji* (Sydney, 1918), pp. 9-10.
47 C.F. Andrews, "India's Migration Problem," *Foreign Affairs*, VIII, no. 3 (April, 1930), 433.
48 The 'labour lines' in Fiji and the 'logies' in other colonies were the terms used for the immigrants' dwellings on the estates.
49 Garnham, *Indians in Fiji*, p. 15.
50 "Emigrant", *Indian Emigration* (London, 1924), p. 13.
51 Peter Ruhoman, *Centenary History of the East Indians in British Guiana, 1838-1938* (Georgetown, 1939), pp. 102-3.
52 *Ibid.*, p. 103.
53 N. Gangulee, *Indians in the Empire Overseas: A Survey* (London, 1947), p. 21.
54 W. Kloosterboer, *Involuntary Labour Since the Abolition of Slavery* (London, 1960), p. 16.
55 Ali, *Girmit*, p. xiii.
56 *Ibid.*, p. xxvii.
57 Hazareesingh, *Indians in Mauritius*, p. 37.
58 S.B. Mookherji, *The Indenture System in Mauritius, 1837-1915* (Calcutta, 1962), p. 65.
59 Dwarkanath Ganguli, *Slavery in British Dominion* (Calcutta, 1972), p. iv.
60 *Ibid.*, p. 1.
61 Tinker, *New Slavery*, p. 383.
62 Maureen Tayal, "Indian Indentured Labour in Natal, 1890-1911," *IESHR*, XIV, no. 4 (1977), 546.
63 Cited in Shridath S. Ramphal, "Roots and Reminders: Reflections on Slavery, Indenture, Apartheid — and Some Personal Conjunctures." Address to the Commonwealth Society of India, New Delhi, 20 January 1986, pp. 11-12.
64 *Ibid.*, pp. 10-11.

III

THE STRAITS DEMAND FOR INDIAN INDENTURED LABOUR

> If the cultivation of Sugar ... and other valuable exportable produce were to increase greatly or even moderately beyond the present extent, a constant demand for labor would arise.
>
> James Low[1]

Ever since the island of Penang was settled by the British in 1786, European agricultural enterprise was devoted mainly to the cultivation of pepper. But the place of this crop in the economy declined because of falling prices, and, consequently, by the late 1830s the pepper planters turned their attention to more lucrative cultivation.[2] At about the same time, the export of cloves and nutmegs also declined as the plantations devastated by blight were abandoned.[3] This gave rise to official and public concern over the economy of the island and to widespread anxiety for the livelihood of the Malays, Chinese, and Indians who were employed there.[4] Apprehension, however, soon subsided when new employment opportunities were created by some sugar cultivation in Penang and by large-scale planting in Province Wellesley.

Sugar Cultivation in the Straits: Background
Although sugar planting as an agricultural crop was said to have been known to the indigenous Malays from times unknown,[5] immigrant Chinese pioneer settlers were the first who cultivated cane and refined the sugar in quantities sufficient to make it a leading article of export.[6] The first estate they opened was in 1790 in the northern part of Batu Kawan,[7] an island on the fringe of the coast of lower Province Wellesley. The value of sugar as an export crop, however, was not recognized by the Chinese until the first decade of the nineteenth century.[8] Between 1810 and 1820, they opened sugar estates on land cleared in the tiger-infested jungles of Province Wellesley[9] and on the central and southern plains.[10] The industry expanded in the 1820s and 1830s, and by 1835, the Chinese brought a total of 900 acres of land in the Province under sugar cultivation.[11]

In 1841, it was remarked:

> Before many years had passed a colony of petty planters was established, a plain of about 1,000 acres was cleared, on which a population of more than 2,000 Chinese settled, and sugar was manufactured to the extent of from 600 to 700 tons annually

.... The prosperity of the planters, many of whom after a few years carried away a competent fortune to their native country, attested that the employment was lucrative in a high degree.[12]

In Singapore, large-scale sugar cultivation was commenced by two European planters. In 1836, William Montgomerie, Senior Surgeon and formerly honorary Superintendent of the Singapore Botanic Gardens, opened the Kallangdale estate; and Joseph Balestier, American Consul in Singapore (1836-52), began the Balestier estate.[13] Both estates planted an estimated total area of 500 acres.[14] The sugar produced was first exported to Britain in 1841, and later to Australia.[15]

The expansion of sugar cultivation in Singapore was stymied by a combination of several factors. It had long been said that the poor, red soil was unsuitable for growing any commercial crops save gambier and pepper.[16] No money facilities were obtainable by way of loans or advances on growing crops.[17] The terms of land tenure were unfavourable to planters.[18] The ineffectiveness of the police in guaranteeing protection to isolated settlements dissuaded other Europeans from opening new estates.[19] The ravages of tigers compounded the difficulties in obtaining an adequate and suitable labour supply.[20]

In the island of Penang, the sugar industry was begun by Europeans in 1838 with the opening of the Otaheite estate; but it was abandoned in 1848[21] because of the combined effect of several disadvantages. The "far too thin" and marshy land required constant replenishment of its fertility by composts.[22] The absence of extensive alluvial plains and of a reliable source of water to irrigate the fields prevented high productivity. Above all, the cost of labour being "excessively dear", the small yields could not defray the expense of cultivation.[23]

In 1846-47, an unsuccessful venture was made to cultivate sugar on a large scale in Malacca. Some wealthy Malacca Chinese and several Europeans from Singapore and Mauritius applied for about 20,000 acres of land, and, in addition to several private undertakings, two large companies were about to be formed.[24] But the local government was not prepared to entertain such "extensive applications on the instant", and the matter was referred to the colonial authorities in Bengal.[25] By the time the reply came, there was a fall in the price of sugar in the United Kingdom, and the land was never taken up.[26]

Until about 1846, the Straits sugar industry did not suffer unduly from labour difficulties. The Chinese proprietors contracted with their own countrymen who had under their charge hundreds of *coolie-Sinkeh*.[27] The European planters also obtained labour through Chinese contractors, and they employed South Indians as well. In 1848, Balestier, the pioneer sugar planter in Singapore, wrote: "Many labourers come also from the Madras side of India, who let themselves out on the estates".[28]

The Inducement to Increase Sugar Production
Following the Emancipation of slaves in the British sugar colonies in 1838-39, and the ensuing shortage of labour, there was a drop in sugar production. It has been mentioned earlier that in British Guiana, the average tonnage of 57,197 pro-

duced between 1833 and 1838 fell to an average of 31,865 between the years 1838-46.[29] From the British West Indies as a whole, whereas during the period 1829-33, the average annual amount of sugar exported to the United Kingdom was 195,893 tons, the average between 1842-45 was 129,115 tons.[30] This decrease became more keenly felt as the capacity for the consumption of sugar in Britain increased.

Sugar consumption in the United Kingdom during the early nineteenth century was largely confined to the upper and middle classes of society. But in 1846, the British government legislated a new Sugar Duties Act which reduced the tariff on British colonial sugar entering Britain from twenty-one shillings to fourteen shillings per hundredweight.[31] Sugar having become more easily affordable, consumption spread to all levels of British society. Consequently, whereas in the period 1820-29, for instance, annual per capita consumption stood at 17.6 pounds, by 1860-69, it rose to 38.7 pounds.[32]

Related to the increase in sugar consumption was the wider use of coffee. In 1846, coffee consumption in Britain totaled 23.7 million pounds, and by 1850, the amount rose to 28.8 million pounds.[33] This rise in sugar and coffee consumption caused in the Straits "a sudden impetus … to the cultivation of sugar cane, which had hitherto been carried on at a great disadvantage".[34]

The Rise of Sugar Cultivation in Province Wellesley
The first European-owned sugar estate in Province Wellesley, the Arrarendum, was opened by N. Bacon in 1840.[35] Further efforts to cultivate sugar-cane in the Province were frustrated by the difficulty in obtaining land in perpetuity or on long leases.[36] The modification in 1843 of land tenure terms, which gave rise to a more liberal land alienation policy,[37] encouraged those European planters who had been daunted by spice cultivation in the island of Penang to transfer their agricultural enterprise to sugar cultivation in Province Wellesley.[38] Consequently, in 1841, over 6,500 acres of land leased from the Penang government were in European hands.[39]

The reduction of tariff duties by the British government in 1846 permitting Penang sugar to be imported into the United Kingdom on a par with that from Bengal, Mauritius, and the West Indies[40] operated to the disadvantage of the sugar industry in Singapore and in favour of that in Province Wellesley. Sugar manufactured in Singapore (although a British Settlement) could only be admitted into the British market on the payment of the higher duties which continued to apply to this commodity exported to the United Kingdom by foreign countries.[41] There was reason for this. At the time, Singapore was a free port where sugar from China, Java, and the Philippines was first collected and then re-exported to the United Kingdom so that the difficulty in distinguishing local from foreign sugar in the process of transhipment caused the small local produce to be treated as foreign as well.[42] The denial to Singapore of the preferential duty was decisive in checking any further efforts at sugar cultivation there.[43] By 1849, the Balestier estate was shut down, and the Kallangdale estate was advertised for sale in 1852; although it was still in operation in 1860, it functioned on a small scale.[44] The privilege extended to Penang gave an impetus to sugar cultivation in Province Wellesley. Whereas in 1848-49, the amount of sugar and rum produced in the Province and exported through Penang was 54,337 piculs (of 133.3 pounds each) and 166,424 gallons respectively, in 1859-60, exports rose to 88,584 piculs of sugar and 208,671 gallons of rum.[45]

This phenomenal rise was largely due to the "uncommon luxuriance" with which the sugar-cane grew in Province Wellesley,[46] which was itself due to a number of factors. The arable, easily drained alluvial plains extending over most of the cultivable land surface of about 25,000 acres[47] were suitable for sugar cultivation. At high tide, artificial dykes prevented the damaging incursion of the sea.[48] Inland, a network of natural water communications, supplemented by wide canals dug by the planters, reduced operational costs.[49] The cane was loaded into barges and drawn to the factories by buffaloes and mules[50] instead of by the more expensive, more laborious, and precarious means of road transportation. The numerous canals and creeks were usually reliable reservoirs for irrigation, especially during prolonged drought.[51] Even though there was an abundance of bat guano, putrid fish, and other manures,[52] the availability of water, aided by the usually even distribution of rainfall,[53] facilitated flood following – the triennial flooding of the fields – which renewed the fertility of the soil to an extent not achievable by any method of direct manual application. Although exposed to the force of the sea-breeze and some of its crops were occasionally damaged by strong squalls, the Province was an entirely hurricane-free zone;[54] thus, cultivation was relatively free from the vagaries of nature. G.F. Davidson, a contemporary traveller, summed up the suitability of Province Wellesley: "I know no better spot for the culture of sugar and if it does not pay the planters there, those of Penang and Singapore have but a poor prospect."[55]

Of considerable importance to the sugar industry, was the tranquility that Province Wellesley enjoyed. This had not always been so. Up to about the middle of the nineteenth century, the Province was a favourite haunt of pirates who attacked and plundered merchant ships in the Straits of Malacca.[56] Not only did this piracy create great anxiety over the safety of cargo-laden ships that needed a place of victualling, watering, and refitting, but it had threatened to destroy the agricultural potential of Province Wellesley. With the advent of steamships and their advantage of superior speed and greater maneuverability over sailing ships, a campaign of suppression eventually stamped out this "curse of commerce". The Province thus came to be regarded as "the only satisfactory productive possession held by the British in these parts."[57]

The factors favouring sugar cultivation in the Province attracted European investment from outside the Straits Settlements. In 1846, there were five European-owned sugar estates in the Province.[58] In 1856, Edward Horsman, Member of the British Parliament and Privy Councillor, established a block of estates covering a total planted area of 2,700 acres.[59] In the same year, Sir John Ramsden, another Member of Parliament, formed the Penang Sugar Company and took ownership of a large portion of the Straits Sugar Company,[60] both of which operated in southern Province Wellesley. By 1860, a total of 9,074 acres of land in the Province were utilized for sugar cultivation.[61] All of the land was not actually cultivated each year; some was fallowed. By 1861, there were eleven large European-owned factories which were "all supplied with excellent machinery, including 'centrifugals' for drying the sugar, and all modern improvements short of vacuum pans" which were being gradually introduced.[62]

Although much less in extent than sugar growing, tapioca cultivation occupied the less fertile tracts of land. The tapioca plant was so hardy that it was cultivable in almost any soil, and required less trenching and fertilizing than cane.[63] One such estate opened in 1855 by Robert Wilson, a planter previously of Penang, turned out a "great success"; its 700 acres under cultivation was worked mainly by South Indian labourers with a few Javanese and Malays.[64]

For employment on the European-owned sugar estates in Province Wellesley, four ethnic groups may be considered possible sources of labour. The only reliable figures available do not give a breakdown of the employment distribution of these groups. Nevertheless, their relative numbers are indicated in the following table:-

TABLE II
ETHNIC COMPOSITION OF THE POPULATION OF
PROVINCE WELLESLEY FOR VARIOUS YEARS, 1844-60

YEAR	MALAYS	JAVANESE[a]	CHINESE	INDIANS
1844	44,271	N/A	4,107	1,815
1851	53,010	"	8,751	1,913
1860	52,836	"	8,204	3,514

a — The Javanese were included in the floating population of the Straits Settlements.
N/A = No reliable information available
Source: Braddell, *Statistics*, p. 2.

The Malays
The indigenous Malays were not responsive to the sugar planters' overtures for their labour. Reflecting contemporary European opinion, James Low, the Superintendent of Province Wellesley, who, it was said, brought a "sympathetic insight into Malay character",[65] and who had unsuccessfully tried to encourage the Malays to diversify their subsistence economy by offering them free seeds,[66] wrote: "Such is the character of the [Province Wellesley] Malay that, with occasional exceptions, he will rather than take a spade in hand for hire, content himself with a bare pittance not exceeding half of the sum he might gain by labor in the plantation of a planter."[67]

Other reasons explain the refusal of most of the Malays to work on the Province Wellesley sugar estates. For instance, the *penghulu*, the chief or headman of a Malay village, could at any time commandeer his subjects to give free labour under the *kerah* (corvee) system.[68] It functioned thus:

> When the Sultan, or any Raja or chief of sufficient authority, wanted labour for any public or private work – such as the clearing of a river, the building of a mosque or house, the manning of boats for a journey – for then all the men within reach were summoned, through the village head-men, to come and undertake this forced labour ....[69]

Failure to respond to this demand for labour conflicted with Malay *adat*, the customary law, and often entailed enslavement of the offender. Furthermore, the Malays' keen inclination towards sport, especially cock-fighting,[70] was incompatible with the steady demand for labour on the estates. Moreover, European observers believed that confining Malay labourers to either field or factory would generate among them uneasiness and irritability which could culminate in a show of protest by quitting.[71] From the planters' point of view Malay labour would have been undesirably intermittent, unpredictable, and unreliable.

Contrary to the belief among some planters that the Malays were lazy and "incorrigibly idle",[72] the essential characteristic of their attitude to labour was a disinclination to steady employment.[73] Usually, they hardly worked more than three days a week, except when they were attending to their rice fields. Malay attachment to rice cultivation was such that even a positive and greater gain seldom severed this partiality.[74] When they were in dire need for money, they would undertake contracts to fell trees,[75] but for short engagements only.[76] Difficult and dangerous though tree-felling was, the compensatory factor for the Malays was that they worked voluntarily, unsupervised, in a familiar environment, and at their own pace. This work-style was in sharp contrast to that of the indentured estate labourer. He was summoned to work by the bull-horn before dawn,[77] and flogged if he was unresponsive to the call, if he was dilatory in his walk to the field, or if he malingered.[78]

Since the Malay generally preferred to work independently, he could hardly be expected to subject himself to a hierarchy of alien officials on a sugar estate. This would conflict with the traditional canons of Malay society. It was held that no occupation was "worthy of prestige save the one associated with the ruler or his rule."[79] Neither would the Malay tolerate the usually rough control exercised over sugar estate labourers by the tindals, the South Indian foremen. According to Low, the respectable Malay "is highly sensitive to slights and premeditated insult, and he fancies, perhaps rightly, that no law can compensate the injury sustained."[80]

The Malays' inclination towards desultory labour was also due to their wants being few, moderate and simple. Their Islamic belief forbade imbibing alcohol; they ate with temperance; clothing for themselves and their family was inexpensive; and their modest and sparsely furnished dwellings, constructed of materials freely procurable,[81] were aptly adapted to the transitory and impermanent nature of Malay settlement.[82] Furthermore, among villagers there existed a spirit of mutual assistance and neighbourliness in which indigent Malays found ready succour.[83] Moreover, were they to flee their *kampong*, or village, as they often did, in response to hostile invasion, or to escape from undue oppression or insecurity engendered by a ruler's despotism, unoccupied and unclaimed land in the Malay States was so abundant that they could squat wherever they pleased.[84] This probability of sudden flight would not have encouraged the acquisition of many personal possessions. Therefore, there was no need to work regularly to acquire them.

Of the greatest importance, the planters could not secure many Malay labourers because several alternative means of subsistence were available to them. Low observed: "The fact is that the bulk of the non-commercial native population [of Province Wellesley] is composed of independent land-owners, and that those who are not proprietors, are either farmers of land, or persons engaged in various occupations which, unless in times of scarcity, supply all their wants."[85]

Quite contrary to the assertion made by Governor Sir William Robinson, of the Straits Settlements, that the Malays "scrape in cultivating a few plantains or a little padi and bearly [sic] live",[86] evidence confirms that usually they had no anxiety in procuring adequate food. Most Malays in Province Wellesley cultivated some rice.[87] Surplus yields found a ready market among the Chinese mining community of the Malay Peninsula[88] with whom they also plied a petty but lucrative bartering trade.[89] Pepper and other spices for domestic use flourished; and with little cultivation, the soil produced tapioca, sugar-cane, coffee, yams, sweet potatoes, and cocoa.[90] Fruits, maize, and plantains were abundantly available.[91] The sea and numerous rivers and streams provided the Malays with a profusion of fish, their chief animal food.[92] In addition to gaming deer and birds, they hunted the wild ox for its "sweet and wholesome" flesh.[93] They also reared some cattle, which not only provided milk, but also muscular power in the rice fields.[94]

Finally, the wages offered by the planters could not have attracted the Malays. In the 1830s, wages paid in Province Wellesley varied. The Indians were paid about $2.70 per month, and the Malays were offered the same rate or even less.[95] In the 1870s, the daily wage rate for indentured Indians ranged between ten and twelve cents.[96] In addition to this, housing and medical services were provided free of charge. These same conditions were offered to the Malays. By comparison, on a day to day basis, the Malays who could farm and fish and supplement their resources with wages, if this at all became necessary, would have procured more than what the indentured Indians could obtain from their labour. Furthermore, the Malays would have derived more enjoyment out of life than the indentured Indians could have got out of their pittance, considering that all the labour devoted by the latter to the production of wealth for a third party was, as would be seen, semi-servile. It was not surprising that the Malays looked "with wonder, and a hint of contempt at those who think it worthwhile to work for money in the hot sun".[97] Unquestionably, the Malays were imbued with a rooted aversion to contracting themselves to work on alien-owned estates in a country to which they were indigenous. In this regard, they were not unique.

Malay aptitude for desultory work was akin to those of other indigenes whose labour similarly constituted a possible alternative in certain British sugar colonies. In Fiji, for instance, apart from the colonial government's prohibition of the employment of natives in industry[98], the Fijians' "cultural background had made them … ill-suited to the rigours and discipline of plantation labour".[99] Furthermore, an observation made by a prominent British officer of the native Cakobau government could also be applied to the Malay. He is recorded as having said: "The fact is that no Fijian will go from home to be worked from morning to night, upon paltry pay, indifferent fare, and frequently anything but mild treatment, if he can avoid doing so."[100] Like his Malayan counterpart, the Fijian had few wants; he was averse to continuous work; he disliked absence from his family; he preferred to cultivate his own plot of ground; and the keen spiritual affinity he preserved with his commune was opposed to a wandering propensity.[101]

Likewise, the attitudes of the Malays and the native Amerindians of British Guiana towards estate labour were similar in many respects. These autochthonous denizens of the forest were accustomed to an established tradition of a casual life of hunting, fishing, and subsistence farming,[102] which was incompatible with the steady monotony required by the sugar estates. The Amerindians were "industrious only by fits and starts".[103] They had no motive to become materially acquisitive; their main object was "to get through life with as little trouble as possible".[104] Above all, having been retained by the sugar planters to catch runaway slaves, they equated estate labour with slave labour.[105]

Malay repugnance towards working on a sugar estate was transferred into a low esteem of the indentured Indians in Province Wellesley. In response to a question from the Sanderson Committee whether the Malays and these Indians belonged to the same social class, Governor Sir John Anderson, of the Straits Settlements, replied: "I am afraid the Malays would be very indignant if you suggested that."[106] Therefore, the Malays would not be induced to work and live among an agglomeration of people whom they considered socially inferior to themselves.

The Javanese
Available statistics of the nineteenth century do not show the number of Javanese labourers in the Straits Settlements, census reports having included them in the floating population. Nevertheless, the traveller, Isabella Bird, mentioned that in 1883 they were "numerous" in Singapore.[107] A number of these Javanese were transients en route to Java after accomplishing *hadj* (pilgrimage) to Mecca. Usually, they would stop off at the nodal point of Singapore to work for employers who were prepared to pay off the debts the *hajis* owed to shipowners who had transported them to and from Mecca.[108] Other Javanese were those who were in the process of signing contracts at the Chinese Protectorate for employment largely in Borneo and Sumatra.[109] The number of all these Javanese at Singapore for each year between 1886 and 1890 were given as follows:-[110]

1886	.....	2,741
1887	.....	3,589
1888	.....	4,931
1889	.....	4,974
1890	.....	5,133

The majority of these labourers could not be diverted to the Province Wellesley sugar estates. In 1886, Javanese agricultural labourers demanded 24 cents per day;[111] whereas the maximum payable rate on the sugar estates was 14 cents a day to adult indentured males,[112] and between 18 and 20 cents to free labourers.[113] However, a small number of Javanese were introduced to work at Province Wellesley in 1886 as free labourers, but within six months, many of them relinquished their employment due to their thorough dissatisfaction with the purchasing power of their wages.[114]

Most planters regarded the Javanese labourers as good workers, and because of their stronger physique and greater ability to work, they were decidedly superior to the South Indians on the estates.[115] Other planters criticized the Javanese for being slow workers but they added that this was compensated for by their neatness and dedication.[116]

Efforts to create a large reservoir of Javanese labourers were impeded by difficulties encountered in importing them on an organized basis. The Netherlands imperial government had consistently opposed emigration of Javanese labourers.[117] But by the 1880s, growing concern over Java's population pressure on scarce land resources induced a reversal of that policy, but not without caution. When the government allowed a small batch of ninety-four Javanese labourers to be taken to its own colony, Surinam (previously called Dutch Guiana), it was in the nature of an experiment.[118]

In 1887, the Netherlands government extended Javanese emigration to the Straits Settlements, but only on the basis of labour contracts, the enforcement of the terms of which they strictly demanded.[119] But the cost of importing one Javanese labourer being between $57.00 and $67.00, which was about twice or thrice that for importing an indentured South Indian,[120] the planters found the scheme prohibitively expensive. Since this would have conflicted with the planter ethos of making minimum outlay and reaping maximum return, the planters did not pursue Javanese importation any further.

The Chinese

The immigrant Chinese in the Straits had a long established reputation for possessing distinctly superior qualities as labourers. John Crawfurd, Resident of Singapore (1823-26), asserted that compared with the Indians and other Asiatics in the Malay Archipelago, the Chinese were unsurpassed in energy, industry, and intelligence.[121] James Low, who was closely associated with agriculture in the Straits in the 1830s, evaluated the labour of three able-bodied Chinese, working under due supervision, equivalent to that of five Indians or Malays.[122] On one estate, when hoeing was being done, the employer would place a gang of Chinese in the middle position with a corresponding number of Indians and Javanese alongside. An observer made this comment: "Anyone who knows the respective values of the three nationalities for such work will appreciate how the Klings [i.e. the South Indians] and the Javanese must have worked to keep up with the stalwart Chinese."[123] Although the Chinese were considered susceptible to prolonged exposure to the tropical sun,[124] they were said to be of "excellent physique", and had been from childhood accustomed to hard work.[125] Furthermore, they were reputed to be entirely free from caste prejudices.[126] Unlike the orthodox Hindus from India, the Chinese would, therefore, have had no food taboos.

Certain factors tended to depreciate the suitability of the Chinese for employment on European-owned sugar estates. It was said that they would very seldom condescend to work as day-labourers,[127] that is, on a daily as opposed to contract basis which the planters could not always guarantee. So turbulent and intractable could they become that it was surmised that only an exceptional European employer would be capable of controlling a large gang.[128] Under European employers they were said to be too independent and restless in disposition for constant and disciplined service.[129] Cutting or reducing their wages (as was frequently done on the sugar estates) was sufficient reason for them to revolt,[130] one writer said. Since the Chinese "'would no more bear ill-usage than an English labourer'",[131] it would be difficult to imagine them working under the harsh supervision of the Tamil tindals. Finally, the Labour Commission of 1890 found that those Chinese labourers who were still working on the Province Wellesley estates were "inclined to be disorderly, cost more in police supervision and [gave] more trouble".[132]

One of the most important reasons why the European planters of Province Wellesley could not engage Chinese labourers in sufficient numbers was connected to the decline in the Chinese sector of the local sugar industry. The adoption by the European planters of modern technology and managerial expertise in the 1850s wrested the monopoly of the sugar industry from their Chinese counterparts.[133] Thus, in 1858, although 1,000 acres or about a third of the planted area of cane land was still in Chinese hands,[134] in 1861, four-fifths of the sugar produced was by European estates; the Chinese and small holdings accounted for the balance.[135] This control of the sugar industry by the Europeans practically shut out all others except the most skilful and wealthy Chinese planters.[136] Consequently, Chinese sugar labourers gradually gravitated to join their countrymen in the tin mines in the Malay States.[137]

There were several reasons for this decisive trend. First, the Chinese miners were more liberally paid. As opposed to the possible maximum of $3.60 per month an indentured labourer could earn on a sugar estate between 1876 and 1884,[138] and $4.20 between 1885 and 1903[139], the average Chinese miner could earn from $3.50 to $4.50 per month in 1851;[140] between $6.00 and $8.00 by 1879;[141] and from about $9.00 in 1896 to about $13.00 in 1898, and about $22.50 in 1899.[142] Second, the miners were paid on the basis of their output.[143] This would have given them a direct interest in their work. Any extra work done beyond their normal tasks would be correspondingly rewarded with additional wages. Thus, their pay was commensurate with their production and productivity. On the other hand, as will be seen later, the average Indian indentured sugar worker did not earn more than the fixed daily wage, and, at times, even this was denied him. Finally, the Chinese contract-gang system enabled the miners to regulate their work according to their own liking. It was they, not the employers as on the estates, who organized the daily schedule. A typical day's work is illustrative of the comparatively simple and easy method of working.

From daybreak to 7 A.M. they are employed in emptying the mines of the water which accumulates during the night. From 7 to 8, they rest and breakfast. At 8, the process of digging out the earth and ore is commenced. At 11, they go to dinner, and return to work again about 1 P.M. At 5, their labours cease for the day.[144]

The total number of hours thus worked was eight. By contrast, the indentured estate labourer was under legal compulsion to do ten. He was required to work from 6 A.M. to 11 A.M. when he was allowed to prepare his meal, and from 1 P.M. to 6 P.M. But as had often happened, he was compelled to work later without any extra remuneration.

From about the 1870s onwards, the Straits government considered the Chinese in the Straits a threat to security as well as to British political hegemony mainly because of the rapid growth in their population. With the expansion of the tin-mining industry and the voluminous rise in Chinese immigration that followed, the numerical disparity between the Chinese and the other ethnic groups in the Straits became quite noticeable as the following table shows:

TABLE III
POPULATION OF THE STRAITS SETTLEMENTS SHOWING
COMPARATIVE ETHNIC COMPOSITION FOR
VARIOUS YEARS BETWEEN 1871-1911

ETHNIC GROUP	1871	1881	1891	1901	1911
Chinese	104,615	174,327	222,969	274,207	369,843
Eurasians	5,772	6,904	6,991	7,623	8,072
Europeans	2,429	3,483	4,422	4,484	7,368
Indians	33,390	41,268	52,637	56,645	82,055
Malays	159,453	194,042	210,387	214,538	240,206
Others	2,438	3,360	15,499	14,752	14,531

Source: H. Marriot, "Population of the Straits Settlements and Malay Peninsula during the last Century," *JSBRAS*, No. 62 (December, 1912), 35: E.M. Merewether, *Report on the Census of the Straits Settlements 1891* (Singapore, 1892), p. 1; J.R. Innes, *Report on the Census of the Straits Settlements, 1901* (Singapore, 1910), p. 1.

The steady rise in the Chinese population prompted Sir Frederick Weld, Governor of the Straits Settlements, to remark:

> I am ... anxious for political reasons that the great preponderance of the Chinese over any other race in these Settlements, and to a less marked degree in some of the

Native States under our administration, should be counterbalanced as much as possible by the influx of Indian and other nationalities ....[145]

An increased volume of Indian immigration, under proper safeguards, Sir Frederick asserted, would conceivably be of mutual advantage to both planters and labourers.[146] The planters, he added, would get the labour they needed for current cultivation and future expansion; and from a humanitarian aspect, the immigrants, by diligent and industrious application of their labour, would be enabled to live in comfort and prosperity under favourable conditions and in a congenial climate.

The demand for Indian labourers in the Straits Settlements was expected to serve a dual purpose. They were needed as a bolster for the sugar industry as well as a countervailing political expedient to off-set the numerical preponderance of the Chinese. J. Norman Parmer rightly observed: "From Weld's administration onward, the Indians were cast in the role of a counterpoise to the Chinese."[147] By importing large numbers of Indians, the British would be multiplying the population and dividing it at the same time. It was hardly likely that the Chinese and the Indians, differing ethnically, religiously, and culturally, and generally following divergent economic pursuits, would unite in revolt against the British. The Labour Commission of 1890 remarked that the Indians were British subjects, accustomed to British rule, and docile.[148] This latter aspect of the Indian characteristic was confirmed by the Sanderson Committee: "All the evidence which we have received goes to show that the Indian indentured labourer, though resentful of anything which he considers injustice, is, if properly treated, perfectly, docile and easily managed ...."[149] It has been said that because the Indian immigrants in the Straits lacked the self-reliance and capacity of their Chinese counterparts, they were not generally recalcitrant.[150]

Indians in Malaya
Indian indentured labour migration to the Straits Settlements could be described as another link in the long historical chain that bound India and Malaya. India's contact with the Malay world, it is widely believed, probably preceded the commencement of the Christian era.[151] This connection was inevitable because of their relative geographical situation. Out-stretched from the body of mainland Asia, they strategically imposed themselves athwart the sea-routes of the east-west trading systems. India's role as an intermediary for western goods heading for the east, and for eastern cargoes aiming at western markets afforded her merchants the opportunity of learning the secrets of international trade. With the establishment of trading routes, Indian merchants, emboldened by a spirit of adventure and goaded by their economic needs, sailed to distant trading stations.[152] The Bay of Bengal soon became a highway of communication for traders, and, in their wake, for scholars and religious missionaries. It was thus that Indian navigators sailing due east came to discover the advantages of making landfall at Kedah on the Malay Peninsula from where they utilized the monsoon to return home.

The region surrounding the lofty and distinctive Kedah Peak soon became an important trading centre for Indian merchants. The necessary organization of trade there gave rise to the settlement of a number of Indians, mainly Tamils from South India. When Francis Light founded Penang in 1786, he reported that the greater portion of the South Indians at Kedah had been inhabitants of long standing, and that some of them had been born there.[153]

With the establishment of Penang by the British, there was a gradual change in the role of Indians in Malaya. Until around that time, the supply of merchandise by Indians on their own initiative was predominant; afterwards, they immigrated primarily to supply labour.[154] In 1790, Francis Light attributed the production of great quantities of fruits, coconuts, pepper, gambier, and sugar-cane to the labour of Chinese, Malays, Siamese, Burmese, British settlers, and immigrants from South India.[155] Four years later, he wrote:

> The second class of our inhabitants consists of the Chooliars [Chulias] or people from the several ports on the Coast of Coromandel [i.e. the east coast of Madras Presidency] …, they are all shopkeepers and Coolies, about one thousand are settled here, some with families, the vessels from the coast bring over annually 1,500 or 2,000 men, who by traffic and various kinds of labour obtain a few dollars with which they return to their homes and are succeeded by others.[156]

From the beginning of the nineteenth century, there were frequent references to Indian labourers in the Straits. George Leith, writing during his Lieutenant-Governorship of Penang (1800-3), mentioned Indian "coolies" customarily working one, two or three years on certain estates, and then returning to Madras Presidency.[157] In 1820, John Crawfurd, Resident of Singapore (1823-26), wrote of Indians employed on Penang estates on a "day-labour" (as opposed to piece-work) basis.[158] Writing in 1835, James Low, the Superintendent of Province Wellesley, mentioned Indians working on "hire" on sugar and other estates in the Province.[159] Joseph Balestier, the first American Consul in Singapore, and a pioneer sugar planter of the late 1830s, said many labourers came from South India and "let themselves out on the estates".[160]

There is also the testimony of C.W.S. Kynnersley, a Straits magistrate whose duties brought him into close contact with Indian labourers for more than thirty years during the second half of the nineteenth century. In the discussion following a paper delivered by A.W.S.O' Sullivan, Indian Immigration Agent and subsequently Assistant Colonial Secretary, Straits Settlements, Kynnersley said that in 1844 a gang of ninety-seven Indian labourers was brought into the Straits from Calcutta.[161] This importation, he added, was in the form of an experiment, and was necessitated by the demand for suitable labourers to work on expanding European sugar estates in Province Wellesley.

Finally, the last known major reference to Indian labourers in the Straits before regulated indenture began in 1872 was made by G.W. Earl, author, voyager, and adventurer. In 1862, he referred to the Straits Settlements as the "favourite resort" of many South Indians; they arrived at Penang in August and September (the height of the monsoon season) in "queer looking brigs and barks" mainly from the South Indian ports of Cuddalore, Karikal, Nagore, and Negapatam.[162] The majority of these Indians, Earl added, were employed on the sugar and coconut estates in Province Wellesley as labourers.

The term "labourers" ought to be defined. Many persons from Madras Presidency emigrated to the Straits not only to labour in the restricted sense of the word, but also to work at trades. Thus, fishermen, barbers, domestic servants, housekeepers, goldsmiths, etc. came to earn a livelihood in the colony. These were termed "free" labourers and were distinguished from those indentured in this respect: whereas the former emigrated on their own account, the latter were recruited largely through the inducement of a cash advance, in addition to having their passage and subsistence paid. They then entered into a contractual agreement – an indenture – not merely to labour but to repay all expenses incurred in their emigration. In this study, unless otherwise stated, the term "labourers" refers to the indentured Tamils of Madras Presidency who were engaged in this manner to work on the European-owned sugar estates in Province Wellesley.

Tamil Suitability for Sugar Cultivation
Of the Tamils' suitability for sugar-cane cultivation, there was a divergence of opinion. Some planters in the West Indies, (whose Indian indentured labour force imported between 1838 and 1916 comprised mainly people from North India) criticized the Tamils' inability to acclimatize as quickly as the North Indians.[163] In the Straits, the Tamils would find themselves in a climate basically not very different from their own. In Madras Presidency, the daily average temperature ranged between extremes of 70 and 91 degrees Fahrenheit.[164] In Province Wellesley, the mean temperature was 79½ degrees Fahrenheit.[165] A number of West Indian planters claimed that the Tamils were not as hard-working and industrious as the North Indians, and that their productivity was low and their mortality high.[166] Furthermore, a report from Jamaica during indenture there reads: "Generally speaking, the Bengal coolies are doing well here, but the Madrassies are, for the most part, very inferior, and there are many habitual and professed beggars and vagabonds amongst them …."[167] Finally, a writer who observed the Tamils during indenture in British Guiana described them thus: "Indolent, dirty, and vagrant in their habits, the Madras coolies were inapt [*sic*] at the work for which they were intended, irregular in their attendance, and migratory in their ways; numbers abandoned the estates to which they were appointed to crowd about the town begging, and filling the most menial situations …."[168]

Some other views of the Tamils were complimentary. A number of planters in British Guiana believed the Tamils were physically superior to their North Indian counterparts and that their aptitude for cane-work surpassed that of fellow Indians.[169] Other West Indian planters held that the types of cane-work in which the Tamils excelled were confined to cleaning canals of weeds and to retrieving canes that had fallen off the punts into the canals, to which their early experience on the Madras sea-coast either as boatmen or fishermen had naturally adapted them.[170]

In the Straits, the Tamils enjoyed a favourable reputation. A local writer observing them said they belonged to an "active, industrious race".[171] They would, therefore, be imbued with a spirit of acquisitiveness; they would be reliable labourers, regular in attending to their work, and amenable to working hard and even beyond their normal tasks, which would enable them to save money and make remittances to their families in India. It was also held that the Tamils were quick to learn their work.[172] This depended on the previous occupational experience of those recruited, on their aptitude and temperament towards regular agricultural work of the kind required of them, and on their state of health and physical prowess. Their reputation of being easily adaptable to the Straits environment,[173] would not only help them to acclimatize and learn their work more quickly, but the process of social orientation could be less traumatic. One planter summed up the qualities of the Tamils thus:

> As general all-round estate coolies I believe the people of this nationality, as imported direct from India, to be second to none in the world and I should advise the intending planter to secure as many of them as he can possibly find work for. Quiet, amenable to discipline, very quick to pick up and adapt themselves to any kind of work, ... they are ... the best of servants to a just master, and they will often settle down on an estate and remain there content with considerably lower wages than they might procure elsewhere, if they are treated with fairness and consideration.[174]

Fair and considerate treatment was not the only factor that would tend to gratify the Tamil labourers. Their contentment also lay in their getting an adequate amount of suitable food (which included betel-nut)[175] and, more importantly, regular pay.[176]

Of the Tamils' being "amenable to discipline" as stated above, there were corroborative views. In Madras Presidency they were said to be "peaceable, quiet and submissive".[177] In the Straits they were regarded as "most amenable to the comparatively lowly paid and rather regimented life of estates," and were "obsequious, servile being[s]".[178] Finally, the Labour Commission of 1890 was convinced that the Tamils were well-behaved.[179] This view is sustainable. During the whole of the regulated indenture period (1872-1910), only on one occasion were the Indians in Province Wellesley reported to have disturbed the peace. In 1879, an attack was made by a "mob of coolies on a manager, the first perhaps ever made by Klings, and which proved almost fatal."[180] Despite the favourable reputation enjoyed by the Tamils in the Straits, the demand for Indian labour could not be automatically met because of characteristic Indian inertia.

Indian Reluctance to Emigrate
Various authorities supported the conventional stereotype that the average Indian peasant would not voluntarily emigrate overseas permanently. Bowness Fischer, who observed Indian overseas migration for many years as the British Consular Agent at Karikal in South India, wrote: "The native of India is not naturally inclined to emigrate .... Even under the most desperate circumstances he always leaves his native land with an idea of returning to it."[181] An official of the government of India reiterated that those Indians who emigrated, whether of the labouring or agricultural classes, always contemplated eventual return to their native vil-

lages.¹⁸² After the terrible famine in Madras Presidency in 1876-78, the commissioners appointed by the Madras government to enquire into its effects declared: "Even under the abnormal circumstances which the year developed, ... many fugitives have returned to the districts."¹⁸³ For the decade preceding 1898-99, nearly 84 per cent of the emigrants originating in Madras Presidency returned to their homes.¹⁸⁴

The transient nature of Indian labour migration is illustrated by the traffic to Ceylon (now Sri Lanka). From the 1830s onward, South Indians working on the coffee plantations would return to their native villages as soon as the crop ended.¹⁸⁵ From 1843 to 1851, although an annual residue of about 30 per cent took up more or less permanent residence, the rest of the immigrant labourers returned to India.¹⁸⁶ From 1852 to 1915, an average of 69 per cent of the South Indian immigrants in the colony returned to their native places.¹⁸⁷

Similarly, of Indians emigrating to Burma, it was said: "'Bonafide agricultural labourers will not go. They will go for six months to great distances and return to

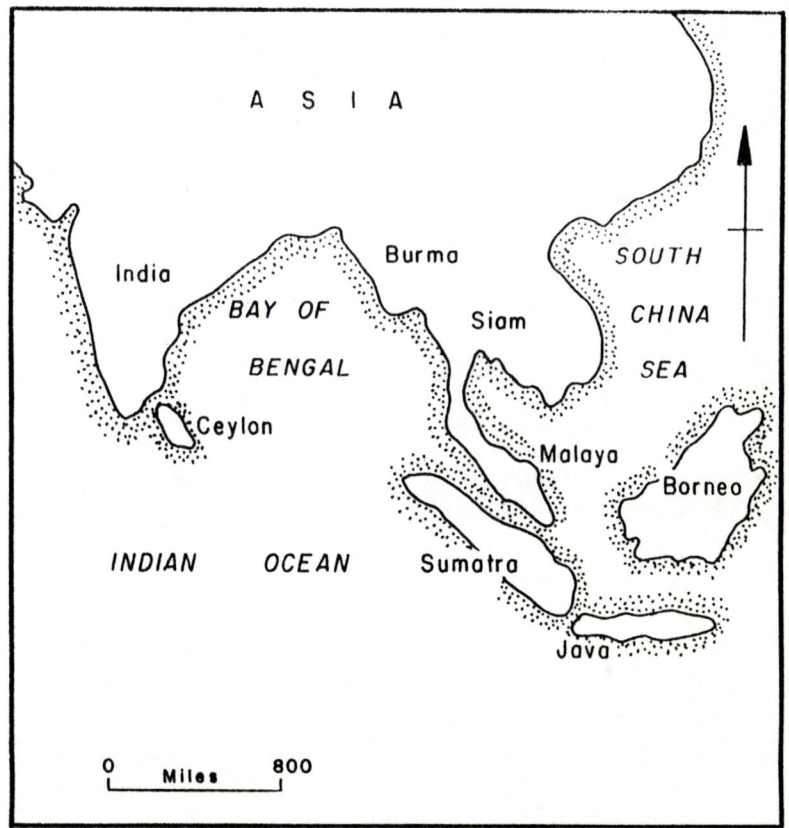

Fig. 3 — THE SITUATION OF INDIA AND MALAYA

their families, but will not export themselves with their families.'"[188] In the 1870s, of the approximately 150,000 Indian labourers in Burma, a great majority of them were temporary or seasonal workers; only a small number actually settled.[189] From 1875 to 1915, an average 82 per cent retro-migrated to India.[190]

Of emigration to the more distant British colonies, the Governor-General of India is recorded as having said:

> The people of India as a whole will not emigrate ... Those who leave their homes ... never cease to look forward to returning eventually to their villages .... We have little doubt that were the West Indian Colonies and Mauritius as near the fields whence the emigrants are drawn as are the Central Provinces and British Burma it would be found that few who emigrate thither would remain as permanent settlers.[191]

The number of those who returned to India from distant sugar colonies is shown in the following table:-

TABLE IV
THE NUMBER OF INDIAN LABOURERS DEPARTING FROM MAURITIUS AND THREE BRITISH WEST INDIAN COLONIES BETWEEN 1842-70

COLONY	ARRIVING	REMAINING	DEPARTING	%
Mauritius	315,401	217,983	97,418	31
British Guiana	79,691	72,070	7,621	10
Trinidad	42,519	38,538	3,981	9
Jamaica	15,169	13,321	1,848	12
Total	452,780	341,912	110,868	24

Source: Geoghegan, *Emigration from India*, pp. 66-67.

Among the reasons that could be adduced for the low number of migrants leaving these colonies for their homeland[192] were the dissipation of nostalgia after five years of indenture and a further five years of "industrial residence", which qualified them for a free or assisted return passage; the acquisition of a family, a home, landed property and livestock; the making of new alliances; the renunciation of the right to repatriation through commutation of the entitlement to a free passage to India for a grant of land; the large number of deaths and the low birth rate; the fear of ridicule and shame in India that usually accompanied a repatriate's inability to demonstrate material progress; and the loss of caste. Probably the greatest discouraging factor was fear of the long and often arduous voyage. By sail, the voyage from Mauritius took some three weeks, and from the West Indies, about three months. By comparison, to the Straits Settlements, the voyage by sail lasted only about ten or twelve days; and when a steamer service was introduced in 1887, it seldom occupied more than five days. Herein lay one of the crucial reasons why the Province Wellesley planters adopted the indenture system.

Sugar and Indenture

The table above illustrates that the nearer the immigrants were to India, the higher the number retro-migrating. The relatively close proximity of Province Wellesley to the Madras coast and the frequent communication across the Bay of Bengal made returning to India comparatively easy and inexpensive. With the established trend of immigrants repatriating as soon as crops were reaped or when they had fulfilled their contractual obligations, unless there was adequate recruitment, the employers could find themselves now with a full complement of labour, and then suddenly with a depleted labour force. The following table illustrates the transient pattern of Indian immigration into the Straits Settlements for the only three years for which such statistics are available. The figures include indentured as well as free labourers.

TABLE V
ARRIVAL AND DEPARTURE OF SOUTH INDIANS
FROM PENANG, 1867-69

YEAR	ARRIVING	DEPARTING	%
1867	2,922	1,451	50
1868	3,253	1,138	35
1869	3,969	1,572	40
Total/Av.	10,144	4,161	41

Source: Compiled from C.O. 273/45. Enclosure in Sir Harry St. George Ord, Governor, S.S., to the Earl of Kimberley, Secretary of State for the Colonies, no. 39, 24 February 1871.

Unless a sizeable number of the labourers arriving in the Straits were bound by legally enforceable contracts, such transient migration could not be tolerated in the sugar industry. Many planters argued that some system of contract was necessary, for unless they could be certain of having a labour force "bound down to them at command at certain seasons, there was risk of losing an entire crop."[193] Were the supply of labour ample, the cogency of this argument would cease, for the loss of one set of labourers by a strike, desertion or otherwise could be replaced by drawing from the general labour market. As will be seen in Chapter V, the inadequacy of the labour supply provided a strong reason for adopting the indenture system.

The sugar planters' aversion to free labour was principally due to its mobility and consequent unreliability. The following report of a Malayan coffee planter aptly illustrated the general attitude of Tamils not under indenture:

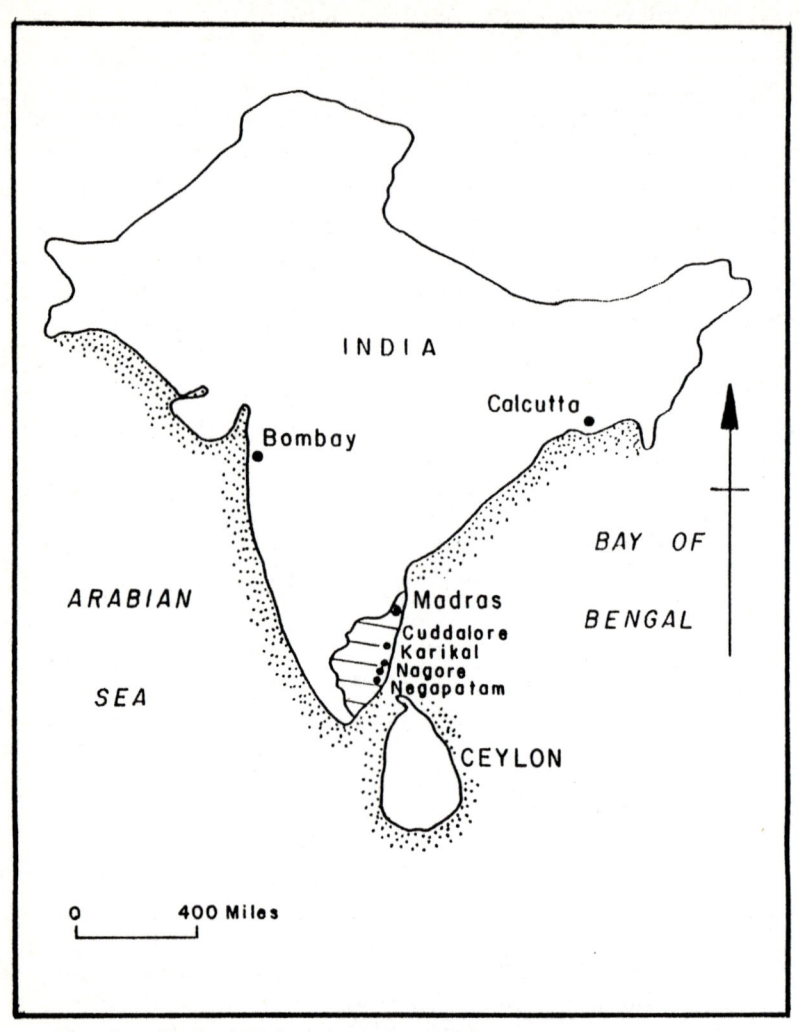

Fig. 4 THE SOUTH INDIAN PORTS OF DEPARTURE DURING PRE-REGULATED INDENTURE

> This is the paddy harvest season; Tamils are fond of reaping the paddy for the Malays by whom they are paid in kind. Six labourers disappeared together from one of these estates without saying anything to the Manager, leaving their wives and children at home on the estate. After a fortnight, they returned with two cart loads of paddy .... They have been as far away as the Province to cut paddy, and now on their return they come to the Manager and request that money for their cart hire be advanced to them. Next morning instead of turning out to work they say they are tired and their hands are sore from reaping paddy and they must rest for a few days. In the meantime the coffee trees are full of crop and there are not sufficient labourers to pick it. The Manager can do nothing but sit still and wait until the coolies are inclined to work.[194]

Similarly, without a captive labour force the sugar planters would have no guarantee that propitious weather conditions would be fully exploited for essential operations such as draining, damming, weeding, soil turning, and planting. In the reaping season, the cane might not be harvested when the sucrose content was highest. Late harvesting would result in stunted ratoons,[195] and it would also delay flood fallowing. All of this would not only disturb the ecological rhythm of the crop, but factory hands would not be fully utilized; sugar production targets might not be achieved; agreements with export markets might be jeopardized; and profits might slump.

The Straits planters had two other reasons for adopting the indenture system. First, it was the surest way of recouping the cash advances made to the recruits in India as well as the cost of their importation. Second, whereas in the other colonies the sugar industry was the dominant and, in some cases, the only source of employment, in Province Wellesley and moreso in the adjoining Malay States, there were numerous and often more lucrative job opportunities beckoning the indentured sugar workers.

The Straits planters' adoption of the indenture system, therefore, perpetuated the symbiosis that coupled it with sugar. One writer rightly observed: "Sugar meant labour – at times that labour has been slave, at other times nominally free".[196] The planters' insistence on indentured labour implied an intention to retain a strong hold on that labour. The issue was not one of having a labour supply or no labour supply; it was a question of having a labour supply anchored to the estate for a specified period of time. Such a labour supply would enable the planters to subjugate, manipulate and intimidate their labour force.

References

1 Captain (later Lieutenant Colonel) James Low. Madras Army; sent on political mission to Perak, 1826; Superintendent Province Wellesley, 1830s; Police Magistrate Singapore, 1840-43; returned to England, 1850. Source of quotation in caption: James Low, *A Dissertation on the Soil and Agriculture of the British Settlement of Penang or* Prince of Wales Island, in the Straits of Malacca; including Province Wellesley on the *Malayan Peninsula* (2nd ed., Kuala Lumpur, 1972), p. 158.
2 For a detailed discussion, see Jackson, *Planters and Speculators*, Chapter 6.
3 Ooi Jin-Bee, *Land, People and Economy in Malaya* (London, 1963), p. 200.
4 *Penang Gazette,* 28 July 1838.
5 Low, *Dissertation,* p. 83.
6 J. Thomson, *The Straits of Malacca, Indo-China and China* (London, 1875), p. 27.
7 James Low, "An Account of the Origin and Progress of the British Colonies in the Straits of Malacca," *JIA*, IV (1850), 378.
8 Thomson, *Straits of Malacca*, p. 27.
9 *Penang Gazette*, 4 September 1841.
10 William H. Newell, *Treacherous River: A Study of Rural Chinese in North Malaya* (Singapore, 1962), p.18.
11 Low, *Dissertation*, p. 49.
12 *Penang Gazette*, 4 September 1841.
13 J. Balestier, "View of the State of Agriculture in the British Possessions in the Straits of Malacca," *JIA*, Vol. II (1848), 147.
14 Jackson, *Planters and Speculators*, pp. 134-35.
15 L. Wray, *The Practical Sugar Planter* (London, 1848), p. 125.
16 J. Crawfurd, *Journal of an Embassy to the Courts of Siam and Indo-China* (London, 1828), p. 534.
17 Balestier, "State of Agriculture", p. 147.
18 *Singapore Free Press*, 13 October 1836.
19 G.W. Earl, *The Eastern Seas* (London, 1837), p. 357.
20 Paul Wheatley, "Land Use in the Vicinity of Singapore in the Eighteen-Thirties," *MJTG*, II (March, 1954), 64.
21 Braddell, *Statistics*, p. 13.
22 Balestier, "State of Agriculture", p. 141.
23 William Hunter, "Plants of Prince of Wales Island," *JSBRAS*, No. 53 (September, 1909), 56.
24 Jackson, *Planters and Speculators*, p. 137.
25 Braddell, *Statistics,* p. 18.
26 *Singapore Free Press*, 27 August 1846.
27 Tam Kim Hong, "Chinese Sugar Planting", p. 30.
28 Balestier, "State of Agriculture", pp. 142-43.
29 Adamson, *Sugar Without Slaves*, p. 163.

30 Burn, *The British West Indies*, p. 127.
31 W.L. Mathieson, *British Slave Emancipation, 1838-49* (New York, 1967), pp. 141-56; Noel Deerr, *The History of Sugar*, Vol. II (London, 1949-50), p. 438.
32 Deerr, *History of Sugar*, Vol. II, p. 532.
33 Tinker, *New Slavery*, p. 28.
34 J.R. Logan, "Journal of an Excursion from Singapur to Malacca and Pinang," *Miscellaneous Papers Relating to Indo-China and the Indian Archipelago*, 2nd Series, Vol. 1 (1887), p. 18.
35 James Low, "British Colonies in the Straits of Malacca", p. 378; Tan Kim Hong, "Chinese Sugar Planting", p. 27.
36 L.A. Mills, *British Malaya, 1824-67* (Kuala Lumpur, 1966), p. 190.
37 *Singapore Free Press*, 29 June 1843.
38 Braddell, *Statistics*, pp. 13-14.
39 Jackson, *Planters and Speculators*, p. 139.
40 G.F. Davidson, *Trade and Travel in the Far East* (London, 1846), pp. 41-42.
41 J. Cameron, *Our Tropical Possessions in Malayan India* (2nd ed., Kuala Lumpur, 1965), p. 338.
42 I.H. Burkill, *A Dictionary of the Economic Products of the Malay Peninsula*, Vol. II (London, 1935), pp. 1937-38.
43 Balestier, "State of Agriculture", pp. 143, 150.
44 Braddell, *Statistics*, p. 18; Jackson, *Planters and Speculators*, p. 137.
45 Braddell, *Statistics*, p. 18.
46 G. Leith, *A Short Account of the Settlement, Produce and Commerce of Prince of Wales Island in the Straits* (London, 1804), p. 80; Low, *Dissertation*, p. 49.
47 Low, "British Colonies in the Straits of Malacca", p.378.
48 H.C. Prinsen Geerligs, *The World's Cane Sugar Industry: Past and Present* (Manchester, 1912), pp. 70-71.
49 Wray, *Sugar Planter*, p. 126.
50 F. Campen, "Cane Cultivation in the Straits Settlements," *Timehri* (New Series), IX (1895), 99-102.
51 A. Wright and H.A. Cartwright, eds., *Twentieth Century Impressions of British Malaya* (London, 1908), p. 369.
52 Balestier, "State of Agriculture", p. 142.
53 The annual mean rainfall in West Malaya was just over 100 inches. See John W. Henderson, *et al.*, *Area Handbook for Malaysia* (Washington, 1970), p. 16.
54 Low, *Dissertation*, p. 1.
55 Davidson, *Trade and Travel*, pp. 41-42.
56 J.H. Moor, *Notices of the Indian Archipelago and Adjacent Countries* (Singapore, 1837), p. 15; F.A. Swettenham, *An Account of the Origin and Progress of British Influence in Malaya* (Revised ed., London, 1948), p. 126.
57 Cameron, *Malayan India*, p. 327.
58 Jackson, *Planters and Speculators*, p. 141.
59 *Ibid.*, p. 143.
60 *Ibid.*

61 Braddell, *Statistics*, p. 13.
62 G.W. Earl, *Topography and Itinerary of Province Wellesley* (Penang, 1861), p. 27.
63 Thomson, *Straits of Malacca*, p. 29.
64 Earl, *Topography*, p. 25.
65 Isabella Bird, *The Golden Chersonese and the Way Thither* (London, 1883), p. 323.
66 Low, *Dissertation*, p. 8.
67 *Ibid*.
68 J.M. Gullick, *Indigenous Political Systems of Western Malaya* (London, 1965), p. 31.
69 Swettenham, *British Malaya*, pp. 142-43.
70 Wright and Cartwright, *Impressions*, pp. 124-25.
71 Arnold Wright and Thomas H. Reid, *The Malay Peninsula* (London, 1912), pp. 315-17.
72 Sanderson, *Report on Emigration*, C5193, p. 33.
73 C.A. Vlieland, "The Population of the Malay Peninsula," *The Geographical Review*, XXIV (1934), 67; PDARC, no. 4, September 1871.
74 Low, *Dissertation*, p. 80.
75 Wright and Cartwright, *Impressions*, p. 205.
76 *Straits Times*, 31 July 1886.
77 C.O. 273/71. Enclosure in Sir Andrew Clarke, Governor, S.S., to the Earl of Carnarvon, Secretary of State for the Colonies, no. 397, 25 December 1873.
78 MPP, vol. 275, November 1874.
79 Syed Hussein Alatas, "Occupational Prestige Amongst the Malays in Malaysia," *JMBRAS*, XLI, Pt. 1 (July, 1968), 151.
80 Low, *Dissertation,* p. 176.
81 W.E. Maxwell, "The Malay Peninsula: Its Resources and Prospects," *PRCI*, XXIII (London, 1872), p. 18.
82 Gullick, *Indigenous Political Systems*, p. 43.
83 T.H. Silcock and Ungku Abdul Aziz, "Nationalism in Malaya," in *Asian Nationalism and the West,* ed. by William L. Holland (New York, 1953), p. 270.
84 Swettenham, *British Malaya*, p. 136.
85 Low, *Dissertation*, pp. 7-8.
86 C.O. 273/93. Sir William Robinson, Governor, S.S., to Michael Hicks-Beach, Secretary of State for the Colonies, no. 78, 26 March 1878.
87 Braddell, *Statistics*, p. 14.
88 Gullick, *Indigenous Political Systems*, p. 31.
89 Low, *Dissertation*, p. 175.
90 Bird, *Golden Chersonese*, p. 7.
91 J.M. Thoburn, *India and Malaysia* (New York, 1893), p. 514.
92 Earl, *Eastern Seas*, p. 185; Swettenham, *British Malaya*, p. 137.
93 Cameron, *Malayan India*, p. 346.
94 J.A. Kruyt, "Address Delivered before the Indian Society on the Straits Settlements and the Malay Peninsula," *JSBRAS*, No. 28 (August, 1895), 40.

95 Low, *Dissertation*, p. 9.
96 J.M. Vermont, *Immigration from India to the Straits Settlements* (London, 1888), p. 7.
97 Michael Ardizzone, *A Nation is Born* (London, 1946), p. 18.
98 Ali, *Indenture in Fiji*, p. viii.
99 Lal, "Fiji Girmitiyas," p. 12.
100 See Gillion, *Fiji's Indian Migrants*, p. 2.
101 *Ibid*.
102 Everard F. Im Thurn, *Among the Indians of Guiana* (London, 1883, reprinted New York, 1967), pp. 227-54.
103 Brett, *Indian Missions in Guiana*, p. 230.
104 *Ibid*.
105 Menezes, *Amerindians in British Guiana*, p. 190.
106 Evidence of Sir John Anderson, in Sanderson, *Report on Emigration*, C5193, p. 41.
107 Bird, *Golden Chersonese*, p. 115.
108 C.M. Turnbull, *A History of Singapore, 1819-1975* (Kuala Lumpur, 1977), p. 44.
109 *Report of the Commissioners Appointed to Enquire into the State of Labour in the Straits Settlements and Protected Native States* (Singapore, 1891), p. 36. (Hereinafter referred to as RLC 1890.)
110 R.N. Jackson, *Immigrant Labour and the Development of Malaya, 1786-1920* (Kuala Lumpur, 1961), p. 127.
111 *Straits Times*, 31 July 1886.
112 Ordinance V of 1884, article 47.
113 PP, Vol. LXXII, 1888, p. 12.
114 *Straits Times*, 31 July 1886.
115 RLC 1890, p. 66.
116 *Straits Times*, 31 July 1886.
117 J.W. Jenks, *Report on Certain Economic Questions in the English and Dutch Colonies in the Orient* (Washington, 1920), p. 63.
118 Annemarie de Waal Malefijt, *The Javanese of Surinam* (Assen, Netherlands, 1963), p. 25.
119 A.W.S., *Rubber Estate Values* (Singapore, 1910), p. 85.
120 C.W.C. Parr, *Report of the Commission Appointed to Enquire into the Conditions of Indentured Labour in the Federated Malay States* (Kuala Lumpur, 1910), pp. 2, 41.
121 J. Crawfurd, *History of the Indian Archipelago*, Vol. I (London, 1820), pp. 134-36.
122 Low, *Dissertation*, p. 9.
123 Makepeace, Brooke and Braddell, *Singapore*, Vol. II p. 93.
124 Thomson, *Straits of Malacca*, p. 33.
125 P.C. Campbell, *Chinese Coolie Emigration to Countries Within the British Empire* (London, 1923), p. 89.

126 T.J. Newbold, *Political and Statistical Account of the British Settlements in the Straits of Malacca,* Vol. I, (London, 1839), p. 13.
127 Crawfurd, *History of Indian Archipelago*, Vol. I, p. 136.
128 Maxwell, *Malay Peninsula*, p. 26.
129 *Straits Times,* 31 July 1886.
130 Campbell, *Chinese Immigration*, p. 89.
131 *Ibid.*
132 RLC 1890, p. 66.
133 Victor Purcell, *The Chinese in Malaya* (Kuala Lumpur, 1967), pp. 46-47; Cameron, *Malayan India*, pp. 338-40.
134 T. Braddell, *Singapore and the Straits Settlements Described* (Penang, 1858), p. 3.
135 Earl, *Topography*, p. 30; Cameron, *Malayan India*, p. 331.
136 Thomson, *Straits of Malacca*, p. 28.
137 Purcell, *Chinese in Malaya*, pp. 104-117; Jackson, *Planters and Speculators*, pp. 129-30.
138 See Appendix A in Ordinance I of 1876.
139 See Ordinance V of 1884, article 47.
140 H. Crookewit, "The Tin Mines of Malacca," *JIA* VIII (1854), 113.
141 P. Doyle, *Tin Mining in Larut* (London, 1879), p. 6.
142 W.L. Blythe, "Historical Sketch of Chinese Labour in Malaya," *JMBRAS*, XX, Pt. 1 (June, 1947), 66.
143 RLC 1890, p. 22.
144 Newbold, *Political and Statistical Account*, Vol. II, p. 97.
145 C.O. 273/45. Sir Frederick A. Weld, Governor, S.S., to Sir H.T. Holland (created Lord Knutsford, 1888), Secretary of State for the Colonies, no. 397, 24 September 1887.
146 *Ibid.*
147 J. Norman Parmer, *Colonial Labour Policy and Administration* (New York, 1960), p. 19.
148 RLC 1890, p. 66.
149 Sanderson, *Report on Emigration*, C5192, p. 22.
150 Vlieland, "Population of Malay Peninsula", p. 67.
151 K.A. Nilakanta Sastri, "The Beginnings of Intercourse between India and China," *Indian Historical Quarterly,* XIV (1938), 380-87; D.G.E. Hall, *A History of South-East Asia* (London, 1955), p. 23; Arasaratnam, *Indians in Malaysia and Singapore,* p. 1; Sandhu, *Indians in Malaya,* p. 21.
152 D. Devahuti, *India and Ancient Malaya* (Singapore, 1965), p. 9.
153 T. Braddell, "Notices of Pinang," *JIA* (New Series) V (1850), 9.
154 Arasaratnam, *Indians in Malaysia and Singapore*, p. 1.
155 H.P. Clodd, *Malaya's First British Pioneer: The Life of Francis Light* (London, 1948), p. 61.
156 T. Braddell, "Notices of Pinang," *JIA*, V, No. 1 (1851), 9.
157 Leith, *Prince of Wales Island*, p. 80.

158 Crawfurd, *History of Indian Archipelago*, I, p. 134.
159 Low, *Dissertation*, p. 9.
160 Balestier, "State of Agriculture", pp. 142-43.
161 A.W.S.O'Sullivan, "The Relations between South India and the Straits Settlements," in *Noctes Orientals: Being a Selection of Essays read before the Straits Philosophical Society between the years 1893 and 1910* (Singapore, 1913), pp. 185-86.
162 G.W. Earl, "Industrial Pursuits, Sources of Labour and Markets for Produce," *JIA*, VII (1862), 178-79.
163 *SSGG,* 9 November 1883, p. 1266.
164 Walter Hamilton, *The East India Gazeteer* (London, 1815), p. 506.
165 Newbold, *Political and Statistical Account*, I, p. 104.
166 W.H. Gamble, *Trinidad: Historical and Descriptive* (London, 1866), p. 33; J. Rodway, "Labour and Colonization," *Timehri,* VI (September, 1919), 29; *SSGG,* 9 November 1883, p. 1266.
167 Quoted in Erickson, "East Indian Coolies", p. 142.
168 Henry G. Dalton, *History of British Guiana*, Vol. 1, (London, 1855), p. 472.
169 R.W. Beachey, *The British West Indies Sugar Industry in the Late 19th Century* (Oxford, 1957), p. 100.
170 *SSGG*, 9 November 1883, p. 1265.
171 J.D. Vaughan, *The Manners and Customs of the Chinese of the Straits Settlements* (Kuala Lumpur, 1879), p. 1.
172 *Straits Times*, 31 July 1886.
173 *Ibid.*
174 Quoted in Jackson, *Immigrant Labour*, p. 106.
175 The leaf of the piper betel, chewed with areca nut and prepared lime.
176 *Straits Times*, 31 July 1886.
177 D.A. Thrower, "The Tamils and their Country," *Eastern World*, III (November, 1949), 8.
178 K.S. Sandhu, "Some Preliminary Observations of the Origins and Characteristics of Indian Migration to Malaya, 1786-1957," in *Papers in Malayan History*, ed. By K.G. Tregonning (Singapore, 1962), p. 47.
179 RLC 1890, p. 66.
180 Vermont, *Immigration from India*, p. 17.
181 MPP, vol. 276, 21 June 1875.
182 C.L. Tupper, *Note on Indian Emigration during the Year 1878-79* (Simla, 1879), p. 40.
183 *Review of the Madras Famine, 1876-1878* (Madras, 1881), p. 27.
184 *Moral and Material Progress and Condition of India during the Year 1898-99,* Vol. LVII (London, 1900), p. 705.
185 S. Arasaratnam, *Ceylon* (New Jersey, 1964), pp. 159-60.
186 Sanderson, *Report on Emigration*, C5192, p. 27.
187 Lanka Sundaram, "Indian Labour in Ceylon," in *International Labour Review* (March, 1931), p. 371.

188 See Tinker, *New Slavery*, p. 118.
189 N.R. Chakravarti, *The Indian Minority in Burma* (London, 1971), pp. 10-11.
190 Cheng Siok Hwa, "Indian Labour in the Rice Industry of Pre-War Burma," in *Proceedings of the Second International Conference Seminar of Tamil Studies, 1968*, ed. by R.E. Asher, II (Madras, 1971), p. 343.
191 Quoted in Tinker, *New Slavery*, p. 118.
192 For a detailed discussion, see sub-heading **Decision to Settle** in Chapter I.
193 RLC 1890, p. 55.
194 G.E. Turner, "A Perak Coffee Planter's Report on the Tamil Labourer in Malaya in 1902," *MHJ*, Vol. 2, No. 1 (July, 1955), 24.
195 i.e. fresh shoots from the base of harvested cane.
196 Eric Williams, *Capitalism and Slavery* (London, 1944), p. 29.

IV

THE TRANSITION TO REGULATED INDENTURE

A traffic, which seems to have been but a modified form of slave trade, thus began, which was necessarily, for many years, a small sneaking business ....
C.G. Master[1]

Until recently, a number of writers on Indians in Malaya have suggested without citing any sources that the indentured labour traffic to the Straits Settlements did not begin until some time during the nineteenth century. On the other hand, some primary sources strongly suggest that the movement commenced in an unregulated form shortly after the settlement of Penang in 1786. The uncertainty of the specific date and the very little that is still known of the early traffic is due mainly to sparse documentation. This led some recent scholars on Malaya to make calculated deductions from events that led them to print to an approximate date.

Commencement of Unregulated Indenture
Arasaratnam believed a "limited and irregular movement" of Indian indentured labourers to the Straits Settlements began about 1838.[2] In that year, it will be recalled, the first European-owned sugar factory was opened in Ayer Hitam Valley in Penang;[3] and sugar cultivation on a commercial scale commenced in Singapore.[4] Another writer, C. Kondapi, suggested that South Indians were first imported under three-year indentures to work on Malayan sugar and coffee plantations in 1833.[5] K.S. Sandhu concluded: "... indentured labour migration from India to Malaya could possibly predate 1823".[6] This dating comes closest to the assertion by the Labour Commission appointed by the Straits government in 1890 which revealed that South Indian "indentured coolies" had been arriving in the Straits "from the commencement of the present [nineteenth] century".[7]

Contrary to these datings, the papers of the South Indian Labour Fund Board of Malaya pointed to the "late eighteenth century".[8] In support of this, there is the testimony of J.W.W. Birch, the Colonial Secretary of the Straits Settlements. In 1871, he stated to the Madras government that they were "well aware" that there had been "previous to the nineteenth century" a regular indentured labour traffic from various South Indian ports to Penang.[9]

There is also the testimony of Thomas Heslop Hill, a coffee planter in Ceylon (1868-78) and Protector of Labour in the Straits Settlements and the Federated

Malay States (1901-5). When Hill was asked by the Sanderson Committee whether there was already an Indian indenture system in the Straits when his connections with the colony began, his response was: "Yes. I think it always more or less existed since the importation of [South Indian] labourers began."[10]

The *Penang Gazette* of 2 July 1870 referring to Indian indenture in the Straits stated that the traffic began "nearly a century" before.

Endorsement of late eighteenth century commencement is found in the "Note on Emigration from India" written in 1873 by John Geoghegan, the Under-Secretary to the government of India in the Department of Agriculture, Revenue and Commerce, which was then responsible for emigration matters. Geoghegan wrote of an "uncontrolled ... Tamil exodus" of domestic servants and agricultural labourers to the Straits Settlements, which "had begun before the end of the last [i.e. eighteenth] century."[11] Some of these labourers, he added, were brought by Indian speculators while others were recruited through planters' initiatives. All these labourers, he said, were engaged under the "mischievous system of advances", repayment of which was secured by their entering into a contractual agreement to work for a specified term not exceeding two years.[12]

Finally, there is the assertion made in 1883 by C.G. Master, the Chief Secretary to the government of India. In a review of indenture, he wrote:

> This traffic in fact originated in the restlessness of some of the sturdy Muhammadan (Lubbay) adventurers of Nagore, which is conveniently situated for such purposes on the border land of the French Settlement of Karikal. These men went over to the Straits Settlements, towards the close of the last century, with a small cargo of labourers, whom they had decoyed from the estates of neighbouring Mirasidars, [holders of hereditary lands] .... Labour being in request on the other side of the water, their venture proved successful; and a traffic, which seems to have been but a modified form of slave trade, thus began, which was necessarily, for many years, a small sneaking business, the exact nature of which, owing to the innate advantages of site enjoyed by Nagore and to the encouragement and protection afforded by the neighbouring French territory, long escaped detection.[13]

In summing up, there are stronger indications that an unregulated Indian indentured traffic to the Straits Settlements commenced towards the end of the eighteenth century, probably around 1790. Because of the obscurity that veiled its operations, it may never be known precisely when it began.

Glimpses of Pre-Regulated Indian Indenture
According to a government of Madras report, the labour traffic was conducted thus in September 1870:

> A shipowner advances money to a head maistry (recruiting agent) who employs under him several subordinate maistries. These latter have to go about to villages and persuade coolies to emigrate. This they do by representing, in bright colours, prospects of enrichment and advance. The ignorant coolies believe easily and while some volunteer to go to try their fortune, many are persuaded. The maistries ... get ten rupees a head for every adult coolly they bring, all contingent expenses being paid. A lower price is given for boys who are not in such demand, and a somewhat higher rate for young and good-looking women.

> The coolies thus obtained are kept in godowns (or depots) in Negapatam (or other ports) until a sufficient number is collected. They are then shipped on the shipowner's vessel and accompanied by the head maistry to the port of destination. There they are sold under contract to serve for certain periods. Each man fetches about five pounds; and all expenses of maintenance, passage money, etc., are discharged by the purchaser. The shipowner and head maistry divide the profits ....[14]

In November 1870, the Lieutenant-Governor of Penang, Colonel A.E.H. Anson, learnt that a number of Indian indentured labourers on a certain Province Wellesley estate had been sent to the Butterworth General Hospital in a "very bad condition."[15] Anson immediately visited the estate, and of the labourers there, he gave the following account.

> I found that a most disgraceful and disgusting state of things existed on the estate. I directed that all of those coolies who were suffering, and requiring medical attendance, should be, at once, sent to the hospital. At this the owner jeered at me; and said I could not accommodate so many. However, I undertook to do so, and forty, including two women, were sent there. Many of these, including the two women, had the marks of flogging on their backs. One of the women so marked had her toes sloughing away. The acts of cruelty were too disgusting to describe.[16]

In 1873, Geoghegan wrote:

> The sugar, spice, tapioca, and cocoanut [sic] plantations of Penang have come altogether to depend on Madras [Presidency] for the supply of agricultural labour. This emigration, which in 1871 was said to average 4,000 a year, was chiefly carried on from Nagore and adjacent small ports, and was unregulated by law, except so far as the general Act [XXV of 1859] regulating native craft plying in the Bay of Bengal affected the vessels engaged in the traffic. The labourers were partly introduced by agents on speculation, and partly by "tindals" [estate headmen] ... sent over by the managers of estates to recruit in and around their native villages. The wages are not very distinctly stated .... The term of engagement does not appear to have exceeded two years; and as a large Tamil population has settled down at Penang, and intercourse between that settlement and Southern India was tolerably frequent, the condition of labourers was probably not uncomfortable.[17]

Finally, J.M. Vermont, who arrived in the Straits in 1854 from the West Indies to manage the Batu Kawan estate, gave this account in his *Immigration from India to the Straits Settlements* published in 1888.

> Up to the year 1857 this immigration was entirely voluntary, and unaided by employers of labour here, the only encouragement given by them being limited to engaging the men on their arrival, and advancing the small sum their passage cost them. As years rolled on and the settlements were developed, the demand for this kind of labour so increased, that owners of estates were compelled to hold out further inducements to these people by assisting them with advances to pay their debts and passage money, on condition that they would sign agreements on their arrival, to work on the plantation of their employer for a year, after which time – provided their advances had been repaid – they were at liberty to go where they chose. The rate of wages given was 10 cents per day's work, a full day's wage being given on Sunday provided they had worked six and a half days in the week.[18]

Vermont's assertion of the traffic being "entirely voluntary" coincided with that of Sir J.C. Hobhouse, President of the Board of Control (1835-41), government of

India. He postulated that the traffic was a "purely voluntary movement on the part of the people stimulated by their own wishes and interests".[19]

Contrary to these assertions, Master, the government of India's Chief Secretary, declared there was "a misconception of the real conditions under which this emigration was initiated and carried out".[20] He said the impression conveyed by Hobhouse was "certainly not in consonance with facts, while it implies an analogy between this [indentured labour] movement and the spontaneous emigration of a free and intelligent people in England and elsewhere which is fallacious and illusory."[21]

Since the beginning of the labour traffic from South India, most of the immigrants had been working at Penang. But as the European sector of the Province Wellesley sugar industry started expanding from about 1846, the Indian population there began to increase as the following table shows. The figures include the number of indentured labourers as well.

TABLE VI
INDIAN POPULATION OF PENANG AND PROVINCE WELLESLEY **FOR VARIOUS YEARS BETWEEN 1812-71**

YEAR	PENANG	PROVINCE WELLESLEY
1812	7,044	72
1820	8,198	338
1830	8,858	N/A
1833	N/A	1,087
1842	9,681	N/A
1844	N/A	1,815
1850	7,840	N/A
1851	N/A	1,913
1860	10,618	3,514
1871	18,611[a]	5,000 (approx.)

a – includes population of Province Wellesley
N/A = No reliable figures available
Source: Braddell, *Statistics*, p. 2; Marriot, "Population", pp. 38-39.

For 1867, 1868 and 1869, the number of Indian indentured labourers contracted to the Province Wellesley planters was 1461, 1626 and 1985 respectively.[22]

The Embargo on Labour Emigration
Labour emigration from South India went on undisturbed until 12 March 1870 when W.J. Hathaway, the sub-Collector (or administrative head) of the South Indian district of Tanjore, who was stationed at Negapatam, published the following story in the *Tanjore Gazette* of 12 March 1870: "Many cases have come to notice which show that there is a regularly organized system in this district of kidnapping men and children and taking them down to coolie godowns in Negapatam, to be shipped from there to Pinang and other places which are thus regularly supplied with men as coolies and girls as prostitutes."

In support of his contention, Hathaway cited a case which occurred in 1869 where seven persons were convicted for being involved in what he described as a "nefarious traffic" of kidnapping.[23] Hathaway did not give any details of the case itself but the sentences imposed ranged from ten to eighteen months rigorous imprisonment in addition to fines of fifty rupees each. The *coolie maistry* (i.e. the labour recruiter), who was the chief offender in the case, was sentenced to two years' similar imprisonment and was fined 100 rupees.[24]

An Indian newspaper reported: "An organized system of kidnapping men and children of both sexes has been discovered and broken up in the Tanjore District. The captives were shipped from Negapatam for Penang and other countries, where the males were employed as coolies and the females sold to a life of prostitution."[25]

Hathaway's determination to prevent a repetition of these abuses found expression in several measures. First, he required the sentences imposed on the offenders to be made public "by beat of tom-tom" in the villages where the kidnapping had occurred and at Negapatam in front of the private emigration depots where the kidnapped people had been held captive. Second, he distinctly warned policemen that they would be prosecuted if found negligent in acting to prevent or suppress this "heinous crime". Third, he enjoined all village magistrates in Tanjore to use their best endeavours to repress the crime. If kidnapping persisted and if it appeared that the magistrate in whose ward it occurred might have had any knowledge about it, an enquiry would be made into his conduct "as much as if it were a case of dacoity or murder." Fourth, he pronounced that the law would interpret all inciting or inducing adults and children to emigrate to the Straits Settlements for the purpose of labour as kidnapping, punishable with imprisonment for seven years, for which the police could arrest without warrant, and no bail would be granted.[26] Fifth, anticipating evasive tactics by the recruiters and shippers, Hathaway pointed out the illegality of shipping labour emigrants from any port other than Madras, Calcutta, and Bombay as was stipulated by article 7 of the Indian Emigration Act XIII of 1864. The penalty he decreed for violation of this stipulation of the Act was a fine of 500 rupees. Finally, he issued a notice warning all shipowners that no vessel would be licensed if there was reason to suspect that it was shipping labour emigrants bound for the Straits under the guise of ordinary passengers.[27]

It seems that there was an impression among the recruiters that this trade could be carried on without fear of punishment, and that the police and the magistrates would not interfere. The steps taken by Hathaway were apparently intended to dispel this mistaken notion, and to show the light in which kidnapping, as newly conceived, would be regarded and dealt with in future. The people themselves would become aware of the illegality of taking cash advances as an inducement to emigrate to the Straits to work. Besides, speculators and shipowners alike would clearly understand the risk they would run by conniving at such unlawful emigration. Once wealthy men were discouraged from supplying the necessary capital, the traffic would most likely cease to exist on any large scale.

Hathaway enforced his repressive measures under Act XIII of 1864. The Act defined emigration as the "departure of any Native of India out of British India for the purpose of labouring for hire in some other place", and went on to declare that British India specifically did not include "the settlement of Prince of Wales' Island [Penang], Singapore, and Malacca".[28] Furthermore, article 4 of the Act stipulated that "contracts may be made with Natives of India to emigrate to any of the British Colonies of Mauritius, Jamaica, British Guiana, Trinidad, St. Lucia, Grenada, St. Vincent, Natal, St. Kitts, and Seychelles, and to the Danish Colony of St. Croix; and it shall be lawful to enable or assist any Native of India to emigrate to any such Colony." The omission of the Straits Settlements from the permitted list of colonies suggests that the labour traffic to the colony had been forbidden since 1864.

The question arises why did the government of India deliberately exclude its own dependencies from recruiting labour in India while emigration was permitted to the other colonies? In the absence of official explanation, some speculation may be ventured. In 1864, the Straits Settlements was still governed by the imperial government of India, and this government had been anticipating the imminent transfer of the administration of the Settlements to the Colonial Office in response to the pressure exerted by the press and the European community in Singapore.[29] The government of India, therefore, omitted the Straits Settlements from the permitted list of colonies with the apparent expectation that when the transfer was affected the colonial government would regulate the indentured labour traffic in accordance with Act XIII of 1864.

The severance of the Settlements from India was not made until 1867, and, at the time, the Act was said to have escaped notice.[30] Apparently, the Straits government had taken immigration from India for granted, the making of labour contracts between planters and Indians having gone on with "perfect freedom" for such a long time. Furthermore, in 1867, Straits officialdom was undoubtedly too pre-occupied with organizing and consolidating the new government, so that immigration matters, being entirely in the hands of the planters, did not warrant their attention. Whatever the circumstances, it was the responsibility of the government of India, as the author of the Act, to advise the Straits government that it had been promulgated.

Reactions from the Straits
The response from the Straits was unanimous disagreement with the action Hathaway took under Act XIII of 1864. The Straits Colonial Secretary, Birch, ar-

gued that it was only by the "merest accident", from the terms in which the Act was conceived, that it was capable of the new construction Hathaway had put on it.[31] Likewise, the planters contended that there was "an accident of legislation" due to an oversight.[32] To Vermont, the prohibition was based on an interpretation of the Act rather than on the Act itself.[33] He added:

> It seems impossible that the framers of the Act 13 of 1864 could have contemplated the prohibition of emigration to the Straits, at the time politically one with India, as well as geographically, historically and socially considered analogous to it; whilst leaving it free to Ceylon and Burmah, and permitting it under certain restrictions, to such distant places as Mauritius and the West Indies. This view of the matter is borne out by the fact that the Act was in force for six years before it was discovered that it would bear such an interpretation.

It is difficult to see how these inferences arose. The Act, after clearly defining what constituted emigration for the purpose of labour, expressly and unequivocally excluded the Straits Settlements from the list of colonies permitted to recruit Indian labour.

In Birch's view, this exclusion had been intended neither to operate against the Straits nor to classify it as a foreign colony for the purposes of the Act.[34] On the contrary, he was of the opinion that the Act was meant to operate in favour of the colony excepting it from the restrictions imposed on the other colonies.[35] This view was apparently strengthened by what had actually occurred in operationalizing the Act, recruitment having been conducted without any interference from the Indian authorities, and the planters had continued to derive their labour from South India for six years after the passing of the Act without any restriction whatever. On this premise, it would seem unfair to have prohibited the traffic and thus cause economic injury to the planters, especially since they were not directly responsible for the perpetration of the alleged abuses. "All the arrangements for collecting and bringing over these immigrants," Birch reported, "were made in India without the knowledge or intervention of the estate managers. All they were concerned with was to bind the immigrants to work".[36]

The *Straits Times* played no less a significant part in opposing the embargo. "What possible reason can there be in 1870 for prohibiting the legitimate emigration of natives of India that has not existed from the moment that Pinang became an integral part of that government? Is it that the transfer of these settlements to the Colonial Office has made us a foreign colony?"[37] This transfer did not render the colony foreign in the sense of, for example, the Dutch colony of Surinam or the French colony of Martinique, both of which were importing Indian labour. When the Straits Settlements became a crown colony on 1 April 1867 and was ruled under a colonial constitution,[38] it was placed in the same category, at least as far as emigration was concerned, as Mauritius and the British West Indian colonies. Although the *Straits Times* had itself hailed the transfer as "the greatest political event which has occurred since the foundation of the Settlement",[39] it seemed unaware of these important implications.

Governor Ord's Enquiry

Disturbed by the claims that the infant colony was the recipient of kidnapped Indian labourers, Governor Sir Harry St George Ord, of the Straits Settlements, personally conducted an enquiry towards the end of 1870 on every estate in Province Wellesley. The result of his enquiry disposed him to refute the allegations of kidnapping in the ordinary sense of he word. He strongly protested to the Madras government dismissing the charges as "unfounded or greatly exaggerated".[40] But to the Secretary of State for the Colonies, he admitted:

> There were a few cases in which boys [and two women] alleged that they had been sent against their will …. I have no doubt but that in some instances advantage has been taken of the discontent of lads with their position at home and of girls or young married women having quarrelled with their husbands or relatives to hold out flattering pictures of the advantages they would obtain in the Straits and to encourage them to emigrate thither.[41]

Although he thus confirmed that recruiters did use deception in procuring recruits, Ord apparently saw nothing singularly sinister in this practice. It seemed to him that any such emigration would be subject to certain hazards and abuses which would also exist in emigration to the other colonies. Indeed, where recruitment had been carried on by local men paid by the results, it could hardly be expected that abuses would not be perpetrated.

Some recruits would have actually invited being coerced. It would not be farfetched to assume that once they had spent their advances, some decided to rescind their decision and refused to emigrate. Wherever this occurred, the recruiters would be faced with three options: they could choose not to return to their employers; they could refund out of their pocket advances given out; or they could use coercive measures to compel reluctant recruits to emigrate. This latter course recruiters could take seemingly with almost entire impunity. Hathaway's admission of some neglect by the police to take active steps to prevent kidnapping[42] leads to the inference that the recruiters were relatively free to secure recalcitrants by the most effective means. This being a strong possibility, Ord's claim that out of the "large proportion" of labourers he had examined only a small fraction had declared being coerced to emigrate could have been an underestimate. Maybe there were others who were too timid or terrified to make such an incriminating accusation. Ord's report revealed no such consideration, apparently because he believed the labourers were aware of their legal rights.

Ord's belief was based on a few incidents which occurred in 1868 and 1869. Twelve complaints were allegedly made by Indian emigrants who were detained on board ship at Penang for non-payment of their fares, and were later released by a writ of *habeas corpus*.[43] Recounting this incident to the Secretary of State, Ord concluded: "This shows that the emigrants are aware of the protection they can claim from the courts of the colony and negatives the presumption that any of them are brought hither against their will."[44] This is rather doubtful. It could hardly be expected that poor and unlettered peasants would be capable of pursuing what would certainly have been for them a complicated and expensive legal process. It was more likely that it was the labour-hungry planter to whom the emigrants were consigned who had secured their release.

Either Ord was using diversionary tactics to convince the Colonial Office of the falsehood of Hathaway's injurious allegations, or he misunderstood or was unaware of the real vulnerability of the average South Indian indentured labourer. For this latter inclination, there was some ground. The description given by Birch, who claimed close observation of Tamils for twenty-five years, indicated why a larger number than contended by Ord could have been forced to emigrate. Birch wrote: "Very few of them can read; and their minds, growing up to maturity in a very narrow circle, and with nothing to rouse their powers, remain in deep ignorance and superstition. But the most painful part of their character is the entire want of independence or what is called honest pride. A common *taluk*[45] peon is to them a terrible personage."[46] Surely, they would be more fearful of a British Governor in the more inhibiting presence of his aides, and of the Attorney-General and the estate managers who accompanied the party. In such formidable company, most of the labourers would have preserved a reticence or would be unwilling to admit being kidnapped. Therefore, it was quite possible that the number of labourers kidnapped was greater than actually discovered.

The language barrier could also have posed difficulties in ascertaining the actual number kidnapped. The enquiry would have depended upon interpreters who, in all probability, at least in some cases, were the tindals, some of whom were also recruiters. Ord had said that the planters had often dispatched their headmen to recruit in India.[47] It would also be recalled that of the seven persons convicted of kidnapping in Tanjore in 1869, two were recruiters. It was quite probable that when the tindals, as recruiters, were confronted with the possibility of losing the advances, they would have preferred to dragoon their recruits into emigrating by utilizing whatever effective means they had at their disposal. Because of fear of victimization, labourers who had been coerced by the recruiting headmen would hardly be expected to accuse them to their face.

The Planters' Protest
Ord's remonstrance against Hathaway's allegations was complemented by protest from the planters. At an urgently convened meeting, they passed the following resolutions:
>   a.   That this meeting has heard with surprise and alarm that the coolie emigration from the Coromandel Coast to the Straits Settlements has been suddenly prohibited, after having existed for upwards of half a century.
>   b.   That a committee be appointed to enquire into the subject of the coolie emigration from India, and the various Legislative Acts bearing upon the subject, with a view of drawing up a memorial to the government in favour of this Colony being placed upon the same footing as Ceylon and British Burmah, with reference to the Legislative Act of 1864.[48]

In the petition addressed to Ord, the planters depicted the economic plight they anticipated and urged his intervention to bring about a speedy resumption of labour emigration.[49] At the same time, they claimed that out of the many thousands of Indian labourers under their employ not one had ever lodged a complaint of having been kidnapped; that women were brought over for prostitution was false; and that a large number of them came over with their husbands and led more reputable and comfortable lives than they had ever done before.[50] Straits records are silent on these issues; no clear evidence is, therefore, available that would corroborate or refute these claims. But the *Singapore Daily Times* observed: "There is one feature in the petition of the planters which strikes us as being peculiar, namely, the credit which they take to themselves throughout for the care and solicitude they have at all times displayed for the well-being of their coolies."[51]

On the other hand, the *Penang Gazette* defended the planters and rebutted Hathaway's allegations. The editor urged the planters to counter the charge of prostitution with an "indignant denial."[52] But he continued rather contradictorily: "Possibly there are isolated cases in which such a 'nefarious traffic' has been practised".[53] In an apparent attempt to diminish the seriousness of even these few cases, the editor postulated that generally the women's new life was a great improvement on that he claimed they had led in South India. Previous to their immigration into the Straits, he asserted, the women were "the very sweepings of the Madras bazaars, wasted with disease, and steeped in every moral iniquity". But after their arrival on the estates, he added, they "become reclaimed ... and in nearly every case marry and live reputable lives, bearing and bringing up children, who, instead of having reason to curse those who induced their parents to emigrate, have every cause to bless the day when they were removed to a better and purer moral atmosphere."

Madras Government's Demands for Labour Protection

In September 1870, the Collector of Tanjore transferred the entire matter to the provincial Madras government. The first step they took was to appoint the sub-collector of Tanjore, H.J. Stokes (who succeeded Hathaway), to enquire into the latter's allegations. In his report of late September 1870, which Master, the Chief Secretary to the government of India, described as "very able and careful",[54] Stokes maintained that the traffic did involve kidnapping of women and minors, which led to a "system of duress or illegal confinement, and, moreover, excessive crowding on board ship."[55] This report persuaded the Madras government to uphold all of Hathaway's repressive measures. Furthermore, the government re-affirmed that labour emigration to the Straits must discontinue with immediate effect.

As matters thus stood, a legal resumption of the traffic was only possible if the Straits government complied with the terms of Act XIII of 1864. Specifically applicable to the Straits Settlements was the following proviso:

> The Governor-General of India in Council may from time to time, by notification ... declare that the emigration of Natives of India shall be lawful to any place other than the places mentioned ... provided that every such notification shall contain also a declaration, that the Governor-General ... has been duly certified that the government of the place to which the notification refers has made such laws and other provisions as the Governor-General ... thinks sufficient for the protection of Natives of India emigrating to such place.[56]

Of the provisions required by the Act before emigration could be resumed, the Madras government insisted on three, pending final arrangements. First, they required the appointment of an Emigration Agent who would be stationed at the port of departure.[57] This officer would be nominated and paid by the Straits government but his appointment would be subject to the approval of the government of Madras. His functions would include overseeing recruitment, arranging such temporary lodging as was required for the emigrants before embarkation, and supplying such medical aid and comforts as might be necessary.[58] Second, the Madras government required the nomination of a proper person, who spoke Tamil, to serve as a Protector of Emigrants at the port of departure.[59] This officer would be appointed and liable to be removed by the Madras government to whom he would be accountable. His salary would be borne by the Straits government; and he would be precluded from holding any other office under government and from following any other profession or occupation while he served as Protector.[60] His main functions would be to "protect and aid with his advice or otherwise all [indentured] Emigrants," and to ensure that all the provisions of the current Emigration Act were duly complied with.[61] Most importantly, he was required to ensure that the recruits emigrated voluntarily. Finally, the Madras government required that emigration should proceed from the port of Negapatam instead of Madras.[62] Unlike Negapatam, Madras was shared by a number of labour-importing countries. Adding Straits recruits to it would not only be inconsistent with the government of India's policy of decentralizing the points of outlet, but it could create a similar or worse crowding situation than that existing at Calcutta. Under such conditions, diseases were more easily transmissible; and the provision of adequate food, water, accommodation, and sanitary facilities would be more difficult.

Locating the port of embarkation at Negapatam instead of at Madras presented three distinct advantages. Competition for recruits in the surrounding districts would be less intensive. Thus, the Straits planters could be fairly assured of a regular and adequate labour supply. Negapatam was closer to the traditional districts where recruitment took place, entailing less travelling expense, inconvenience, and fatigue. If certain recruits were rejected at the depot, their return home would be easier.

In response to the Madras government's requirements, Governor Ord was critical of what he described as the "peculiar nature" of such an "expensive system" of emigration.[63] His estimated cost of salaries for the Agent, the Protector, and a medical inspector of emigrants, excluding ancillary staff, amounted to £2,500 per annum.[64] To avoid this, he sought to convince the Madras government of the great benefit Indian labourers derived from immigrating into the Straits. Furthermore, he added, they found themselves in a climate well suited to their constitution; they were working amongst a population composed of friends and compatriots, and at a kind of work not altogether unfamiliar to them; and their wages were higher than those obtainable in South India.[65]

Had the Madras government relented, Hathaway's efforts to purge the traffic of its illegal concomitants might have been in vain; a lack of administrative unity in Madras Presidency would have become evident; the public would have lost faith in the ability of their rulers to protect them; and the recruiters would have been given tacit encouragement to continue with their evil ways.

Ord's Appeal to the Colonial Office

Meanwhile Governor Ord had appealed to the Colonial Office to bring about a revival of the traffic on an unregulated basis. But his plea was to no avail. One official minuted on Ord's dispatch: "I do not think the Straits Settlements can claim or expect the Colonial Office to press their claim to continue to enjoy the benefits (probably accompanied by serious abuses) of an uncontrolled emigration from India."[66]

The Secretary of State for India, the Duke of Argyll, was initially sympathetic towards the Straits. He admitted there certainly appeared "much force" in Ord's representation of the heavy financial burden regulated emigration would impose on the Straits government. But after further consideration, he was convinced that kidnapping was an undesirable adjunct to emigration and that the removal of the evil could only be expected if the measures demanded by the Madras government were implemented.[67]

The futility of resisting the required terms then became clear to Ord; yet he was still not disposed to comply fully. To the Madras government, he proposed a course intermediate between the terms of Act XIII of 1864 and the absolute freedom of emigration to Ceylon and Burma. As far as personnel was concerned, he suggested merging the functions of the Agent into those of the Protector,[68] obviously to minimize expenses.

This suggestion was not without merit. As the planters then required an average of about 2,000 indentured immigrants per annum, all to be shipped between May and October,[69] it would seem unnecessary to burden the colony with the double expense of a permanent Emigration Agency in addition to a Protectorate especially since the depot would only be utilized for the same period. Even if the two offices were combined (for which the Straits government was willing to remunerate the Protector appropriately), his duties could be justified only for about six months in the year. For the rest of the year, the Straits government considered his services superfluous. This was not so. According to article 16 of Act XIII of 1864, the Protector was also required to inspect on arrival all indentured repatriates at the port to which he was stationed; to enquire into their treatment during the period of their service abroad; and to make a report to the Madras government. Apparently, Ord conceived the performance of these duties as a means of satisfying the curiosity of the Madras authorities, which should, therefore, not be defrayed by the Straits government.

The Madras government, conscious of the distinct nature of the functions they required to be performed by the two officers, objected to Ord's proposal for a merger. They believed a combination of the two offices "would throw most incongruous duties on the covenanted officer whom this Government contemplates appointing as Protector".[70] Indeed, it would seem most inappropriate for an officer of the government of Madras to be engaged in recruiting labourers. The emigrants would blame the Protector, and in effect the Madras government, as the author of any abuses that might be practised on them; and Indian public opinion would do likewise. Furthermore, as the *de facto* employee of the Madras government, the Protector might be required to organize recruiting operations on terms that might be objected to by his government and by himself. It was, therefore, necessary to guarantee the independence of the Protector from any undue influence which the planters or their recruiting agents might attempt to exert over his sphere of operation. It would almost be certain that sooner or later a collision of opinion would arise between the officer executing both functions and the civil authorities at the port of departure. It would also be an inconsistent policy. Emigration to the other colonies was not characterized by a merging of the functions of the Agent into those of the Protector;[71] and there was nothing peculiar about the Straits that specially qualified it for such an unprecedented concession.

At that point, the negotiations were deadlocked: the Madras government relentlessly preserving its protective posture; the Straits government striving to effect a resumption of the traffic on its own terms.

Illegal Recruitment

The denial of fresh supplies of labour from South India threatened the viability of the Straits planting industry. In the early 1870s, European sugar estates in Province Wellesley were spread over the greater part of the cultivated area. Nearly every estate had a steam crushing-mill and a refinery where an "efficient" staff of European engineers was kept constantly engaged.[72] If the labourers were to follow the usual pattern of returning to India at the expiry of their contract, or seeking employment elsewhere, the sugar industry would gradually grind to a standstill. Capital, land, machinery, and the administrative and ancillary staff would then be left idle; some estates might be abandoned; the government would lose revenue; and the attempt to compensate for the short-fall in colonial sugar production would fail.

Certain Indian speculators were quite aware of the acute shortage of labour in the Straits and clandestinely carried on an illegal recruiting business. The recruiters they hired, utilizing their powerful influence, persuaded adults to represent themselves as passengers; and they taught minors to pretend having paternal or avuncular relations on board.[73] These deceptive tactics increased the difficulty of obtaining evidence against recruiters who had abetted the abduction of the recruits.

Attempts made by Madras government officials to establish that some people were being taken to the Straits for the purpose of labour often failed. No written contracts could be found to substantiate agreements; neither would suspected bona fide recruits themselves admit being recruited to work in the Straits. This absence of evidence prevented magistrates from convicting recruiters. They would not betray their illegal trade even under oath; and, similarly, the head recruiters, who kept the godowns, always professed ignorance of the entire transaction.[74]

The efforts of the Madras authorities were not always in vain. In one godown officials discovered two boys and "from the doubtful account they gave of themselves, they were suspected of not being the sons of the men whom they named as their fathers."[75] This suspicion turned out to be true, as the officials learnt shortly after releasing the boys from the godown. Once well clear of it, they named their real fathers who were sent for from their village in Tiruchirapalli (Trichinopoly). The officials believed that the boys would not have voluntarily emigrated but because they had accepted advances, food, and clothing, they had placed themselves in the power of the recruiters.[76] While this incident corroborated Hathaway's earlier claims about the prevalence of kidnapping and contradicted the consistent denials from the Straits, it must be recognized that the recruiters' tactics would have required the boys' complicity. It seems that their reputed "inarticulate ignorance and infantine superstition"[77] had rendered them compliant preys of the recruiter.

The subsequent prosecution of the keeper of the godown for kidnapping and for offences against the emigration Act failed. No evidence could be found to establish the boys' correct age. Neither could it be proved they had been assisted to emigrate for the purpose of labour in the Straits.[78] Similarly, lack of evidence prevented a committal in another case involving a young married woman who had been abducted. The prosecution could not prove that deceit had been used to persuade her to enter the godown.[79] Besides, the husband refrained from prosecuting under section 498 of the Indian Penal Code, which prescribed a penalty for enticing away a married woman with criminal intent.[80]

Once the recruiters found it risky to confine recruits in godowns, they took them directly to the ships to circumvent the police. This was not always successful. The Assistant Superintendent of Police at Tanjore, who was investigating a case of missing children, came upon a vessel about to sail for the Straits and gave the following account of the incident:

> I called all the little boys ... and questioned them closely as to where they were going, where their parents were, and so on. I fancied they had got their stories cut and dried ready for use for they answered satisfactorily enough and they all produced parents, uncles or guardians .... This vessel was laden with coolies and was just ready to start when some kidnapped boys were found on board. The license was immediately stopped and most of the coolies landed. They say the owner lost about Rs. 20,000. Serve him right. If the shipowners did not connive there would be no kidnapping.[81]

The kidnapping of boys, as well as women, was detected also by the Master Attendant stationed at the port of Negapatam. On several occasions, he brought on shore boys and women who at the last moment before the ship sailed were discovered by their relatives, or who had suddenly decided against emigrating. When these were interviewed, they invariably declared that their passage had been paid for them; that they were consigned to certain *chetties* (Indian money-lenders) in the Straits; and that they were under a verbal contract to labour for which they had received advances.[82]

For every boy, the recruiter was paid "less than" the ten rupees offered for men.[83] Despite the lower commission, the recruiters diverted their operations from men to boys. Poor boys roaming the villages would be less aware of the law, more credulous about the promised El Dorado awaiting them in the Straits, and more ready to accept tempting offers of an immediate cash advance, food, and clothing. Their domestic responsibilities, if any, would be less restraining, and it was easier for them to pretend they were going to join parents. On the estates they would be less productive than men, and would earn less. Low wages would delay the repayment of advances; this would ensure a protracted period of indenture during which the boys might develop into robust workers. It was probably for these reasons that, as Stokes, the sub-Collector of Tanjore, said: "Boys are carried off suddenly from their village and are lost to their parents".[84] Of the number of boys immigrating to the Straits, Stokes said he "roughly estimated" about five in every 100 were kidnapped.[85]

The number of women emigrating to the Straits was considerably less than that of men. Contrary to the claim made by Vermont, the manager of the Batu Kawan estate, that a "large number" accompanied their husbands,[86] the Colonial Secretary, Birch, said the proportion of women to men was "usually very small."[87] In support of Birch, the following table shows the sexual composition of passengers, including all categories of labourers, who left South India for Penang, for four years.

TABLE VII
SEXUAL PROPORTION OF ALL INDIAN PASSENGERS
PROCEEDING FROM SOUTH INDIA TO PENANG, 1866-69

YEAR	MALES	FEMALES	RATIO
1866	5,296	321	16:1
1867	3,955	339	11:1
1868	4,387	462	9:1
1869	6,245	768	8:1
TOTAL/AV.	19,883	1,890	11:1

Source: Compiled from MPP, Range 439, vol. 10, 13 September 1870.

This comparatively small number of women, which could be regarded as one of the main causes for the prevalence of prostitution of which Hathaway, the former sub-Collector of Tanjore had complained, was partly due to the difficulty of recruiting them, and also to the policy of the planters. According to them, family immigration was disadvantageous.[88] This may be upheld on economic grounds. The planters' outlay on passages would be greater; more housing and other social facilities would have to be provided; the productivity of the women would normally be lower than the men's; and maternal duties would tend towards irregular work and consequently less production. In the final analysis, profits would diminish. It was this rather short-sighted view of their own interests which ruled out the establishment of a reliable long-term labour force.

No serious consideration was apparently given to family immigration as an investment in the longer term and to the stability family life could give to the labour force. The planters ignored the prospect that families might become satisfied with their new life; that they might acquire immovable property; and that their children might develop a sense of belonging to their environment; all of which would tend to encourage the immigrants to settle permanently on the estates. It was said previously that Indian immigration tended to be semi-transitory. This trend was complemented and encouraged by the colonial sugar planters' policy towards family immigration.

From an economic point of view, it was an astute policy. The primary concern of the Province Wellesley planters was to secure cheap, reliable, and highly productive labour; they were little concerned with the wider aspects of colonialism. As capitalists, they would almost always be motivated by the maximization of their profits. Morally, however, their policy could have the unfortunate effect of spreading promiscuity; diminishing religious and social restraints; and permitting degradation.

The recruiters' difficulty in procuring young marriageable women persuaded them to turn to the married. A Madras official wrote: "Women who have a passing quarrel with their husbands or parents are seduced away by females employed for the purpose, who hurry them on boardship before they well know what they have done."[89] The prevalence of such abuses confirmed the Madras government's determination to decline to permit the continuance of emigration unless legalized and subject to the safeguards imposed by Act XIII of 1864. The only hope of reducing the seduction of married women was if the South Indian recruiters, like their North Indian counterparts, were required by law to observe certain conditions.

In North India, the *arkatis* (or recruiters) were required to enquire into the marital status of their female recruits and to declare the exact nature of that status to the emigration authorities.[90] Failure to do so was punishable by a fine, imprisonment, or confiscation of the licence to recruit.[91] But the recruiters' consistent display of their resourcefulness in their defiance of authority suggests that they would have contrived more ingenious devices to circumvent it.

The Diversion to Karikal

The impediments introduced by the enforcement of Act XIII of 1864 induced the recruiters to divert the "cooly trade" to the neighbouring French port of Karikal. In less than three months in 1871, ninety-two claims were registered by men seeking their wives and children who, they claimed, had been seduced or abducted from their homes and traced to Karikal.[92] The claimants having examined the French emigration depot without finding the missing persons presumed they had already been shipped off to the Straits, or were lying hidden in some illegal depot at Karikal.

Suspicions aroused, the Acting French Emigration Agent and the Commissaire de Police descended upon a native lodging house in which were hidden fourteen British Indian subjects. The *maistry* (or recruiter) escaped, and his recruits, who, it was discovered, had been deceived into engaging themselves to work in the Straits, were, a Madras official believed, "sent adrift to fall in the hands of a more astute and adroit kidnapper."[93] Prosecution initiated by Bowness Fischer, the British Consular Agent at Karikal, of a licensed recruiter of the French Emigration Society for being connected with the establishment of the illegal depot resulted in a fine of fifty francs (about three Straits dollars).[94] "French justice," Fischer observed, "having considered him sufficiently punished."

This "infamous system of emigration" operating through Karikal, Fischer observed, acquired an "impudence and strength which tended to mar, if not destroy, the intentions of Act XIII of 1864."[95] Despite Hathaway's energetic measures, he added, the illicit traffic continued "unchecked, uncontrolled and unlimited with the full knowledge of the French authorities who appeared either unwilling or powerless to control it."

In the midst of the recruiters' infractions of the Emigration Act, the government of India passed a more comprehensive Act VII of 1871 superseding Act XIII of 1864. The new law was applicable to all labour-importing colonies, and its passing was in no way connected with the peculiarities which attended emigration to the Straits Settlements. Its *raison d'etre* was primarily to counteract the "very widespread discontent and disaffection existing throughout the immigrant population" in British Guiana,[96] which had led to the appointment of a Royal Commission of enquiry in 1870. Unlike its predecessor, Act VII of 1871 did not specifically exclude the Straits Settlements from recruiting in India, but its omission from the permitted list of colonies[97] had the same effect. Nevertheless, the repetition of the clause empowering the Governor-General of India to legalize emigration to any "Settlement"[98] made possible a resumption of the traffic to the Straits Settlements if its government would comply with the requirements of the Act.

Regulated Indenture Established
While Ord was on leave, which began on 4 March 1871, he held elaborate discussions with the Colonial Office on the embargo. Upon his return to the Straits on 23 March 1872, he realized that very serious consequences would ensue if a replenishment of Indian labour were denied to the estates for another crop-season.[99] Since Ord had no alternative, consideration for the sugar industry compelled him to accede to the demands made by the Madras government. In May 1872, he indicated to them his agreement to appoint an Emigration Agent in addition to a Protector of Emigrants; to establish a depot at any port required; and to ensure that emigrants would be embarked only on ships licensed by the Protector.[100] At the same time, Ord also declared his intention to pass an ordinance which, he said, by the appointment of proper persons in the colony, "shall secure [to the labourers] complete immunity from any unfair dealing and shall render impossible the recurrence of any of those irregularities which (correctly or not) have been alleged against the present system." He also gave this commitment: "The government of India may rely on the watchful care of this government over any men who may thus be sent over previous to final arrangements being concluded.[101]

Ord's treatment of this issue may be criticized. With considerable military and colonial experience behind him,[102] he "had been accustomed to discipline, to regulations, to taking responsibility and being given a reasonable measure of authority with which to exercise it."[103] With a reputation as "essentially a man of progress";[104] he might have been expected to be more sensitive to the rule of law. Once the illegality of the emigration had been exposed and confirmed, he was surely obliged to conform with the legal requirements.

Ord's attempt to economize is understandable. During his briefing in London before leaving to assume the government of the Straits Settlements in 1867, he was given little guidance on policy except to keep expenses down.[105] His strict adherence to that policy had delayed for over two years what could have been achieved almost immediately, as events soon proved.

The detailed protective measures Ord embodied in a draft ordinance were so convincing that the Madras government telegraphed the Straits on 24 May 1872 proposing tentative arrangements pending final measures. The following is an extract of the telegram:

> All restrictions on coolies proceeding from Negapatam to the Straits will be removed for the present, planters' agents to bring coolies intending to proceed to the Straits before Magistrate, at Negapatam, and state all particulars as to repayments of costs of passage, money-advances, diet during voyage, wages in Straits Settlements, nature of work, duration of engagement, return passage. Magistrate will enter these particulars in a register, copy of which will be sent to the Colonial Secretary to be reduced in individual case into a contract on arrival. Magistrate will ascertain that coolies go willingly and with full knowledge of condition. Magistrate will protect natives from crimping, and prevent desertion of families, passages will be under Indian Passengers Act.[106]

To these proposals, Ord responded thus: "The offer made in your telegram of 24th May respecting coolie emigration is accepted by Straits government."[107] He also telegraphed Lord Kimberley, the Secretary of State for the Colonies, as follows: "Having addressed Indian government respecting coolie emigration as reported in my dispatch 45, they have replied pending legislation emigration permitted temporarily on certain terms which I have accepted."[108]

Upon Ord's acceptance of the proposed conditions, the government of India legalized labour emigration to the Straits by passing Act XIV of 1872 - "An Act to Exempt the Straits Settlements from the Indian Emigration Act 1871." On 4 June 1872, the Madras government enjoined the Tanjore magistrates to remove the existing restrictions on emigration to the Straits. On 6 June, a notification was issued allowing indentured emigration to the colony.[109]

The detailed arrangements for giving effect to the provisional settlement took four years to perfect. After the submission of several preliminary measures, they eventually appeared as the Straits Settlements Ordinance I of 1876 - "An Ordinance for Regulating the Immigration of Native Labourers from British India." This ordinance regulated all aspects of the labourers' employment in the colony. Meanwhile, recruitment of indentured labourers continued apace.

References

1 Chief Secretary to the government of India, 1883. See MPP, vol. 583, 19 March 1883.
2 Arasaratnam, *Indians in Malaysia and Singapore*, p. 11.
3 Deerr, *History of Sugar*, I, p. 187.
4 Balestier, "State of Agriculture", p. 147.
5 C. Kondapi, *Indians Overseas, 1838-1949* (Bombay, 1951), p. 41.
6 Sandhu, *Indians in Malaya*, p. 78.
7 RLC 1890, pp. 36, 40.
8 ARSILFB, 1959, p. 8.
9 C.O. 273/45. Enclosure in Ord to Kimberley, no. 39, 24 February 1871.
10 Evidence of T.H. Hill, in Sanderson, *Report on Emigration*, C5193, p. 429.
11 Geoghegan, *Emigration from India*, pp. 1, 59.
12 *Ibid.*, p. 59.
13 MPP, vol. 583, 19 March 1883.
14 MPP, vols 40-44, 13 September 1870.
15 A.E.H. Anson, *About Others and Myself* (London, 1920), p. 296.
16 *Ibid*.
17 Geoghegan, *Emigration from India*, p. 59.
18 Vermont, *Immigration from India*, pp. 4-5.
19 RLC 1890, p. 36.
20 MPP, vol. 583, 19 March 1883.
21 *Ibid*.
22 C.O. 273/45. Enclosure in Ord to Kimberley, no. 39, 24 February 1871.
23 *Tanjore Gazette*, 12 March 1870.
24 *Ibid*.
25 *Friend of India*, 14 April 1870.
26 *Tanjore Gazette*, 12 March 1870.
27 *Ibid*.
28 See Act XIII of 1864, article 2.
29 See Turnbull, *Straits Settlements*, Chapter IX.
30 Geoghegan, *Emigration from India*, p. 59.
31 C.O. 273/45. Enclosure in Ord to Kimberley, no. 39, 24 February 1871.
32 RLC 1890, p. 36.
33 Vermont, *Immigration from India*, p. 10.
34 C.O. 273/45. Enclosure in Ord to Kimberley, no. 39, 24 February 1871.
35 *Ibid*.
36 *Ibid*.
37 *Straits Times*, 9 July 1870.
38 See Turnbull, *Straits Settlements*, p. 382.
39 *Straits Times*, 21 March 1867.
40 MPP, vol. 272, December 1871.
41 C.O. 273/45. Ord to Kimberley, no. 39, 24 February 1871.

42 *Tanjore Gazette*, 12 March 1870.
43 C.O. 273/45. Ord to Kimberley, no. 39, 24 February 1871.
44 *Ibid*.
45 *Taluk*, a dependency or sub-district (held by a *talukdar*) in South India. A *taluk* peon, a native office messenger, or as in this instance, an orderly of that sub-district, Source: C.A.M. Fennel, *The Stanford Dictionary of Anglicized Words and Phrases* (Cambridge, 1892), p. 755.
46 C.O. 273/45. Ord to Kimberley, no. 39, 24 February 1871.
47 *Ibid*.
48 *Penang Gazette*, 2 July 1870.
49 C.O. 273/45. Enclosure in Ord to Kimberley, no. 39, 24 February 1871.
50 *Ibid*.
51 *Singapore Daily Times*, 7 January 1871.
52 *Penang Gazette*, 2 July 1870.
53 *Ibid*.
54 MPP, vol. 583, 19 March 1883.
55 IEP, nos 1-15, September 1870; Geoghegan, *Emigration from India*, p. 59.
56 Act XIII of 1864, article 5.
57 MPP, no. 1313, 29 September 1871.
58 See Act XIII of 1864, articles 10-12.
59 MPP, no. 1313, 29 September 1871.
60 Act XIII of 1864, article 4.
61 *Ibid*., article 16.
62 MPP, no. 1313, 29 September 1871.
63 MPP, vol. 272, December 1871.
64 C.O. 273/45. Ord to Kimberley, no. 39, 24 February 1871.
65 PDARC, no. 4, September 1871.
66 C.O. 273/45. Minute no. 3119, in Ord to Kimberley, no. 39, 24 February 1871.
67 PDARC, no. 4, September 1871.
68 C.O. 273/47. Ord to Kimberley, no. 55, 15 May 1871.
69 C.O. 273/53. Officers, India Office, Letter from Hon. R.S. Ellis, Chief Secretary, government of Madras, to Colonial Secretary, Straits Settlements, 22 August 1871.
70 MPP, no. 43, December 1871.
71 See Act XIII of 1864, articles 10-16.
72 Thomson, *Straits of Malacca*, p. 28.
73 MPP, Range 439, vol. 10, 13 September 1870.
74 *Ibid*.
75 *Ibid*.
76 IEP, nos 1-15, September 1870.
77 *Ibid*.
78 MPP, Range 439, vol. 10, 13 September 1870.
79 *Ibid*.
80 See *Tanjore Gazette*, 12 March 1870.

81 MPP, Range 439, vol. 10, 13 September 1870.
82 MPP, no. 93, 24 September 1870.
83 IEP, nos 1-15, September 1870.
84 MPP, no. 583, 19 March 1883.
85 *Ibid*.
86 Vermont, *Immigration from India*, p. 9.
87 C.O. 273/45. Enclosure in Ord to Kimberley, no. 39, 24 February 1871.
88 *Ibid*.
89 MPP, no. 583, 19 March 1883.
90 Arthur A. Hill, "Emigration from India," *Timehri*, VI (September, 1919), 48 .
91 *Ibid*.
92 MPP, vol. 272, December 1871.
93 *Ibid*.
94 *Ibid*.
95 *Ibid*.
96 *Report of the Commissioners Appointed to Enquire into the Treatment of Immigrants in British Guiana*, p. 1.
97 See Act VII of 1871, article 23.
98 *Ibid*.
99 C.O. 273/57. Enclosure in Ord to Kimberley, no. 45, 16 May 1872.
100 *Ibid*.
101 *Ibid*.
102 Sir Harry St George Ord (1819-85). Commissioned Royal Engineers, 1837; served in Crimean War, 1854-55; transferred to colonial service, 1855; Lieutenant-Governor of Dominica, 1857; Governor of Bermuda, 1861-66; Governor of the Straits Settlements, 1867-73. Source: Turnbull, *Straits Settlements*, p. 381.
103 Robert Heussler, *British Rule in Malaya: The Malayan Civil Service and its Predecessors, 1867-1942* (Oxford, 1981), p. 5.
104 *London and China Telegraph*, 26 January 1867. Cited in Turnbull, *Straits Settlements*, p. 381.
105 Turnbull, *Straits Settlements*, p. 381.
106 MPP, vol. 273, 15 December 1872.
107 *Ibid*.
108 C.O. 273/57. Ord to Kimberley, telegram, 25 May 1872.
109 RLC 1890, p. 36.

V

RECRUITMENT

> There is no royal road to plentiful and cheap labour. What the community, represented by Government, can do is to eliminate cheating, illegitimate profits, misrepresentation and every such bar to immigration.
>
> RLC 1890

Although the Madras government had lifted the ban on indentured emigration to the Straits Settlements, the Indian authorities would not actively promote recruitment. The policy of the government of India, as expressed by the Secretary of State for India, the Marquess of Salisbury, was "one of seeing fair play between the parties to a commercial transaction, while the Government altogether abstains from mixing itself up in the bargain."[1] In other words, its position regarding emigration was one of "neutrality, more or less benevolent."[2]

This prudent policy was expedient to the emigration of Indians to the Straits Settlements. It shifted the responsibility for the welfare of the emigrants from the Indian authorities to the Straits government and the employers; and it prevented casting upon the first of these the odium of any shortcomings in the process of recruitment which it was unable to prevent. The *Singapore Free Press* quite aptly observed: "The Indian government had properly and naturally exercised paternal supervision towards its subjects of the low, chiefly agricultural classes of the Madras Presidency upon finding the increasing want of labour when there was an insufficiency in the Straits Settlements."[3]

Shortfall in Labour Supply

The recruiting procedure adopted by the Province Wellesley planters differed from that of most of the other British colonies. In these colonies, the governments charged themselves with the task of importing annually the number of Indian immigrants required by individual planters, and allotted the labourers on their arrival in the colonies to the different estates according to the requisitions made. The initial charges connected with the recruitment and passage of the labourers were borne by the colonial governments, and the outlay was eventually recovered from the planters concerned. This procedure effectually obviated the necessity of giving cash advances to intending emigrants as was in the case of the Straits Settlements.

The government of India initially thought it was only under such conditions that emigration from India to the Straits could be put on a sound footing. But the Straits government would not take the responsibility for the procedure adopted by the other colonies. They preferred the system in vogue since the inception of indenture to continue. Thus, up to 1907, (when free passages to the Straits were offered to bona fide Indian agricultural emigrants) each planter indented direct on his agent in India for the number of labourers he required. The agent then sent out the *maistries* (recruiters) with cash advances which, once given to recruits, were later charged to the planter. The intending emigrants then contracted with the Emigration Agent at the depot at Negapatam without any intervention on the part of either the Indian or the Straits government.

The sugar planters' maximum labour requirement has been calculated on the basis of one Indian labourer to every acre of land for cane cultivation.[4] The planters' estimated labour requirement and the number of Indian indentured labourers recruited for various years during indenture were according to the following table:-

TABLE VIII
THE DEMAND AND SUPPLY OF INDIAN INDENTURED
LABOURERS FOR VARIOUS YEARS

YEAR	ESTIMATED REQ'MENT	PRESENT + (Beginning of Year)	ARRIVALS = (During Year)	TOTAL SUPPLY	SHORT-FALL[a]
1880	10,000	1,610	1,191	2,801	7,199
1884	10,000	3,116	1,539	4,655	5,345
1888	10,000	4,584	2,567	7,151	2,849
1890	10,950	4,118	1,529	5,647	5,303
1896	15,650	2,615	1,784	4,399	11,251
1900	9,600	3,995	2,160	6,155	3,445
1905	11,233	1,622	1,087	2,709	8,524
1908	6,480	2,410	1,229	3,639	2,841
1910	5,319	2,282	1,432	3,714	1,605

a = Unindentured labourers were also usually employed on the estates, but their numbers were not consistently provided. The number of indentured labourers who died, deserted, etc. would have reduced further the shortage of labourers.

Source: ARII and Blue Books for relevant years; MPP, no. 25, August 1884.

The shortfall in the supply of indentured labourers was not compensated for by recruitment in North India. The government of India was not absolutely opposed to the Straits recruiting there, but they preferred recruitment to be confined to the South, mainly in Madras Presidency. This policy reflected careful consideration. As about 5,000 Indians, mainly Tamils from Madras Presidency, had already been living in Province Wellesley in 1871,[5] confining recruitment to South India would benefit the immigrants in two ways. It would promote communication between them and South India, which would facilitate dissemination of information regarding conditions of life in the colony; and it would ensure that those newly arrived would find themselves among their own linguistic group, if not among relatives and friends.

From the Straits' point of view, recruitment in North India would necessitate additional arrangements for regulating the traffic and for the temporary lodging, transportation and protection of emigrants. This would involve additional expenses which the Straits government had been trying hard to avoid. Furthermore, North Indian recruits had been accustomed to be contracted (almost exclusively by the more distant colonies), for the equivalent of twenty-five to thirty Straits cents wage a day, together with a free onward and a heavily subsized, if not free, return passage to Calcutta.[6] These conditions were in return for a five-year indenture and a further five-year "industrial residence". Straits recruiters offering between twelve and fourteen cents wage a day without a free passage, even for a three-year indenture, would have found it difficult to compete with their North Indian counterparts, the *arkatis*, especially since recruitment by several British and foreign colonies was already being conducted on an extensive scale in North India. The government of India's preference for the Straits to confine their recruitment to the South implied an intention to distribute emigration outlets rather than concentrate them at one port.

Within South India, of the two major linguistic groups, the Telegus and the Tamils, the Straits planters considered the former less amenable to emigrate to the Straits. Although the Tamils were generally regarded as "a more stay at home folk than the Telegus",[7] the latter were more inclined to emigrate to Burma, which they considered a freer and nearer market, and where many of their relatives and friends had already been living.[8] Besides, compared with the Tamils, the Telegus were regarded as more susceptible to sickness, especially fever,[9] which was endemic even among the Tamils in the Straits. The confinement of recruiting to Tamils thus narrowed the field further.

Methods of Recruitment
The recruiters' first major obstacle was to overcome the Tamil's natural reluctance to emigrate. To do this, the *maistries* often played on his imagination, picturing life in the Straits as consisting of "absolute idleness with curry and rice and arrack [distilled rice wine] *ad nauseam*."[10] The recruiters were so convincing at times that official counsel was often ignored. "The Indian cooly, who is mostly tantalized by the recruiters," remarked the Acting Civil Surgeon stationed at the Negapatam depot, "… hardly gives ear to what is told him in earnest by the Emigration Agent and the Protector".[11] He added that the average recruit preferred to expose himself to the "risk of trying his fortune in a strange land, the description of which, has already been given to him by the recruiters in the most commendable terms." This suggests, as one writer correctly observed, that the *maistries'* "painting unduly optimistic pic-

tures of life and conditions of work on the estates" had far more to do with the recruit's wanting to leave India than the belief that he could earn more wages than he could at home.[12]

Where the *maistries* offered financial incentives, it seems that there was a deliberate intention to deceive. Usually, they described the wage rates in Straits currency[13] of which the recruits reportedly possessed little or no concept. "Not one coolly in fifty," declared the Protector of Emigrants, W. Austin, "has the faintest idea of the amount of wages he had contracted to serve for."[14] When asked by the Protector what they expected to earn, one man would say four rupees a month, another five rupees, another six, and ten, and so on.[15]

As part of the campaign by the government of India to protect recruits against trickery it had since 1873 required recruiters to be approved and registered by the Emigration Agent and licensed by the Protector.[16] The description of each such recruiter was then publicized in the particular district in which he was to operate. Each recruiter was required to wear a badge bearing the following inscription in English and in the vernacular of that district: "Recruiter of Emigrants for the Straits Settlements."[17] This helped to establish the bona fides of the recruiters and to ensure their respectability; it rendered recruiting by non-authorized persons difficult and illegal; it enabled the police to distinguish between bona fide Straits recruiters and crimps recruiting for places to which emigration was prohibited; and it also saved the recruiters from interference and possibly blackmail at the hands of the police and other subordinate officials. Of greatest importance, the licensing of recruiters gave the Madras government, acting through the Protector, a hold over them which it could not obtain in any other way, and made it possible to punish fraudulent recruiting.

The Madras government still feared that the respectability the badge gave the recruiters was "capable of mischievous misapplication by unscrupulous and designing natives", especially since the majority of Tamils upon whom they exercised their calling were illiterate "superstitious and susceptible rustics".[18] They, the Madras government reckoned, were too liable to identify the recruiters with the subordinate officers of government, and to believe that their services were "peremptorily required by the Sirkar (i.e. the government), of whom too many of them had the most untutored and most unsatisfactory conception."[19]

The licensing of recruiters did not totally eradicate abuses. In the application for a licence, the applicant stated his own and his father's name, his age, caste, colour and height, any distinguishing marks, and the name of the village and district to which his family belonged.[20] Although a magistrate was required to countersign the application,[21] this was no guarantee of honest dealing. Madras government officials claimed that the magistrate's signature conferred a "fictitious power" upon the holder of the licence, which often gave rise to a "dangerous and demoralizing system of proxies which was found difficult to detect or control."[22] The officials explained that although the individual who presented himself for a licence might be a man of the most satisfactory respectability, many of the persons who actually used it were an "eager, callous, and too often utterly unscrupulous race of men".[23] Many cases were reported where the head recruiter, while enjoying ease in his village, engaged subordinates to do the field work.[24]

The apprehension which this state of affairs aroused, prompted the Madras government to limit the validity of recruiting licences to one year.[25] This measure was ineffective. The power of withdrawing licences did not give adequate control over those who used them, and fear of its loss was not sufficient to induce recruiters to carry on their business honestly. The Chief Secretary to the government of Madras observed:

> There is not an honest recruiter in Southern India, and if there was he would speedily become dishonest as soon as he began recruiting. I believe that if you offered a merely nominal wage, and a sufficiently high commission you would get some coolies all the same. They would be bamboozled from their homes by false promises and then terrorized until they would not call their souls their own, and perhaps if necessary drugged - it often happens.[26]

Of the recruiters' dishonesty, there is sample evidence. One immigrant claiming he had been a grass cutter and shepherd in India, said the recruiter had told him he would be sent to join his brother in Burma.[27] Instead, he was taken to Province Wellesley where he discovered to his deep chagrin that he was required to use the *changkol*, or hoe, which he could not; that he was indentured for three years, of which he was initially unaware; and his pay was far less than he had been led to expect, which led to his utter disappointment.[28] Another recruit, previously a bill-collector, claimed that the recruiter had promised to get him clerical work on an estate, but on arrival in the Province, he was compelled to use the *changkol*, which he could not because of an old injury to an arm.[29] In 1897, the Protector of Immigrants wrote: "Most of the coolies I examined informed me that when they were engaged in India they were not told they would be required to labour on an estate and do *changkol* work but that they would get similar work to that on which they were engaged in India, such as shopkeeping and cart driving."[30]

Referring to the labourers' disappointment in their expectations, a coffee planter in Malaya, Thomas Hill, who subsequently became the Protector of Labour (1901-5), said that those few indentured labourers who were literate used to send "such miserable letters" of their experiences to their relatives at home that indentured emigration became increasingly unpopular.[31] On another occasion, Hill had challenged the Province Wellesley planters to instance a single case of an indentured labourer having induced any relation or friend of his own to emigrate under indenture. "Needless to say," he added, "my challenge was never taken up."[32]

Competition with Ceylon and Burma
One crucial factor which led to the shortfall of labourers in the Straits Settlements was competition in South India from mainly Ceylon and, to a lesser extent, Burma. Compared with the Straits, immigration into these colonies was as shown in the following table:-

TABLE IX

COMPARATIVE FLOW OF INDIAN LABOURERS INTO BURMA,
CEYLON AND THE STRAITS SETTLEMENTS, 1880/81-1888/89

YEAR	BURMA	YEAR	CEYLON	STRAITS SETT. (All labs.)	PROVINCE WELL. (Indentured)
1880/81	6,682	1881	54,204	6,648	879
1881/82	8,020	1882	51,640	9,728	1,452
1882/83	22,075	1883	39,055	10,429	1,448
1883/84	12,659	1884	45,962	15,904	1,539
1884/85	5,993	1885	46,665	21,461	1,025
1885/86	7,616	1886	39,907	20,064	1,915
1886/87	24,642	1887	72,660	16,892	2,666
1887/88	38,956	1888	81,710	19,867	2,567
1888/89	38,014	1889	64,459	18,032	1,965
TOTAL	164,657		496,262	139,025	(15,456)

a = Many of the labourers going to Ceylon were for periods of less than one year.
Source: ARII 1881-89; RLC 1890, pp. 42-44.

Ceylon

Emigration to Ceylon was facilitated by some general factors. Under the authority of Act XIII of 1847, the government of India allowed unrestricted emigration of Indian labourers to the colony because it was "geographically, historically and socially considered analogous to the Continent of India."[33] Besides, the advantage of "uninterrupted intercourse from time immemorial",[34] and the substantial Tamil population that had already settled there[35] (see later), and Ceylon's unique position in its proximity to the reservoir of labourers in lower South India specially favoured recruitment.

Several specific factors were also responsible for the disparity between immigration into Ceylon and the Straits. Foremost, compared with the Straits, economic conditions in Ceylon were far more attractive. In the 1880s, Tamils employed on the coffee estates of Ceylon were paid the equivalent of eighteen Straits cents a day; and, furthermore, the cost of living was said to be lower than in the Straits.[36] At about the same time in Province Wellesley, male indentured labourers could hardly earn more than between ten and twelve cents a day. With the usually insatiable demand for labour in Ceylon, although it was highest during the July-December coffee harvesting season,[37] Tamils could normally find temporary employment there at any time during the year. This was convenient for those not wanting to settle permanently or to work for a fixed length of time. The achievement of these advantages was facilitated by the *kangany* system of recruitment. *Kangany* was the Tamil term used to designate a foreman (or headman) of a gang of labourers working on a plantation, and sometimes on some construction. Usually, the labourers under his supervision were those whom he himself had recruited.[38]

The *kangany* system of recruitment for Ceylon held several advantages over indentured recruitment for the Straits as conducted by the *maistries*. Unlike the *maistries*, the *kanganies* were not subject to any emigration law and were not required to be licensed. In theory, anyone approved by the planters could recruit. Unlike indentured recruits, *kangany* recruits were not subject to the time-consuming and often expensive exercise of appearing before a magistrate to declare their intention to work in Ceylon. Neither was there any medical examination to ascertain their fitness and bona fides as agriculturists. On the other hand, a slightly incapacitated indentured recruit or anyone who appeared below sixteen or above forty-five years of age was liable to be rejected at the emigration depot. The purely patriarchal character of the *kangany* system, and the fact that there were usually relations of kinship within each batch of recruits,[39] would have tended to discourage desertion. In contrast to indentured recruitment, the number of labourers engaged would be normally sustained. The *kangany* system's chief advantage over its counterpart lay in the difference in the method of engagement. Whereas indentured recruits were bound by legally enforceable written contracts, violation of which implied a prison sentence, the *kangany* recruits were either engaged on the basis of a promissory note or a verbal agreement.

Unlike the Straits government, the government of Ceylon promoted Indian emigration on a large scale. In 1859, the latter introduced an additional schooner service subsidized at about the equivalent of eleven Straits cents per person per crossing.[40] In the 1860s, Ceylon's emigration subsidy in terms of Straits currency stood at $65,000, and by 1896, it was increased to $97,000.[41] By comparison, it was not until 1887 that the Straits Settlements, together with the Malay States of Perak, Selangor, and Johore, agreed to introduce a jointly subsidized steamer service from Negapatam, but the outlay was only $30,000 yearly.[42] In the meanwhile, for the 1,200 mile, ten-to-twelve day voyage by sail from Negapatam to Penang, indentured recruits were charged $9.00 without subsistence.[43]

Of the traffic to Ceylon, there were a few good reports. Emigration officers in the government of India were convinced that the *kangany* recruited labourers were generally well-treated, and as they said, they would not interfere with "this perfectly voluntary emigration to an easily accessible market … with which intercourse is constant, and whence return is easy.[44] Governor Sir William Gregory, of Ceylon, was also satisfied. In 1872 (while recruitment for the Straits was still suspended because of abuses in the recruiting system), Gregory enthused: "I am … able to state that almost universally the treatment of the coolies will stand the closest investigation, and that the relations between them and their employers are of the most cordial description."[45] Gregory's assertions should be taken *cum grano salis*. Apparently, Gregory saw or knew only the more complimentary aspects of the traffic to Ceylon and ignored the "unscrupulous avaricious" *kanganies* who, as was reported, often misappropriated travelling allowances intended to be spent on recruits,[46] and who often defrauded the labourers they had recruited.[47]

Notwithstanding, the advantages held out by Ceylon continued to attract more labourers than the Straits Settlements until the twentieth century. The Tamil segment of the immigrant population in Ceylon which, in 1871, stood at 534,339, rose to 951,740 in 1901.[48] In sharp contrast, in 1871, in the Straits Settlements, the total Indian population was 33,390; and in 1901, it increased to 56,645,[49] of which 5,344 were indentured at Province Wellesley at the beginning of the year.[50]

Burma

The greater number of labourers immigrating into Burma than to the Straits Settlements may be ascribed to better inducements and facilities. In the 1870s, the approximately four-day voyage by steamer from South India to Burma cost about $3.25 (in Straits currency), which was a little over a third of the fare by sail from Negapatam to Penang, the cost being about $9.00.[51] Even when the Straits inaugurated a steamer service in 1887, the five-to-six day journey cost indentured labourers about $10.00, and they complained of being underfed and overcharged.[52]

The relatively freer mode of Burma's recruiting system was more to the South Indians' liking. Whether the Burma-bound recruits paid their own passage, or whether it was defrayed by a labour contractor (who was styled *maistry* in Burma, although he functioned more like a *kangany*), there was no prolonged restriction on their freedom. At least until 1890, the cost of living in Burma having been said to be lower than in the Straits,[53] the labourers would have been able to rid themselves of any debt they might have incurred sooner than it would have taken the average indentured labourer in the Straits. Thus, the Burma *maistry* could rarely exercise protracted thraldom over his recruits. At any rate, any temporary loss of liberty would be less irksome than the three-year indenture in the Straits. The introduction of any legally binding contractual agreement for South Indians arriving in Burma, the Chief Commissioner of Burma believed, would materially check the influx of Indian recruits.[54]

Recruits for Burma were offered a wide range of employment to choose from. They could engage themselves in clearing forests and swamps; in building towns, roads, and railways; in agriculture as rice farmers; and in the timber industry.[55] Women could work either as domestic servants or as casual rice-mill hands.[56] On the other hand, all the Province Wellesley indentured recruits were destined to work on sugar estates, though in the out-of-crop season some of them were engaged in cultivating and peeling tapioca. Once they were bound to an employer, they could legally change neither him nor their employment. Any premature release from their written contracts was possible only if they could repay their debts to their employer (which was hardly practicable because of their low wages) or through permanent incapacitation or death.

Of the greatest importance, emigration to Burma was more remunerative. According to some Madras officials wages in Burma were so "ample" that many labourers who had spent two or three years there were known to acquire savings varying from $80.00 to $120.00.[57] In contrast, in the entire period of indenture in the Straits, not a single indentured labourer was reported as having saved so much money. Emigration to Burma was, there, more conducive to making those South Indians who were imbued with a spirit of enterprise more independent members of society. The advantages could not have been unknown in the Indian villages. The prosperous condition in which emigrants returned was likely to excite envy and admiration and to stimulate the traffic to Burma.

Emigration to Burma was not without disadvantages. The *maistries* often exploited illiterate labourers by misrepresenting the terms of their verbal agreement; and the desire to earn maximum wages in minimum time caused overstrain and debility which, together with appalling living conditions, led to many deaths.[58] It was believed that in Rangoon, Indian immigrants who were "lodged in slum tenements ... suffered conditions infinitely worse than any experienced in the coolie lines on the [colonial] sugar plantations".[59] The government of Burma's public acceptance of direct responsibility for inviting Indian emigrants was not accompanied by an undertaking to guarantee their protection and proper housing and medical attendance,[60] all of which were assured to the indentured recruits in the Straits.

Despite these drawbacks, Indian emigration to Burma continued to outstrip the traffic to the Straits. By 1901, there were 568,263 persons of Indian extraction in Burma,[61] 190,000 of whom had been born in Madras Presidency.[62] In contrast, in the same year in the Straits, the total Indian population was 56,645;[63] of this, 5,344 were under indenture in Province Wellesley.[64]

It seems that the people of South India had understood that the advantages of emigrating to Ceylon and Burma outweighed the disadvantages. Before a similar state of things could be expected in respect of the Straits, indentured emigration had to become popular among the people of South India. This could have been guaranteed by the best of all advertisements, that is, a flow of returning labourers in good health and with money to their credit. Until this state of affairs was reached, the Province Wellesley planters would have found it difficult to compete successfully not only with these colonies but with the more distant ones as well.

Competition with more Distant Colonies
The shortfall in the indentured labour supply in the Straits Settlements was to some extent also due to competition in Madras Presidency from the far-off colonies. For instance, between 1875 and 1882, the British West Indies, Mauritius and Bourbon (Reunion) recruited 24,473 emigrants.[65] To Martinique and Guadeloupe, 9,305 recruits, the majority of whom originated in Madras Presidency, were dispatched between 1872 and 1883.[66] To Natal, some 21,400 South Indians were recruited between 1860 and 1903.[67]

Despite that to these colonies the recruits were contracted to work for five rather than three years as required by the Straits, the daily wage rate offered was higher. In the Straits, up to 1902 the highest rate paid was fourteen cents. In the other colonies, it was between the equivalent of twenty-five and thirty Straits cents.[68] Whereas Straits recruits were required to repay the cost of their outward passage and to pay their own fare back to India, the recruits for the more distant colonies were offered a free outward passage, and if they worked another five years after completing their first indenture, they would be entitled to a heavily subsidized or, as was the case in some colonies, a free return passage. Indian emigration officials often asserted that the denial by the Straits Settlements of free outward and return passages to their recruits was an important factor that restricted emigration to the colony.

The Return Passage Issue
The issue of the provision of a free return passage to India deserves special attention because it had considerable effect on the recruitment of indentured labourers for the Straits. Quite apart from the fact that the government of India had specified that the Straits government should make provision in the labour ordinance for a free return passage for each indentured immigrant upon the expiry of his contract,[69] there were good reasons why the Straits government should have adopted such a policy in its own interest. The apparent attitude of the average Indian villager towards emigration was such that the guarantee of a return passage would have tended to reduce his reluctance to leave his home. It also meant that the eventual return of himself and his family would not depend upon his prospering in his oversea venture. This would have greatly reduced the risks involved in accepting indenture. If he were to become incapacitated for any reason, his ability to pay his passage would not have prevented his repatriation — a matter of concern for the intending labourer, and also, one would imagine, for the Straits government who would otherwise have to support him in his destitution. Any intention to desert towards the end of the expected indenture period would have been diminished, both by reducing the need to earn a credit sufficient to pay for a passage and by the fear of losing the free passage entitlement. Nothing more would have favourably affected recruitment than the regular return of considerable numbers of relatively successful emigrants with good reports of the Straits. The Indian government having been prepared to agree to five-year contracts if the right to a return passage had been written into them,[70] the cost would not have been high and the supply of labour would have been less constrained. As some labourers would have chosen to remain in Malaya and others would die, the cost of providing free return passages would have been even further reduced.

Advertisements
The shortfall in the supply of indentured labourers induced the planters to advertise for Tamil labourers by means of public notices of which the following translated version appeared in 1890.

WANTED COOLIES

Many coolies are wanted for Province Wellesley, near Penang, to work on coffee, tapioca, and sugar plantations.

1. As soon as they arrive in Penang they must enter into a written agreement to work for three years. After three years they can either come away or remain to work on the estate.

2. Those who work on an estate will receive for the first year, males, about $3.60 (i.e. about Rs. 8—2 ans.) a month. If they do extra work they will receive higher wages at the above rates.

Houses, fuel, and land for gardens will be given free. All expenses incurred in going to the estates, such as trainage [sic], feeding expenses, passage money, and a cloth will be given free. Besides this, as soon as they arrive on the estate they will be presented with one month's provisions and $1. There are shops and a good supply of water. There are doctors, who speak Tamil. Rice is sold at market price. Fish, fowl, sheep, vegetables, etc., can be got at cheap rates. Cloths, etc., are taken from here and sold at cost price. The country is quite similar to our own places, and comfortable. Many of our own countrymen are working on each estate.

3. There is a Protector, and under him Assistants, who are appointed by the Government to enquire into the welfare of the coolies and to see that they are well treated.

4. Fortnightly steamers run to Penang; they are comfortable, and good food on board is given. They carry Doctors and Inspectors to look after the coolies.

5. Province Wellesley, which is adjacent to Penang, is much healthier than Perak, Sungei Ujong, etc. We hear that the water supply in Perak, Sunjei Ujong etc. is not good as in Province Wellesley; moreover, fish is not obtainable, and everything is dear: a fowl which costs ¼ rupee or 5 annas in Penang will cost R. 1 or Rs. 1¼, and rice which in Penang can be bought for R. 1, will cost Rs. 1¾ in those places. As these countries have been newly opened, the climate does not agree with the people, and causes fever and dysentery.

We think that on account of these difficulties they offer better wages and a shorter term of contract. But if both wages and expenses and comforts are compared, Penang seems a better place for coolies.

(Signed) GANAPATHY PILLAY AND CO.,
Agents for Planters, Penang.
Negapatam, 16th December, 1890.[71]

The part of this advertisement setting out the terms of employment was misleading in several ways. First, labourers could not necessarily "come away" after three years. If they had not worked six days of every week for thirty-six months, or if they had not liquidated all their debts to their employer, they would be legally bound to continue working until they had fulfilled both contractual obligations. Second, the manner in which the payment of wages was expressed could be interpreted by intending male and female recruits that they would receive a guaranteed monthly net wage of $3.60 and $2.40 respectively. In practical terms, male and female labourers were paid the full daily rate of twelve and eight cents respectively only if they had satisfactorily completed two tasks of work. Furthermore, as will be seen in the analysis of wages in Chapter VIII, the average labourer did not earn pay for more than an average of 20.5 days per month during his or her first year of employment. Thus, the actual gross wage would have been less than the amounts presented in the advertisement. Third, the cost of emigrating from the point of recruitment to the estates was not "free". Initially, "all expenses incurred" were borne by the employers, but each labourer was legally required to repay through monthly deductions from his wages the cost of his importation up to a maximum of $12.00. Fourth, while it is undeniable that housing, fuel, and garden plots were provided free, no evidence is available to support the statement that "as soon as ... [the labourers] arrive on the estate they will be presented with one month's provisions and $1." Finally, the advertisement failed to mentioned the nine-hour work-day; the almost universal use of the *changkol* (or hoe) of which the labourers repeatedly expressed their utter dislike; and criminal punishment of any labourer who violated the contract. In short, Ganapathy Pillay and Company, the Indian recruiting agents, were guilty of using deception to attract labourers. Commenting on this advertisement, the Labour Commission of 1890 rightly observed: "The reference to the Native States, which reads like the attempt of an agent for the Colony to forward his own interests at the expense of others, sufficiently indicates the character of the people to whom we now trust our recruiting."[72]

A recruiting agent of the Madura Shipping Company in Negapatam commenting on advertisements such as that above as a means of attracting recruits for indenture in the Straits said they would not improve recruitment unless the rates of waves were put on a par with those offered by the other colonies. He added: "The great thing is to get a good name among the emigrants and the rest is easy."[73] Undoubtedly, good wages, which made possible some savings, combined with favourable reports of living and working conditions, would themselves have been powerful advertisements, averting the expense of hiring agents and utilizing posters. The ex-Protector of Labour, Thomas Hill, agreed that public notices such as shown above were not as effective as the good reputation of an estate and the popularity of the employer.

Stricter Selection of Emigrants
Following numerous complaints from the planters regarding the disappointing quality of a large percentage of immigrants received, in 1891, the Straits government instructed the Superintendent of the emigration depot at Negapatam, Dr Hardaker (who was appointed in 1890), to make a careful selection of recruits by eliminating those who were physically unsound and unaccustomed to agricultural labour.[74] In addition to complying, from 1892 Hardaker required every intending emigrant to use the *changkol* "until the sweat ran off his back".[75] However expedient this was, it was imposed under artificial conditions, and the large number of injuries that later occurred while labourers used this implement in the field sug-

gests that the test did not always provide an accurate measure of an ability to use it skillfully.

The stricter medical examination and the *changkol* test often resulted in "many rejections."[76] As the rejection of some recruits sometimes led to the refusal of others to emigrate,[77] the already reduced number was diminished further still. Following Hardaker's introduction of the two screening procedures, there was a sudden decline in emigration as shown in the following table. To some extent also, a significant influence working against indentured recruitment from the early 1890s was competition from the *kangany* system of recruitment. This is discussed below.

TABLE X

THE EFFECT OF THE STRICTER SELECTION OF EMIGRANTS ON THE VOLUME OF INDENTURED IMMIGRATION INTO PROVINCE WELLESLEY, 1890-1900

YEAR	IMMIGRANTS
1890	1,529
1891	2,644
1892	1,192
1893	1,189
1894	1,053
1895	719
1896	1,784
1897	1,766
1898	1,792
1899	1,347
1900	2,160

Source: ARII 1890-1900

Competition with Kangany Recruitment

The inadequate supply of indentured labourers to Province Wellesley was also affected by competition from the *kangany* system of recruitment. This system was introduced into the Malayan Native States by coffee planters who had come from Ceylon. Precisely when this system began in Malaya, like the commencement date of unregulated indenture, is also uncertain. But the probable date is generally held to be sometime in the 1860s, if not earlier.[78] It did not begin to compete with indentured recruitment until after the establishment of large-scale commercial coffee cultivation in the Malay States around 1890.[79] During the "rubber rush" in Malaya from about 1903,[80] the competition became a serious threat to indentured recruitment.

In Malaya, the *kangany* and his functions were described as follows:-

> The Kangani [sic] system of the coffee and post-coffee era involved a short-term contract, generally verbal rather than written, which could be dissolved at a month's notice on the part of either party. It received its name because of the important role of the kanganis, or headmen, who in theory were foremen on estates or senior mem-

bers of families, but in actuality were often only 'coolies of standing'. The kangani ... was both recruiter and field foreman, at least in the case of those he recruited. He was sent by an employer or association of employers to bring back his friends, neighbours and relatives in his home village and taluk [sub-district]. The kangani, on behalf of his employers, undertook to provide food, clothing and transit for the recruits in connection with the overseas trip. Frequently he was empowered to discharge their local debts or to leave money with their relatives. Considerable responsibility rested on him to choose the right sort of recruits and as compared with indenture there was a somewhat better chance that whole families or neighbourhood groups would come together.[81]

Although some of the advantages of *kangany* recruitment over indentured have already been discussed in relation to Ceylon,[82] because of its importance it stands some repetition here. *Kangany* recruitment for Malaya was less subjected to restrictions, government control, and inspection.[83] In theory anyone could recruit and be recruited. Whereas the indentured recruits entered into written, legally enforceable contracts with their employers, *kangany* recruits were, at least in theory, "free". The *kangany* usually recruited labourers of a superior physical quality.[84] Otherwise, he stood to lose his supervisory position and esteem and even money, as his employer would return unfit recruits at the *kangany's* expense. The *kangany* recruited a certain proportion of women as well.[85] In terms of the local need for a sexually balanced labour force and the imperial desire for permanent settlement of Indian immigrants in Malaya, this dimension of the system had the benefit of encouraging family emigration and consequentially tended to create stability on the estates. Compared with the influence of the *maistry,* which ceased as soon as the recruit entered the depot at Negapatam, that of the *kangany* over the emigrants they recruited was more elaborate. As most of the recruits were the *kangany's* relatives, friends or neighbours and as he had negotiated their engagements, conducted their journeys, and superintended their labour, he was better able to secure loyalty and to prevent desertion. *Kangany* recruited labourers were provided with free housing and medical services comparable to those provided for indentured Indians at Province Wellesley.[86] But the coffee and rubber planters of Malaya did not consider the cost of providing these facilities as a part of the labourers' wages; thus, their wage rates were higher. Most importantly, compared with the *maistry*, the *kangany* opened the way which the labourers he had recruited could earn much higher wages. In 1903, for instance, the daily rate of wages at which indentured immigrants were recruited was 25 and 20 cents for adult males and females respectively.[87] By contrast, in the same year (because of the flourishing coffee industry), planters in Perak and Kedah offered 30 cents wage a day; those in Pahang, 35 and 40 cents to male and an average of 20 cents to female recruits.[88]

However superior was *kangany* recruitment compared with indentured, it was not without limitations. As the *kanganies* went several times over the same recruiting ground, they were occasionally unproductive.[89] This created an erratic labour supply. *Kanganies* were often opposed by the *maistries*, who feared that this type of competition was detrimental to their livelihood.[90] In South India, employers resisted the operations of the *kanganies*; and if they persisted in poaching recruits, the *kanganies* were reported to the police and arrested for crimping.[91] Straits officials claimed that the *kanganies* used objectionable methods to recruit; and that "the best of them are always ready to misrepresent facts to the coolie and to terrify them with all manner of lying threats."[92] From the planters' point of view, the worst feature of the system was the occasional absconding of *kanganies*.[93] Planters thus lost not only the hope of fresh supplies of labour, but also the money entrusted to the abscondees.

In the final analysis, the success of the *kangany* system of recruitment would be best illustrated by the comparative flow of immigrants. As the following table attests, the Tamils preferred *kangany* recruitment (for coffee and later rubber estates) to indentured recruitment (for the Province Wellesley sugar estates). The figures in the centre column do not reflect a diminished demand for sugar estate labourers in Province Wellesley. Between 1901-7, the average annual demand was around 9,000.[94]

TABLE XI
COMPARATIVE FLOW OF INDENTURED AND *KANGANY* LABOURERS, 1901-07

YEAR	INDENTURED (Province Wellesley)	*KANGANY* (Malay States)
1901	1,023	2,000
1902	830	1,474
1903	364	1,858
1904	784	3,375
1905	1,087	7,429
1906	857	19,177
1907	1,397	21,260
TOTAL	6,342	56,573

Source: ARII 1901-7; Sandhu, *Indians in Malaya*, p. 308.

The question naturally arises why the sugar planters did not follow the example of the coffee and rubber planters and adopt *kangany* recruitment instead. The sugar planters considered the authority exercised by the *kanganies* over the labourers they had recruited prejudicial to the relationship between employers and their employees.[95] They alleged that the *kanganies* often screened labourers' idleness and connived at greater delinquencies.[96] The Province Wellesley planters disliked this interposition which they claimed caused "many irregularities" and, furthermore, "much discontent" among themselves.[97] But most importantly, the sugar planters would not offer the wage rates paid to *kangany*-recruited labourers; and they disapproved of the system because *kangany* recruits were "free". The strongest hold the sugar planters could have had on such labourers was a one-month, verbal agreement dissoluble by either party at a month's notice. Such an agreement would have been severely detrimental to the sugar planters' interests.

Problems in Recruiting Districts

The insufficient number of indentured recruits for the Province Wellesley estates was also due to some extent to certain specific problems in the districts from which they were mainly drawn. The recruiters hardly extended their sphere of operations beyond Tanjore, Tiruchirapalli (Trichinopoloy), Madurai (Madura), Salem, and Coimbatore. The further inland they went, the greater was their expense in bringing down their recruits to the depot at Negapatam, where there was always the possibility of some being rejected, which implied loss of commission. Rather than going among the vast and indigent population of Nilgiris or South Arcot or North Arcot, where "the very name of the Straits" was unknown to the people,[98] the *maistries* preferred to pick up recruits within a narrow radius.[99] Within these areas, the *maistries* were generally unpopular because of their reputed dishonesty. In some areas, according to one Madras government official, they were looked upon with "positive detestation".[100]

In 1880, Madras officials asserted that there was no permanent shortage of employment in the Presidency.[101] They, however, admitted that occasionally certain portions of the people felt prompted to seek employment beyond the limits of the Presidency. In 1900, they contended that there were ample fields of labour within short distances where the unemployed could find either temporary or permanent work.[102] There is hardly any data to disprove this.

However, it would first be useful to establish whether there was any burdensome overpopulation in Madras Presidency by examining the following table:-

TABLE XII

MEAN DENSITY OF POPULATION PER SQUARE MILE IN INDIA AND MADRAS PRESIDENCY AT CENSUSES BETWEEN 1881-1911

YEAR	INDIA	MADRAS PRESIDENCY
1881	141	317
1891	159	351
1901	163	397
1911	175	456

Source: E.A. Gait, *Census of India, 1911*, Vol. I (Calcutta, 1913), p. 84.

The appreciable rise in the mean density of the population of Madras Presidency since 1881 drew a claim from Madras officials that in no part of the Presi-

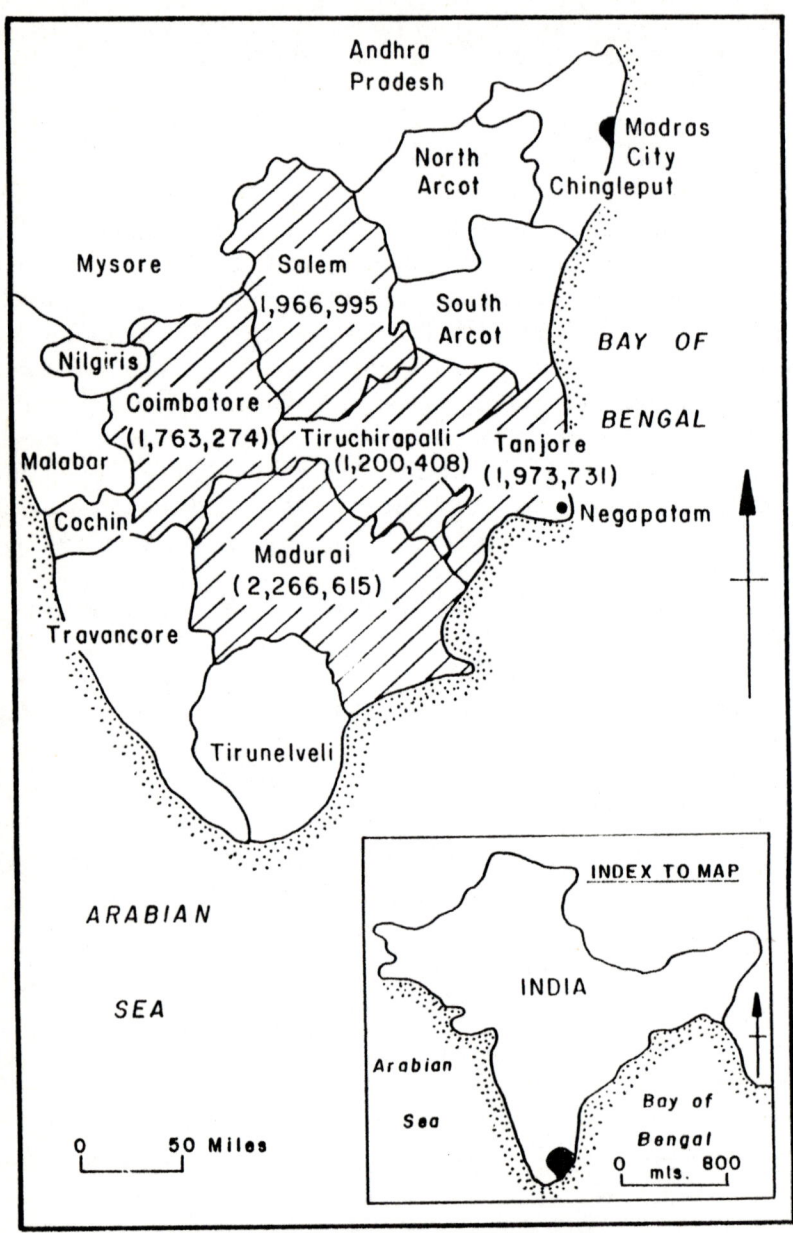

Fig. 5 – THE MAIN DISTRICTS OF ORIGIN OF INDENTURED RECRUITS AND THEIR POPULATION IN 1871–1872

dency did the population "seriously press upon the means of subsistence."[103] In the absence of other evidence, some skepticism must be maintained over such pronouncements and indeed over all those made by government officials that living standards had improved.

Certain developments taking place in the two districts mostly drawn upon by the Straits recruiters would have tended to discourage the people to part with their freedom for a three-year indenture. For instance, Tanjore, which carried the highest mean population density of 572 between 1881 and 1901,[104] was by 1902 said to be "fully cultivated," and owing to a new river irrigation system, which increased soil fertility, chronic food shortage was "practically unknown."[105] Similarly, in Madurai, following the completion of some extensive irrigation works in 1902, there was a return to "comparative prosperity", and the local demand for labour had increased.[106] Consequently, wages were increased, and at the same time, the price of rice decreased.[107] Official reports showed that during the 1901-11 intercensal period, favourable agricultural conditions enabled the unemployed labouring classes throughout the Straits recruiting districts to obtain employment near their homes, and fewer found it necessary to seek a livelihood elsewhere.[108]

Commenting on Malayan efforts to recruit Tamils, in 1900 the *Times of India* said the people looked askance at the "promised life of ease and plenty."[109] In 1902 one Malayan coffee planter equipped with offers of thirty to forty cents daily wage said rather disappointedly: "These ... people are too well off in their own homes to think of leaving them, except for some very special reason".[110] Governor Sir Frank Swettenham, of the Straits, asserted that the Tamils either preferred to remain at home on half the wages they could earn in the Straits or to emigrate to other places where they could earn very much higher wages.[111]

Hard pressed for Labour, the Province Wellesley planters dispatched more tindals than usual to recruit. As headman of a gang, the tindal would be able to select the recruits on the basis of their agricultural background; and more importantly, the planters expected him, like the *kangany,* to induce his relatives, friends, and neighbours to emigrate. But the *maistries*, fearing loss of commission, resented the encroachment upon an area they considered to be their preserve.[112] One of the more successful strategies they used in discouraging the people from being recruited by tindals was by telling them that they would be taken to a country other than the Straits.[113] As the Labour Commission of 1890 observed, the *maistries* had formed "a close 'ring,' with a practical monopoly of the [recruiting] business."[114]

The Tamil Immigration Fund
Up to 1907, the Province Wellesley planters had arranged with various recruiting agents at Negapatam to supply them the requisite labourers. With the more extensive development of the coffee industry in the Malay States in the 1890s and the progressive expansion of the rubber industry from about 1903, the need to stimulate recruitment had become so pressing[115] that a semi-official body termed the Indian Immigration Committee, consisting of government officials and private employers' representatives, was appointed in 1907 to advise the government on this question.[116]

Having consulted with the Planters' Association of Malaya, the Committee's deliberations were embodied in the Tamil Immigration Fund[117] Ordinance of September 1907; and the Indian Immigration Departments of the Straits Settlements and of the Federated Malay States were amalgamated.[118] The object of the legislation was to provide funds for the expenses of the scheme and to prevent desertion, reckless competition for labour, and crimping of one employer's labourers by another through the offer of higher wages and better conditions of work. An assessment based on the number of days worked by the Tamil labourers under the employ of each planter was then levied. The proceeds thus accrued were deposited into the Fund from which were defrayed the general expenses of recruitment.[119]

The principal items covered by the Fund included the cost of recruits' train fares from village to depot; food and medical attention at the depot; steamship passages and food on the voyage to Penang; transport charges to places of employment; recruiting allowances to the employers by whose agents or *kanganies* the labourers were recruited; the cost of repatriating destitute labourers to India; and the maintenance of a home at Kuala Lumpur for decrepit Indian labourers.[120]

This new system broke down the monopoly of the *maistries* and covered much of recruitment costs, part of which indentured labourers were required to repay. In the 1860s, they were required to repay sums between $5.00 and $7.00 which included advances;[121] but by 1890, the cost of their recruitment, including cash advances, often exceeded $20.00.[122] Between 1876 and 1884, they were legally required under article 59 of Ordinance I of 1876 to repay the entire amount; but from 1 January 1885, the repayable amount was fixed by article 42 of Ordinance V of 1884 at a maximum of $12.00, apparently to encourage emigration. With the introduction of the Tamil Immigration Fund in 1907, all bona fide Tamil labourers landed on the estates practically free from financial obligations, except where advances had been made under indenture.

The scheme did not attract as many indentured labourers as it did other types of Tamil agricultural labourers. Whereas for the years 1908-10, indentured recruits for Province Wellesley numbered 1,229, 1,117 and 1,432 respectively,[123] the other types numbered 41,807, 38,807 and 74,593 respectively.[124]

References

1. PHRAD, no. 24, February 1880.
2. Sanderson, *Report on Emigration*, C5194, p. 99.
3. *Singapore Free Press*, 29 September 1897.
4. Low, *Dissertation*, pp. 9, 52-53.
5. Estimated on the basis of figures provided in Braddell, *Statistics,* p. 2; Marriot, "Population of the Straits", pp. 38-39.
6. PSSLC, Paper no. 11, 24 April 1903, p. C72.
7. *Ibid.*, p. C92.
8. PDARC, no. 87, 25 December 1902.
9. Wright and Cartwright, *Impressions*, p. 127.
10. MPP, no. 658, 14 May 1881.
11. MPP, vol. 3746, 15 November 1890.
12. S. Nanjundan, *Indians in Malayan Economy* (New Delhi, 1950), p. 21.
13. MPP, vol. 1555, 6 January 1880.
14. MPP, no. 658, 14 May 1881.
15. *Ibid*.
16. MPP, vol. 274, July 1873.
17. MPP, no. 39, February, 1874.
18. *Ibid*.
19. *Ibid*.
20. MPP, vol. 274, July 1873.
21. *Ibid*.
22. *Ibid*.
23. PHRAD, no. 6, February 1880.
24. PRAD, no. 41, 15 April 1880.
25. *Ibid*.
26. PSSLC, Paper no. 11, 24 April 1903, p. C70.
27. RLC 1890, Appendix B, Inspection no. 3, n.p.
28. *Ibid*.
29. *Ibid*.
30. IEP, no. 67, July 1897.
31. Evidence of T. H. Hill, in Sanderson, *Report on Emigration*, C5193, p. 430.
32. PSSLC, 21 October 1897, p. C186.
33. Tupper, *Note on Indian Emigration*, p. 7.
34. RLC 1890, p. 43.
35. "Emigrant", *Indian Emigration* (London, 1924), pp. 1,5.
36. C.O. 273/130. Enclosure in Sir Cecil Clementi Smith, Acting Governor, S.S., to the Earl of Derby, Secretary of State for the Colonies, no. 541, 29 December 1884.
37. Bertram Bastiampillai, "Social Conditions of the Indian Immigrant Labourer in Ceylon in the 19th Century, with Special Reference to the Seventies, and some Comparisons with Conditions in other Colonies," in *Proceedings of the First International Conference Seminar of Tamil Studies,* (Madras, 1966), I, p. 682.

38 Sanderson, *Report on Emigration*, C5193, p. 27.
39 *Ibid.*
40 Evidence of E.V. Carey (a Selangor planter), in RCII 1896, p. xi.
41 *Ibid.*
42 PP, vol, LXXII, 1888, p. 12.
43 MPP, Appendix A, November 1875.
44 Tupper, *Note on Indian Emigration*, p. 7.
45 *Ibid.*
46 Bastiampillai, "Indian Labourer in Ceylon", p. 695.
47 Sanderson, *Report on Emigration,* C5193, p. 28.
48 *Ibid.*, p. 27.
49 Marriot, "Population of the Straits", pp. 32-33.
50 ARII 1901, p. 12.
51 MPP, Vol. 276, 1 July 1875.
52 MPP, vol. 652, 17 October 1888.
53 RLC 1890, p. 43.
54 PRAD, no. 35, August 1884.
55 Chakravarti, *Indian Minority in Burma*, p. 8.
56 *Ibid.*
57 PHRAD, no. 5, February 1880.
58 Cheng Siok Hwa, "Indian Labour in Burma", pp. 342-43.
59 Tinker, *New Slavery,* p. 273.
60 MPP, no. 583, 19 March 1883.
61 Chakravarti, *Indian Minority in Burma*, p. 15.
62 *Imperial Gazeteer of India*, Provincial Series, (Madras, 1908), p. 26.
63 Marriot, "Population of the Straits", p. 33.
64 ARII 1901, p. 12.
65 Saha, *Emigration of Indian Labour*, p. 73.
66 Xavier S. Thani Nayagam, "Tamil Migrations to Guadeloupe and Martinique, 1853-1883," in *Proceedings of the Second International Conference Seminar of Tamil Studies*, ed. by R.E. Asher, II (January, 1968), pp. 372, 375.
67 PSSLC, Paper no. 11, 24 April 1903, p. C94.
68 *Ibid.*, p. C72.
69 See MPP, no. 43, February 1874.
70 *Ibid.*
71 Quoted in George Netto, *Indians in Malaya: Historical Facts and Figures* (Singapore, 1961), pp. 24-25.
72 RLC 1890, p. 44.
73 PSSLC, Paper no. 11, 24 April 1903, p. C85.
74 *Ibid.,* p. 81.
75 E.V. Carey, "Notes on a Trip to Negapatam," *Selangor Journal*, III (1895), 44.
76 Letter from Ganapathy Pillay and Company, in evidence of J.M. Vermont, in RLC 1890, Appendix A, p. 72.
77 PSSLC, Paper no. 11, 24 April 1903, p. C85.
78 MPP, nos 40-44, 13 September 1870; R.K. Jain, *South Indians on the Plantation*

Frontier in Malaya (New Haven, 1970), p. 198; Sandhu, *Indians in Malaya*, p. 89.
79 Parmer, *Colonial Labour Policy*, pp. 7-8.
80 From about 1903, the expansion of the motor industry and the concomitant need for pneumatic rubber tyres, especially in the U.S.A., Germany and the United Kingdom, caused a sharp rise for the demand for rubber, which consequently created a greater need for labour to increase output in Malaya. See J.H. Drabble, *Rubber in Malaya, 1876-1922* (Kuala Lumpur, 1973), Chapter II.
81 Sandhu, *Indians in Malaya*, p. 90.
82 See earlier in this Chapter.
83 Evidence of Sir John Anderson, Governor, S.S., in Sanderson, *Report on Emigration*, C5193, p. 42.
84 PSSLC, 12 March 1901, p. C157.
85 Evidence of Sir John Anderson, in Sanderson, *Report on Emigration*, C5193, p. 43.
86 IEP, no. 2278, December 1884; Jackson, *Immigrant Labour*, p. 104.
87 ARII 1903, pp. 4-5.
88 PSSLC, 29 April 1903, p. B36; Jackson, *Immigrant Labour*, p. 104.
89 ARII 1896, p. 4.
90 Evidence of T.H. Hill, in RLC 1890, Appendix A, p. 1.
91 Evidence of T.H. Hill, in Sanderson, *Report on Emigration*, C5193, p. 429.
92 PSSLC, Paper no. 11, 24 April 1903, p. C72.
93 Evidence of Sir Frank Swettenham, in Sanderson, *Report on Emigration*, C5193, p. 405.
94 See Table XI.
95 Parmer, *Colonial Labour Policy*, pp. 22-23.
96 Evidence of J.M. Vermont, in RCII 1896, p. i.
97 *Ibid.*
98 PSSLC, Paper no. 11, 24 April 1903, p. C73.
99 ARII 1895, p. 2.
100 PHRAD, no. 6, February 1880.
101 PHRAD, no. 5, February 1880.
102 PRAD, no. 16, March 1900.
103 *Ibid.*
104 H.H. Risley and E.A. Gait, *Census of India, 1901*, Vol. I (Calcutta, 1903), p. 98.
105 *Imperial Gazeteer of India*, (Tanjore), p. 118.
106 ARII 1902, p. 1.
107 PP, vol. LVII, 1904, p. 31; ARII 1902, p. 1.
108 Gait, *Census of India*, 1911, vol. I, p. 35.
109 *Times of India*, 4 April 1900.
110 Turner, "Tamil Labourer", p. 23.
111 Evidence of Sir Frank Swettenham, in Sanderson, *Report on Emigration*, C5193, p. 403.
112 RLC 1890, p. 41.

113 Evidence of T.H. Hill, in RLC 1890, Appendix A, p. 1.
114 RLC 1890, p. 45.
115 On 7 February 1896, the *Straits Times* observed: "Without Indian labour much of the planting enterprise which now promises to be such a source of wealth to the country must cease to be remunerative."
116 G.E. Turner, "Indian Immigration," *MHJ*, I, No. 2 (December, 1954), 81-84.
117 Later styled the "Indian Immigration Fund".
118 PSSLC, 17 September 1907, pp. B133-35.
119 Sanderson, *Report on Emigration*, C5193, p. 34.
120 ARSILFB, "History of the Indian Immigration Fund," (Kuala Lumpur, 1959), pp. 9-12; Turner, "Indian Immigration", p. 82; R.L. German (Compiler), *Handbook to British Malaya* (London, 1937), p. 131.
121 Vermont, *Immigration from India*, p. 5.
122 RLC 1890, pp. 45-46.
123 ARII 1908-10.
124 *General Report on the Administration of the Presidency of Madras, 1901-10; Indian* Immigration Committee: Minutes of Meetings, 1907-10.

VI

THE EMIGRATION PROCESS

> Indeed, the wonder is that ... [the government of India] has not closed the ports long ago to the emigration of indentured labour until the whole of the recruiting system has been purged of its malodorous concomitants.
>
> John H. Harris[1]

Unless the Tamils who had been recruited to work under indenture in the Straits Settlements were brought to the Negapatam port of departure on the day of sailing, the recruits had to be accommodated, fed, and otherwise provided for in a depot. This was usual because the recruiters could not procure a full complement for the emigrant ships all at once, and because sailings were irregular. Since 1878, the government of India required by law a number of specific procedures to be carried out. While the recruits were detained at the depot, and during the voyage to Penang that followed, their treatment was prescribed by the Indian Emigration Act V of 1877 and by the Indian Passengers Act XXV of 1859.

The Sifting Process
When Act V of 1877 came into force on 1 January 1878, it required the recruiters to take every recruit to the Civil Surgeon of the district in which the recruitment had taken place. This officer would examine the recruit and either reject him or certify that he was in a fit state of health to proceed to the Straits and to work there.[2] This medical examination was a necessary and beneficial measure imposed by the government of India. The Province Wellesley planters had repeatedly remonstrated with their agents against the apparent lack of care in selecting recruits. For instance, of the 350 indentured immigrants who arrived at the Malakoff estate in 1873, the *Singapore Daily Times* observed: "Not quite 50 were good men such as are usually imported, and of the remainder, the greater part were suffering from hereditary and other diseases said to be incurable; while the whole, it seems could only be compared to a lot of beggars picked up from our streets."[3] The manager of the estate, Walter Knaggs, immediately sent a letter to his agent at Negapatam, Messrs Oliver and Company, which in part reads: "I cannot too strongly impress upon you that this constant shipment of weak Coolies not only entails loss on the Estate, but by filling the Hospitals, and leading to constant deaths, it is inflicting serious injury on the cause of Immigration to this place."[4]

When Knaggs realized the ineffectiveness of his remonstrances he immediately ordered his agent "*not to send me any more*".

Intending emigrants who had been certified fit by the District Medical Officer were taken by the recruiters to the Negapatam depot where the Protector of Emigrants conducted a screening interview. This was desirable. It had often happened that recruits had been tempted to emigrate for the most inadequate reasons. Debt, domestic discord, and a transient discontent with their lot often rendered those with a weak will easy prey to "an insidious maistry."[5] Since no rule or statute could eradicate this inbuilt weakness in the recruiting process, it was incumbent upon the Protector to check the recruits' motives before they entered into a contract.

The manner in which the recruits were interviewed at the depot often frustrated the beneficent intention of the Emigration Act V of 1877. The Act required the Protector to explain to "each emigrant" individually the terms of the contract; and to ascertain whether he understood the nature of the agreement as regards the rate of wages, the locality of the estate, the period and nature of service, and the arrangements as to the food to be supplied to him; whether he had been induced to emigrate by any coercion, undue influence, fraud or misrepresentation; and whether he was willing to fulfill the terms of the contract he was about to sign.[6] Article 39 of the Act specifically required this exercise to be conducted by the Protector of Emigrants in the presence of the Emigration Agent.

According to Madras government officials, the interviews were often carried out in the presence of the *maistries*.[7] Madras officials claimed that the recruits were "hushed by the awful presence" of the *maistries*.[8] The recruits, "these most docile of people" as the officials described them, would answer the questions they had been taught by the *maistries* to expect with the "most delightful readiness."[9] D.G. McConechy, an official of the Madura Shipping Company, which was commercially connected with Indian emigration to Malaya, revealed: "The coolies are so terrorized by the recruiters that they say 'yes' to everything."[10] When recruits had "taken the shilling", a Madras official once observed, "many of them believed that they had forfeited their right of personal liberty."[11] Those recruits who had been liberated from the depot through the intercession of parents or relatives were pursued and maltreated by the recruiters and relieved of their clothes; and "their earrings were snatched from their ears."[12] Therefore, it could not be expected that the recruits would accuse the *maistries* of any deception that might have been practised on them or to declare their unwillingness to emigrate.

Those recruits whom the *maistries* believed showed symptoms of unwillingness to emigrate or in any other way proved refractory, were regularly withheld by the Emigration Agent from the examination until they signed the contract in response to coercion.[13] Anyone who used coercion to persuade a recruit to enter into a contract to emigrate to the Straits was liable to be punished with imprisonment for a term of up to three years.[14] No evidence has been found of any Emigration Agent having been prosecuted for committing this offence against the Emigration Act. Recalcitrant recruits who were discovered contemplating desertion from the depot after signing the contract, were "cooped up all day … to be taken under guard like prisoners morning and evening to walk and sit as their keepers bade them."[15] The planters resented this. They did not want the depot to be "a sort of prison, with locks on the door and bar [*sic*] to the windows, and guards to prevent escape"; they said they had always maintained that it was to be a "place of shelter to which the recruits might freely go."[16]

When one Province Wellesley planter, E.L. Roberts, visited the depot in 1882, the recruits complained to him "bitterly of their unpleasant imprisonment," and said they were "worried by the watchmen at every turn, and treated generally as if they were sheep."[17] Another planter, E.V. Carey, of the Selangor Coffee Planters' Association, said the conditions at the depot suggested to the recruits "the idea of forced service."[18] The Medical Officer stationed at the depot declared that the recruits, especially the women, many of whom were without husbands, usually became "demoralized, discontented and riotous", which he feared "might ooze out ... and work harm on the estates."[19] Despite the misgivings of Roberts and Carey, the recruits were confined to the depot in the planters' own interest. As some time usually elapsed between the recruits' admission into the depot and their embarkation, if they were allowed to roam about, the Emigration Agent could lose track of them, and the planters could lose the money advanced.

There had been several occasions when recruits were detained at the depot for many weeks, sometimes for months.[20] The main reasons were a lack of a full complement, irregular sailings, bad weather, and the illness of some of the recruits. During such periods, according to the Collector of Tanjore, the recruits were "treated like slaves."[21] Recruits, naturally, resented this. Many who were unable to desert, "behaved ill out of desperation," and were consequently sent to the courts. A Straits planter who observed this added that those recruits who were convicted were not returned to the depot after their sentences expired, and that the Emigration Agent never heard of them or their debts again.[22] This was to the planters' disadvantage. Not only did they obviously lose the monies advanced to the abscondees, but their escape held out a temptation to others to misbehave as a means of freeing themselves from their liabilities. Some immigrants who became disgusted with their wearisome life at the depot and could not desert or otherwise rid themselves of it would inform the Protector that they had changed their minds and did not wish to emigrate.[23] This seemed an easy way out. But as only a few took advantage of it, the majority were apparently afraid of reprisals from the *maistries*.

Recruits who tried unsuccessfully to abscond or who failed to convince the Protector that they had been misled by the *maistries*, were forcibly embarked. K. Tambisammy, the Tamil manager of the Rawang tin-mines in Selangor and a Straits government contractor, reported: "The recruiters, are scoundrels to a man; they not only make gross misrepresentations to the intending emigrants, but even employ force to bring them over .... I have myself seen men dragged from the depot to the steamer by force in the presence of the Police Officers, who raised no remonstrance."[24]

Although Section VIII of the Indian Emigration Act V of 1877 required the Protector of Emigrants and the Emigration Agent to be present at each embarkation to ensure that emigrants went voluntarily, it appears that they were either unwilling or unable to carry out this duty effectively.

The Provision of Food

The system of providing recruits with food at the depot was a major cause of grievance among them. According to article 8 of Act V of 1877, it was the Protector's duty to ensure that recruits were properly fed. This important responsibility was entrusted by the planters to their agents, some of whom engaged food contractors. These prepared food, almost exclusively rice, in huge cauldrons and served it as if, a Madras official said, "the place were a jail", which, he added, "the coolies utterly abhor."[25] One Province Wellesley planter believed that if the labourers were fed like that on the estates "not one man would remain".[26] The Straits Protector of Immigrants said he would not on any consideration have allowed it.[27] So the anomaly existed of the Protector at Negapatam allowing an abuse which the Protector in the Straits would not countenance.

Disappointed with food contractors, the planters instructed their agents to purchase suitable food from the bazaars. But the recruits accused the agents of buying inferior food.[28] It could not be ascertained what checks existed on whether the agents spent on food the full amount budgeted for it. Nevertheless, although the planters believed it was a duty the agents "had heart in", the temptations involved made it seem likely that the accusation did contain some truth. Some doubt was removed when the Collector of Tanjore recommended improvement to the diet by the inclusion of a greater proportion of nutritious food such as pulse or salt-fish or millets, and by allowing more for taste by "meliorating the lamentable deficiency in variety".[29]

Substitution of Recruits

Despite repeated protests from the planters there were numerous criticisms of the general quality of the indentured immigrants arriving in the Straits. In 1879 (the year after a Medical Officer was appointed to the depot), the Principal Civil Medical Officer (P.C.M.O.) of the Straits Settlements, described some immigrants as the "dregs of humanity swept from the highways and by-ways".[30] Every batch, he claimed, contained a number of "utterly useless characters," varying from a small percentage to a fourth or even sometimes a third of the whole.[31] One planter, J. Lamb, said some immigrants could be distinguished by their "very low, often semi-idiotic type of physiognomy."[32] A few of these, he believed, had been beggars or scavengers.[33] Other planters described some of the labourers received as being "poor in physique, abject, and lacking in vitality."[34] On several occasions during 1880, Governor Weld protested to the Emigration Agent against the arrival in the colony of a number of indentured immigrants in a "condition unfit for labour."[35] Enquiry was made on every such representation, but always with the result that the Emigration Agent was able to assert that he had personally exercised "all possible care in regard to this point."[36] He maintained that the emigrants sent to the Straits had left Negapatam "strong and in good health."[37]

Later reports showed that generally the quality of the immigrants continued to be unsuitable for sugar cultivation. The Commission of 1881 (which was appointed by the Straits government to enquire into the cases of alleged ill-treatment of Indian immigrants in Province Wellesley) found many instances of non-agriculturists such as Brahmins, shopkeepers, weavers, etc. and even boys under ten years of age.[38] Some planters told the Labour Commission of 1890 that among the labourers they received were those who were "inferior, both in physique and ability to perform agricultural or outdoor labour."[39] The Commission itself described some of the labourers received as "miserable fellows who have legs like pencils, baggy knees, and pot bellies".[40] When these were required to use the *changkol*, the Commission said: "They lose heart and strength, deteriorate into 'hospital birds' and swell the death-rate."[41]

For the apparent disparity in the state of the labourers' health between their departure from Madras Presidency and their arrival at Penang, Madras officials blamed the effects of the voyage. They contended that the ten to twelve days at sea were enough to produce very ill-effects upon the emigrants, many of whom, they claimed, probably suffered from sickness and whose material comforts were not much attended to on board a native ship.[42] As will be seen later, there is some evidence to support the latter part of this contention.

The Emigration Agent admitted that the voyage caused injurious effects on the emigrants, most of whom, he discovered had never sailed before and were consequently sea-sick during the entire journey.[43] He added: "It is therefore absurd to say that the stamp of cooly sent is inferior". In support of this, the Labour Commission of 1890 declared that a large proportion of immigrants arrived "utterly unfit" to work because they had been "prostrated by the discomforts of the sea-voyage".[44]

On the other hand, the Straits P.C.M.O., Dr M.F. Simon, disagreed with these contentions. He discounted the possibility that the sea-voyage could have had any serious adverse physical effect on the emigrants beyond temporarily upsetting them, for which they might require treatment or a few days' rest.[45] He, however, conceded that if the immigrants were neglected upon arrival on the estates while still under the effects of the voyage, they could suffer permanent harm.[46]

The consistent claims that only healthy, able-bodied emigrants had been admitted into the depot, and diseased and debilitated immigrants were received from native-owned sailing ships, led to the belief that a surreptitious system of substituting rejects for bona fide emigrants had been introduced at some stage between admission into the depot and arrival at Penang. It was difficult for the depot authorities to detect how this evasion was perpetrated. Some officials suspected the *maistries* of bribing the watchmen; others believed illegal entries were gained into the depot by diverting the watchmen's attention.

There were three other distinct possibilities. First, following complaints from emigrants over their jail-like incarceration, the Collector of Tanjore requested the Emigration Agent to allow them occasional freedom outside.[47] During these short interludes, it was quite possible for a number of substitutions to be effected. Second, the small craft which ferried batches of emigrants to the ships, which for reasons of draught were usually anchored on the roadstead, could have been substituted by others containing the rejects. Finally, on the Negapatam-Penang voyage, many emigrant ships were captained by South Indians, most of whom were said to be in collusion with Indian speculators and recruiters.[48] It was suspected that after some of these ships were cleared at Negapatam, the captains veered to some other South Indian port or rendezvous where they embarked rejected recruits. When the native-owned barque *Sri Ranganayaji* once took fifteen instead of the usual ten or twelve days to reach Penang and arrived with more passengers than she had embarked at Negapatam, the suspicions regarding the vessel's illegal trade were confirmed.[49]

Other evidence implicated the *Sri Ranganayagi*. The Straits Medical Officer and the Protector of Immigrants described a large number of the 171 immigrants disembarked from this vessel in 1880 as "old, weakly and diseased".[50] But the Chief Surgeon at Negapatam indignantly maintained that the contingent he had sent comprised "a particularly good lot of men", and that the assertion made in the Straits was "most ridiculous".[51] He claimed that he himself had passed the emigrants; that the Civil Surgeons who had assisted him had exercised the "greatest care" in examining them; and he had rejected those who had the slightest appearance of weakness or who were over forty years old.[52] In support of his contention, he quoted the Protector of Emigrants as having described that shipment as containing a "capital batch of emigrants."[53] The conflict in views between the Negapatam and the Penang officials concerning that batch of emigrants suggests either that one view at least was incorrect or that something drastic had occurred during the voyage to change the emigrants' state of health.

Corroborative evidence tended to substantiate the Straits officials' claims that there was frequent substitution of "decrepits" for those passed at the depot. "Vague rumours" to this effect were said to have been verified by an (unquoted) statement voluntarily made on oath by Mootoosammy, one of the emigrants who had been aboard the *Sri Ranganayagi,* and who was hospitalized at the Butterworth General Hospital immediately after arrival at Province Wellesley in 1880.[54] Besides, the discovery by the Commission of 1881 of many instances of non-agriculturists among the indentured immigrants led to their conclusion that the "practice of substitution was sometimes resorted to."[55]

Despite the regulations contained in the Indian Emigration Act V of 1877, embarking the emigrants at Negapatam afforded ample opportunity for evasion. Recruits could not be received on board unless they produced the embarkation pass issued to them by the Emigration Agent and countersigned by the Protector.[56] There was no guarantee that the emigrants embarked were the same ones certified at the depot. The passage ticket did not state the passenger's name; it merely read "one adult" or "one minor."[57] Therefore, anyone to whom a *maistry* had given a ticket, and who could manage to elude the port authorities could represent himself as an indentured emigrant.

Manifests provided by the Emigration Agent to the captains of vessels and which were intended to prevent substitution, were found to be "erroneous and perfectly unreliable, fictitious names appearing in the return."[58] To verify such returns on board would have imposed an enormous amount of work which would be harassing even under favourable circumstances. When hundreds of passengers of all sorts were in the company of animals in an open roadstead and had to be dealt with individually to ensure that person, name, and number corresponded, the confusion was said to be "indescribable."[59]

An added difficulty was that a certain proportion of the ordinary passengers did not "appear on the scene until the eleventh hour."[60] The Harbour Master or the Emigration Agent could not be expected to furnish reliable manifests as it was quite impossible for either of them to do so within the twenty-four hours before the ship sailed. Besides, some ordinary passengers did not purchase their tickets for the crossing until the "last minute". This was due to the keen competition among the shipping companies which led many passengers to wait until the fares were reduced. Mustering such a heterogeneous crowd on board a vessel under ordinary circumstances would have been extremely difficult; doing so during the monsoon when the passengers would be nearly all sick would have been impracticable.

Illegal Emigration from Karikal

However lax the formalities at Negapatam might appear, some Indian speculators and their *maistries*, preferring to take no risks, transferred their *locus operandi* to the adjacent French port of Karikal. That was illegal. The Emigration Act V of 1877 declared only four ports – Negapatam, Madras, Calcutta, and Bombay – from which British Indian subjects might be exported for the purpose of labour. Since the Protector of Emigrants could not exercise any direct control over the *maistries* in foreign territory, the speculators and their *maistries* were thus free to neglect and oppress the emigrants with impunity.

According to Madras officials, these Negapatam speculators, who were the principal perpetrators of the illegal trade from Karikal, included "perhaps the keenest and most eager traders" of Madras Presidency; they were men who "would do anything and dare anything in the pursuit of gain."[61] They were anxious to make Karikal the headquarters of their trade, the port not being controlled by British Indian authority. This increased the chances of their competing successfully with their French rivals. Not unexpectedly, they would not relinquish their illicit trade until, Madras officials said, they had "exhausted every trick and subterfuge that their experienced ingenuity could suggest to them."[62]

That a system of illicit emigration from Karikal to the Straits had long existed, more or less fitfully, there was no doubt. Since about 1870, the year in which the Madras government declared indentured emigration to the Straits illegal, Madras officials reported the operation of the traffic as follows. Steamers plying between Karikal and Penang conveyed as passengers persons who in reality were British Indian indentured emigrants.[63] Besides allegations constantly made by Bowness Fischer, the British Consular Agent stationed at Karikal, and the personal discovery in June 1871 by the French Emigration Agent of one of his recruiters' involvement in the trade,[64] there was the testimony of Captain Wilhelm of the French brig *Macassar*. In August 1871 (when indentured emigration to the Straits was still suspended), Wilhelm's declaration to Fischer and to the Collector of Tanjore that his mission to Karikal was principally for "coolies", who he understood had been recruited in the Tanjore district for labour in the Straits,[65] confirmed the suspicion. Some Karikal speculators who were also engaged in shipping across the Bay of Bengal, "frankly admitted" to Fischer that a large proportion of the passengers they had been transporting to the Straits were *de facto* indentured emigrants from British India.[66] In mitigation of their admission, they declared their willingness to submit to any rules and pay any fees that might be demanded of them if the traffic were recognized by the French authorities, and if the same status was accorded their business as was enjoyed by Indian emigration to the French colonies. The French authorities at Karikal would not agree to the latter suggestion. They were anxious to have the illegal traffic to the Straits terminated. They believed if another line of emigration was permanently established at Karikal, the ensuing competition for emigrants would eventually destroy emigration to the French colonies in the West Indies.

There was little doubt about this possibility because compared with emigration to the French colonies, the traffic to the Straits presented certain advantages. By sailing vessel, the voyage to Guadeloupe and Martinique lasted around ninety days;[67] Penang could be reached within a maximum of twelve days. The engagements contracted by emigrants proceeding to the French colonies were of five years' duration;[68] Penang-bound emigrants were required to sign three-year contracts. It is true that the French colonies paid twice or nearly thrice the equivalent wage rates offered by the Straits planters, but this was in return for the longer contract. It is also undeniable that the French contracts stipulated free passages to and from the colonies. But the planters in Martinique and Guadeloupe would not defray the cost of repatriation until the labourers had completed their first contract and had served a further five-year "industrial residence", which was nothing other than a euphemism for another term of indenture.

In the final analysis, the greater number of British Indian labourers emigrating to the Straits than to the French colonies suggests, admittedly not very convincingly, that emigration to the former colony was more popular. Between 1878 and 1883 (when Tamil emigration to the French West Indies was discontinued), a total of 5,012 labourers emigrated to Martinique and Guadeloupe.[69] For the same period, a total of 6,998 indentured recruits emigrated to the Straits Settlements.[70] Although of this number it could not be ascertained precisely how many British Indians were illegally taken to the Straits via Karikal, there could be no doubt that the French were anxious to see the illegal traffic terminated.

One of the most notorious aspects of the illegal emigration from Karikal to the Straits was overcrowding on board ship. In 1881, the German-owned *Septima* had on board 482½ passengers,[71] with another 190 awaiting embarkation; when all boarded, she would have had an excess of 72½ passengers beyond her licensed capacity, and 222½ above what should have been her actual maximum capacity.[72] A survey of the *Septima* conducted by British consular officials stationed at Karikal revealed that she did not have the required superficial minimum accommodation for the 600 passengers she was licensed to carry; her actual capacity being 450.[73]

When the matter was reported to Madras government officials and due investigation was made, they discovered that at the time of licensing the vessel the captain had included the dimensions of the whole saloon and of the officers' cabins as passengers' accommodation.[74] According to the officials, not only was this "contrary to the existing practice at British Indian ports, and inconsistent with the spirit and intention of the Native Passengers Act XXV of 1859," but it was "disallowed and reprobated by express orders" of the government of India.[75]

Commenting on the labour emigration from Karikal to the Straits, a French official at Karikal described it as a "veritable (slave) traffic in disguise. Passengers who set out for Penang were not really free labourers, who were conscious of what they were going to seek far off, but many of them were caught by any bait and tricked by any greedy and unscrupulous trader."[76] Fischer acknowledged these emigrants needed guidance and protection. The only effective course open to him in this regard was to urge the French authorities to repress the abuses with a firm hand while extending to the Straits-bound emigrants the same humane and enlightened security offered to their own recruits. All that was required, he asked them, was to try and distinguish between those who were bona fide passengers and those who had been inveigled into a contract, and to punish "with exemplary severity" those who had induced the latter to impersonate ordinary passengers.

The system operating at Karikal was hardly capable of achieving this end. According to an agreement signed between the government of India and the local French authorities on 2 September 1864, which was intended to control the movements of "interlopers", all persons departing from Karikal were obliged to be furnished with passports.[77] The simple system of obtaining one facilitated the illicit trade. An Indian, no matter who, could present himself at the Karikal Police Court, ask for a passport, pay the required fee, and could go where he liked; "no disagreeable questions were asked as to his antecedents; no enquiries were made as to his future livelihood."[78] It was true that two "intelligent" individuals had to testify to the applicant's bona fides, but this, Madras officials asserted, was a "mere formality."[79] The same two persons, they added, would vouch for any number of applicants from any part of Madras Presidency.

Under such a loose system abuse was quite possible, and it would not be in the interest of the Karikal police to check it. It seems an anomaly that British Indian subjects should be permitted to leave India questioned only by an undoubtedly disinterested junior official of a foreign government. As a native of Karikal was said to resemble a British Indian native of Madras Presidency "as much as one pea resembles another",[80] it would still have been impossible for that official to tell whether an intending emigrant, who no doubt had been thoroughly tutored by the *maistry* before he applied, was a British or French subject if he positively declared himself the latter.

The facility with which the *maistries* could induce the average Tamil recruit to say anything when he was confronted by authority was well known in official circles. Fischer asserted: "The *maistries* tutored them to tell the most palpably purposeless falsehoods with the most astounding assurance, and so powerful appears to be the sway the recruiters exercise over their minds that they not infrequently tell these lies even if it is their evident interest to tell the truth."[81] To expect the Commissaire de Police would sift the testimony of each of the many persons who applied to him for passports in the course of a busy day was asking too much. His duties were "too multifarious and too onerous".[82]

Victualling during the Voyage from Negapatam

Those Indian speculators who preferred to process their recruits legally through the depot took little care for the emigrants' nutritional needs on the voyage. Since 1872, the Madras government had authorized the following daily diet for each emigrant while on board:-[83]

Rice ...	1 lb.
Daal (split-peas soup) or saltfish...	4 ozs.
Onions, turmeric, chillies, or other curry-stuff ...	2 ozs.
Salt	½ oz.

Instead of implementing this diet, the speculators imposed their own. One of the worst cases of under-rationing reported by Dr J.T. Veitch, the Colonial Surgeon stationed at Penang, involved the barque *Neelayathatchy*. After she arrived at Penang from Negapatam with a batch of 147 indentured recruits on 28 October 1874, Veitch inspected the immigrants and reported that the labourers had the "appearance of being a half-starved lot and [that] many of them were miserably thin and wanting in that development which would render them serviceable as estate labourers."[84]

On the basis of the immigrants' testimony, Veitch concluded that the major contributing factor to their condition was the inadequate food supplied to them on board. The daily allowance had consisted of three coconut shells of boiled rice and about half a pint of water.[85] This "altogether insufficient quantity of food," the Surgeon declared, "was an act of gross inhumanity". It was a contravention of article 8 of Act XXV of 1859 on the part of the speculators to deny emigrants adequate food and water. Failure to comply with the Act was liable to a maximum fine of twenty rupees (about nine Straits dollars) for every passenger who had thus suffered privation. It could not be ascertained whether anyone was charged.

In 1875, the testimony given by three indentured immigrants at the request of the Straits Colonial Surgeon provided more interesting light on conditions on board emigrant ships. The translated evidence of Jonas reads:

> I came from the Coromandel Coast. I left Negapatam on 6th October [1874]. I don't know the name of the ship. That man (pointing to Saiboo Kundoo) was the nacoda [captain]; there were more than 140 coolies on board. We received each day about 11 or 12 o' clock three coconut shells of boiled rice; the coconut shell was a little larger than the one now shown me. We also received a tin of water, the size of one now produced. For the first two days and after we sighted Penang we received a little larger tin of water; and if we asked for more the cook beat us. We only received rice and water once a day. We had salt water into which we squeezed some tama-

rind. I did not complain to the captain. If I received five coconut shells of rice it would have been sufficient. When I complained to the malim [the ship's officer] he said he had to be careful with the water lest it be calm. For five days there was calm and no rain. Kadersa, the man who shipped us on board at Negapatam put on board for our use large salt fish, ghee, coconuts, dhall [daal], and vegetables. We only get small salt fish, bringall [aubergine], and pumpkins. There was no headman on board but the coolies cooked for us …. Kadersa did not say how much food we are to have everyday. He said we would get what we want on board.[86]

Another indentured immigrant, Yacoob, gave basically similar evidence and added that the twenty ordinary passengers "got as much rice as well as other things from the cook as they asked for".[87] His complaint against the "bad and insufficient quantity of food" produced no effect. The captain told him to be content with what he was served. Yacoob's body began to itch, which he said was due to the overcrowding. "There was no room to lie down and we had to take by turn to take our rest." He admitted sailing on "a good number of ships before but had never been treated like this."

Kessuwayah's testimony confirmed Jonas'. In addition, in response to his complaints, the captain told him the vessel was "in calm", and if no breeze sprang up he would order less rations. "I said in that case I will certainly die. He said he will throw me into the sea." Of the food, Kessuwayah said: "The cooks and free passengers eat up all what Kadersa put for us on board."[88]

In the 1870s, for the voyage by sail from Negapatam to Penang, emigrants were charged $13.00 with ration,[89] which was then considered a very high price. The Lieutenant-Governor of Penang, Colonel A.E.H. Anson, argued on the basis of his investigations that the cost of the passage without ration by sailing ship for ordinary passengers did not exceed $9.00.[90] Thus, for subsistence on the voyage, the emigrants were charged $4.00 although they were usually deprived of the greater part of the food to which this charge entitled them. Assuming that the vessels took twelve days to reach Penang, the daily rate of diet would cost each emigrant about thirty-three cents. But as they received only one meal a day, consisting usually of rice with a little pumpkin or curry, Anson reckoned that its actual cost did not amount to more than six cents a day or about seventy-two cents for the voyage.[91] Thus, the speculators realized a profit of about $3.00 on each emigrant. This would add three months to the period which the labourers were placed under deductions to repay their debt, which would in most cases be added to the time they would take to work out their contract.

In 1882, one recruiting agent, on instructions from some planters, made a contract with Captain Menzell of the steamship *Meenatchy*, and it was only then that some improvement in the immigrants' condition became noticeable. Two main reasons were responsible. The ship was apparently chosen with serious concern for the emigrants' welfare as its description given by one planter suggests.

> The ship is perfectly ventilated, with eighteen inches ports all round. Besides this there are two large centrifugal air pumps, worked by machinery, to throw fresh air below, and force out any impure air that might otherwise accumulate in bad weather. In places where, if not looked after, uncleanliness might occur, continuous and co-

pious streams of water are continually flowing, and I can certify that not the cleanest railway station in England is free from impure odors [sic]. Sir Frederick Weld visited the ship and expressed himself greatly pleased at her completeness for the purpose of carrying native passengers.[92]

This steamer was much faster, reducing the voyage from twelve to five days. Its speed and reliability would eliminate any delays occasioned by storms and calms. The abridgement of the voyage and its superior comfort should ensure that the emigrants would land in a better physical condition. The cost of the passage and provisions having been reduced to the equivalent of about $10.00, the immigrants would be enabled to repay their debts to their employers sooner, and to save more. From the planters' point of view, there was also the advantage that the importation of labourers would not be restricted to the monsoon season.

The second reason was that Menzell held himself personally responsible to ensure that the emigrants were properly fed and cared for during the voyage. Madras officials reported they were served two "good" meals daily with sufficient pure water.[93] Consequently, their condition was so satisfactory, compared with previous arrangements, that all indentured emigrants recruited by that agent were subsequently conveyed by the *Meenatchy* under Menzell's captaincy.[94] By contracting with him to victual the emigrants, the planters secured their recruits from semi-starvation, and protected them from the additional cost which the speculators would have exacted.

Government-Controlled Depot

There were improvements at the Negapatam depot as well but not until the Straits government assumed control over it in 1890. Since a number of recruits had to travel considerable distances and needed rest in preparation for the voyage, the Superintendent, Dr Hardaker, persuaded the Straits government to enlarge the existing building. Previously, with room for only about 200 persons, resort had often been made to private godowns. Invariably, these were of "ill repute, filthy, insanitary, overcrowded, and wretched."[95] Whenever outbreaks of cholera occurred in the town of Negapatam, the disease usually broke out in these godowns as well. When the afflicted inmates were transferred to the depot as accommodation allowed, the disease was naturally introduced there also.[96]

In 1892, the Straits government erected two temporary supplementary sheds; and in 1895, construction of a new depot was completed. A visiting Province Wellesley planter reported it was "a large airy building kept scrupulously clean, and the accepted recruits were as fine looking a lot of men and women as one could wish to see".[97] In 1901, the Collector of Tanjore was inspired to note of the depot thus: "A most striking change for the better".[98] He found several improvements in the supervision of the recruits; more buildings were being constructed; and the recruits were in a "hale and hearty condition".[99]

References

1 Member of the British Anti-Slavery and Aborigines Protection Society, 1910. Quoted in Harris, *Coolie Labour*, p. 3.
2 *Singapore Daily Times*, 21 January 1874.
3 C.O. 273/71. Enclosure in Sir Andrew Clarke to the Earl of Carnarvon, no. 397, 25 December 1873.
4 *Ibid.*
5 MPP, no. 40, February 1874, p. 59.
6 See Act V of 1877, Chapter VII.
7 MPP, Appendix, September 1881.
8 MPP, no. 1313, 29 September 1881.
9 *Ibid.*
10 PSSLC, Paper no. 11, 24 April 1903, p. C70.
11 IEP, nos 1-15, September 1870.
12 MPP, Range 439, vol. 10, 13 September 1870.
13 MPP, Appendix, November 1881.
14 See Act V of 1877, article 40.
15 MPP, Appendix, November 1881.
16 PSSLC, 30 April 1897, p. B45.
17 MPP, no. 372, 14 June 1882.
18 Evidence of E.V. Carey, in RCII 1896, p. ix.
19 MPP, no. 372, 14 June 1882.
20 *Ibid.*
21 *Ibid.*
22 *Ibid.*
23 *Ibid.*
24 Evidence of K. Tambisammy, in RLC 1890, Appendix A, nos 170-71, n.p.
25 MPP, no. 372, 14 June 1882.
26 *Ibid.*
27 *Ibid.*
28 *Ibid.*
29 *Ibid.*
30 PSSLC, 24 July 1879, p. C143.
31 *SSGG*, 24 October 1879, p. 962.
32 PSSLC, 24 July 1879, p. C142.
33 *Ibid.*
34 MPP, no. 909, 16 June 1880.
35 C.O. 273/105. Weld to Kimberley, no. 259, 7 December 1880.
36 MPP, no. 1314, 29 September 1881.
37 *Ibid.*
38 *Report of the Commissioners Appointed for the Purpose of Enquiring into the Cases of Alleged Ill-Treatment of Indian Immigrants Employed on Certain Estates in Province Wellesley* (Singapore, 1881), p. 7. (Hereinafter referred to as *Report of the 1881 Commission*).

39 RLC 1890, p. 45.
40 *Ibid.*, p. 33.
41 *Ibid.*, p. 45.
42 MPP, no. 909, 16 June 1881.
43 PSSLC, 17 October 1881, p. C42.
44 See RLC 1890, Appendix A, p. C108.
45 Evidence of Dr M.F. Simon, in RLC 1890, Appendix A, p. C108.
46 *Ibid.*
47 MPP, no. 372, 14 June 1882.
48 MPP, vol. 1555, 24 February 1880.
49 *Ibid.*
50 C.O. 273/105. Weld to Kimberley, no. 259, 7 December 1880.
51 MPP, vol. 1555, 24 February 1880.
52 *Ibid.*
53 MPP, no. 909, 16 June 1880.
54 *Ibid.*
55 *Report of the 1881 Commission*, p. 7.
56 See Act V of 1877, article 34.
57 PRAD, no. 4, March 1886.
58 *Ibid.*
59 *Ibid.*
60 *Ibid.*
61 MPP, vol. 346, 21 July 1878.
62 *Ibid.*
63 Tupper, *Note on Indian Emigration*, p. 8.
64 MPP, no. 547, 10 December 1874.
65 MPP, vol. 276, 1 May 1875.
66 *Ibid.*
67 Xavier S. Thani Nayagam, "Tamil Emigration to the Martinique," *Journal of Tamil Studies,* I, No. 2, Pt. 1 (October, 1969), 81
68 MPP, vol. 276, 1 May 1875.
69 Nayagam, "Tamil Migrations to Guadeloupe and Martinique", p. 375.
70 ARII 1879-83.
71 Children were counted as half passengers.
72 MPP, no. 1025, 29 July 1881.
73 *Ibid.*
74 MPP, no. 1314, 29 September 1881.
75 MPP, no. 1025, 29 July 1881.
76 *Ibid.*
77 MPP, vol. 276, 1 May 1875.
78 *Ibid.*
79 *Ibid.*
80 PRAD, no. 4, March 1886.
81 *Ibid.*

82 *Ibid.*
83 MPP, vol. 1555, 27 October 1880.
84 MPP, vol. 276, 29 January 1875.
85 *Ibid.*
86 MPP, vol. 276, 29 January 1875.
87 *Ibid.*
88 *Ibid.*
89 MPP, Appendix A, November 1875.
90 MPP, vol. 276, 1 July 1875.
91 *Ibid.*
92 MPP, no. 372, 14 June 1882.
93 MPP, vol. 1925, 15 January 1882.
94 *Ibid.*
95 MPP, vol. 276, 7 October 1875.
96 *Ibid.*
97 *Singapore Free Press*, 3 September 1895.
98 IEP, vol. 6135, October 1901.
99 *Ibid.*

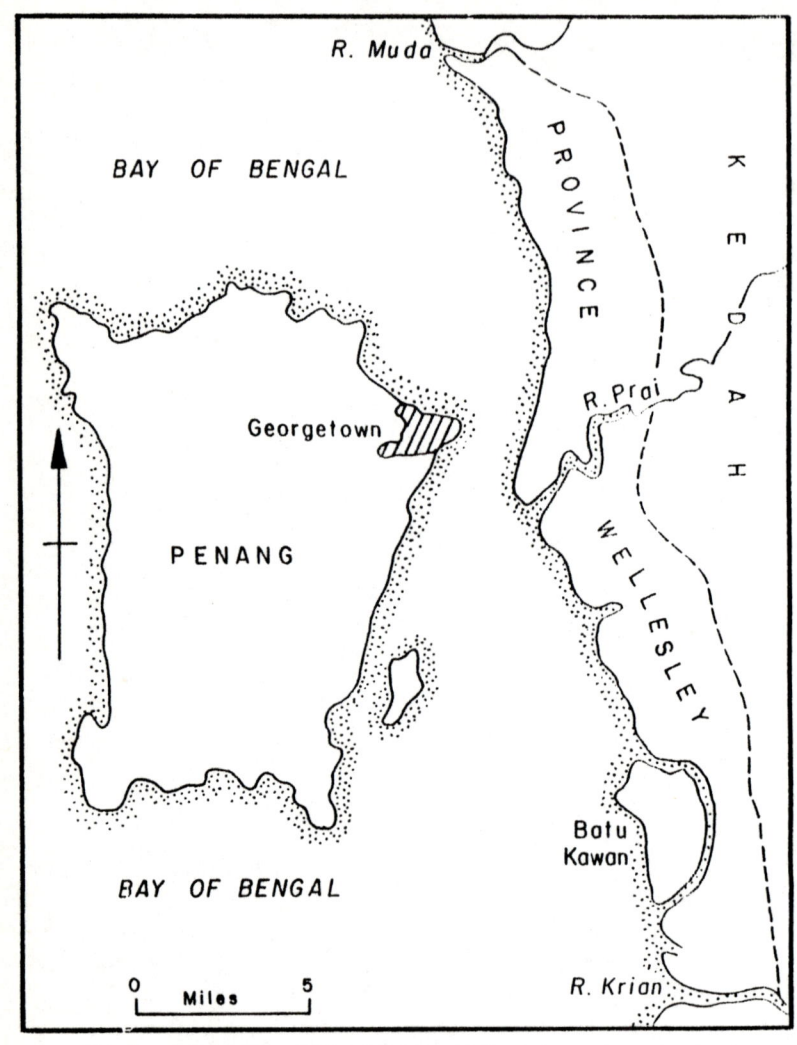

Fig. 6 — PENANG AND PROVINCE WELLESLEY DURING INDIAN INDENTURE

VII

THE CONDITIONS OF LABOUR

On their arrival to this country they are disabused of the fairy tales they heard regarding these parts before they departed from their own homes .... This especially applies to the statute Immigrant coolie.

Henry A. Haviland[1]

During the negotiations in 1872 with the government of India for a resumption of indentured emigration, the Governor of the Straits Settlements, Sir Harry Ord, had committed himself to pass a labour ordinance which, *inter alia*, would incorporate comprehensive measures for the protection of Indian indentured labourers in the colony.[2] The draft ordinance submitted by the Straits government in April 1872 was not approved by the government of India. Since further negotiation was required, the recruitment of urgently needed labourers was delayed. In order to protect the planting interest of Province Wellesley, Ord[3] tried to persuade the government of India to remove the embargo by pledging this assurance: "The government of India may rely on the watchful care of this government over any men who may thus be sent over previous to final arrangements being concluded".[4] This undertaking convinced the government of India of the benevolent intentions of the Straits government, and the ban was lifted. When Ord announced the news to the Legislative Council, he reiterated his commitment thus: "We [the Straits government] would do all that the Indian Government could ask for the health and safety of the coolie, and are perfectly prepared to do it."[5] These pledges were not long afterwards dishonoured by a number of scandalous events.

The Tassek Incident
On 24 October 1873, an incident occurred on the Tassek estate which cannot be attributed to any default of the employer. Its significance lay in the chain of events which it precipitated. A sixteen-to-eighteen-year-old Indian indentured labourer, Kurapen, was reported to have fainted while at work and later died in the field.[6] "The faintness was no doubt caused by exposure to the sun in a debilitated condition,"[7] concluded Dr J.D.M. Coghill, Acting Colonial Surgeon in charge of the Butterworth[8] General Hospital, who performed the autopsy. At the inquest held on 26 October 1873, Coghill testified that the post-mortem revealed that Kurapen had not eaten for twenty-four hours before he died.[9] He believed if the labourer

had been promptly and properly attended to after he fell, he would have survived.[10]

One of the other witnesses summoned to the inquest, Sharmaniden, gave the following translated description of the incident:

> I am a coolie on the Tassek Estate. The day before yesterday [i.e. 24 October 1873] at 6 p.m. the tindal told all the Coolies to go home as work was done and told two of us, myself and Sillen to go and bring deceased home slowly as he was unwell. We went to where he was in the 30 field. We came up to him and calling him to come home he cried and said he did not want to go. We took his hands, he resisted saying he had a stomach ache and did not want to go home on a Cart coming by. And as I could not see I said to Sillen I must go home first, you watch and if he does not come tell the Tindal. And I went home. I met the Cart after I left deceased and Sillen. I did not tell the Tindal as I left Sillen to do that.[11]

Three other labourers testified,[12] and on the basis of all the evidence, the coroner, J.B. Hewick, pronounced that Kurapen had died from "natural cause aggravated by neglect and exposure."[13]

The Province Wellesley police were suspicious of the circumstances surrounding Kurapen's death, and Sharmaniden and Sillen were prosecuted on a charge of causing Kurapen's death by negligence. At their trial held at the Supreme Court on 7 November 1873, the judge terminated the case prematurely when he found that, as he said, "although there was a moral, yet there was no legal liability on the part of the two labourers to see the deceased home."[14]

The Alma Affair

Present at the Sharmaniden and Sillen trial was the manager of the nearby Alma estate, Walter Knaggs, who suddenly left the enquiry for his estate from where he hurriedly sent five of his labourers to the Butterworth Hospital. Eight days later, on 15 November, the Magistrate of Police and Chief Executive Officer of Butterworth, F.H. Gottlieb, was on a visit to the Hospital when his attention was drawn to the fact that five labourers had been received on 7 November 1873 from the Alma estate in a "moribund condition". Gottlieb immediately requested the Acting Colonial Surgeon, Coghill, to furnish him with a report on these labourers. Coghill responded on 16 November and in the covering letter to his report (which is presented herein later) he observed:

> The significant fact ... that these unfortunate persons were only sent to Hospital on the very day on which an enquiry was being held ... concerning the death of a young Cooly belonging to Tassek Estate who died of debility aggravated by exposure, want of food and the absence of medical treatment, and at which the Manager of Alma Estate was present, is pregnant with meaning.[15]

Apparently Knaggs had anticipated a suspicion of motives and had tried to pre-empt any accusation against his sincerity. In a letter to Gottlieb dated 18 November, Knaggs claimed: "The fact of my sending these men to the Hospital, shows that my action in the matter was 'bona fide'". "Setting aside the important question of humanity," he added, "motives of economy alone would always prompt me to do so if I were sure of getting them back again – as the maintenance and superintendence of the sick on the Estate cost more than the charges at

Butterworth." [16] The fact that Knaggs took sudden action during the trial of Sharmaniden and Sillen suggests that his real intention was to forestall the possibility of his own prosecution should any of his labourers die from negligence or other causes that would arouse suspicions of neglect.

The condition of the five Alma estate labourers left no doubt that their health had been grossly neglected. Coghill's report of 16 November 1873 to Gottlieb reads:

> The female Tylamah and the lad Ramsamy were almost moribund on admission and were mere skeletons covered with skin, the girl died of exhaustion on the 9th instant and the boy this day, while the third Periaya is at the present moment rapidly sinking. [He died later in the day of 16 November 1873] These two lads were only kept alive by the most liberal use of stimulants and nourishing food. The fourth boy Asha Kee is in a very critical state but I do not apprehend any immediate danger. The fifth case, Robert, injury to the great toe, is almost well. I may add that the three boys from Alma have stated that they were compelled to work when sick.[17]

In addition to these labourers, by 9 December 1873, the Lieutenant-Governor of Penang, Colonel A.E.H. Anson, under whose administration Province Wellesley fell directly, recorded that more patients had been received and who exhibited a great want of medical care and attention.[18]

Since these labourers had cost the Alma estate $22.00 each to import (which they were required to repay through monthly deductions of $1.00), and since they were all first-year immigrants, a large portion of their debt would have been still outstanding. Furthermore, apart from humanitarian considerations, when labour was so much needed, it is difficult to understand why in the planter's own interest the labourers' health was allowed to deteriorate like that.

Knaggs did offer an explanation, and even tried to exonerate himself. In his letter to Gottlieb dated 18 November 1873, Knaggs claimed that upon his recent arrival as manager of Alma, he had found "a bad state of things existing;" and that upon taking charge, he immediately established "a comfortable infirmary" for the accommodation of the sick; that the apothecary he had engaged to attend to his sick labourers had removed to Penang and could no longer perform that duty; that he could not procure the services of a regular medical practitioner for under $50.00 per month; that he was awaiting the permanent appointment of a Medical Officer in Province Wellesley to supervise the infirmary; and that to send labourers to the Butterworth Hospital was "simply to lose them" as well as the $22.00 he had expended in importing each of them. "This only," he added, "and not any niggardly spirit of economy, is the cause of my not sending my sick people to Butterworth until absolutely necessary, unless they express a wish to go there."[19]

From the sources available, it was not possible to test the authenticity of Knaggs' assertions except for sending labourers to Butterworth was "simply to lose them". Gottlieb confirmed that Indian indentured labourers had indeed "escaped from the Hospital here, thus causing loss to the Proprietors."[20]

The circumstances surrounding the death of Periayah, Tylamah, and Ramsamy prompted Gottlieb to request the coroner, Hewick, to conduct an inquest. In his evidence to the inquest held on 17 November 1873, Coghill said:

The female [Tylamah] and Periaya [sic] had been ill four months before being sent to Hospital, and Ramsamy nearly 2 months. The immediate cause of death in the case of Ramsamy was debility and in that of Periaya, dysentery. Had the men received the requisite medical care and treatment at the beginning of their illness I believe they would in all probability have recovered – their youth being vastly favorable to such a termination. Another Cooly Ahseekee, aged 16, is now in a very critical state, and I would recommend his statement of being compelled to work when ill to be taken down as fatal collapse may at any moment step in.[21]

The "Dresser"[22] stationed at the Butterworth Hospital, W.H. Dickson, also testified. *Inter alia*, he said both Ramsamy and Periaya, two days before their death, had told him how they had been "compelled to work when ill." Ramsamy, he added, had told him that he had been ill for thirty eight days, during which he was made to work, first in the field until he was incapable, and then he was sent to peel tapioca roots. Periayah had been ill for four months previous to his admission to hospital, and "had also been made to work during that period."[23]

The last witness to testify was Asha Kee (Ahseekee). His translated testimony reads:

> I am a Coolie on Alma Estate where I have been employed for about a year - I was ill for 15 days previously to my being sent to the Butterworth Hospital. I had been ill 4 or 5 days when I told the Kranny [or kerani, the estate's payroll clerk] who sent me to the Estate Hospital, where I continued twelve days, but getting no better I was sent down to Butterworth Hospital by the Kranny.[24]

In his verdict, the coroner found that "the deceased Ramsamy and Periaya died from debility and dysentery aggravated and brought to a fatal termination by the want of requisite Medical care and treatment at the beginning of their illness."[25] The inquest could not recommend prosecution of anyone because as the Acting Solicitor-General pointed out: "There is no legal provision ... to oblige proprietors to make better provision for the sick Coolies on their Estates."[26]

Colonel Anson was indignant at this whole affair. In a letter to Knaggs dated 9 December 1873, he wrote: "I have ... to call your most serious attention to the wretched condition in which some of [your] Coolies ... have been received at the Butterworth Hospital, and in the name of humanity to solicit that you will take immediate measures to make better provision for the labourers committed to your care." In Anson's final paragraph, he added: "Under these circumstances it will be a matter for consideration of this [Penang] Government whether it will not be desirable to communicate with the Government of India with the view of putting a stop to the further recruiting of Coolies for your Estate."[27] Anson's mood was retributive. He was disposed to request a curtailment of a labour supply for Alma even if Knaggs' pecuniary interests would consequently be jeopardized.

Knaggs' apprehension must have mounted when he realized the implications of Anson's contemplation. He immediately responded to appease the Lieutenant-Governor, repeating most of the reasons he had given Gottlieb why he ought to be exculpated.[28] In his conclusion, he pleaded with Anson thus: "With regard to the concluding paragraph of your last communication I beg to express a hope that you will not allow me – a stranger – to be sacrificed for the abolition of a system which I found existing here on my arrival; and that you will not adopt a course fraught with such serious consequences both to myself and others without mature enquiry and deliberation." In a postscript, he further implored Anson to appoint a commission of enquiry "*at once* ... so that the state of things may be ascertained as they exist *now*; and before it can be said that any alteration has been made in the working economy of the Estate."[29]

In order for him to determine the course he ought to pursue, Anson appointed a Commission of Enquiry comprising three Straits government officers. For convenience, their report has been divided into two aspects. Briefly, the favourable findings were: – there were no signs of physical ill-treatment; there was an adequate supply of water which was obtained from an excellent spring quite convenient to the labourers' dwellings; there was no attenuation among the labourers except what arose from natural causes; and (as the Commission was told by an unidentified estate official), the diet for the sick at the infirmary "consisted of fowls, bread, rice, curry, and eggs."

The uncomplimentary features of the report were: - the physical condition of the labourers was "generally inferior"; the labourers stinted themselves in food because after paying the monthly installment (of $1.00) towards the liquidation of their advances and passage money, they had little money left with which to buy ration; medical attention was not provided on the spot for many cases; and the neighbourhood of the labourers' dwellings was "freely sprinkled with animal and human ordure."[30]

After this report was submitted to Anson, there was no further mention in the available records of the Alma affair. It was, therefore, not possible to ascertain whether Anson had requested the government of India to debar Alma from recruiting. Six years later, in 1879, (when the first detailed statistics on Indian immigration to the Straits Settlements were provided in the first Annual Report), the estate was employing 154 indentured Indians.[31] Thereafter, a continuous stream of Indian indentured labourers flowed into Alma.

There were several sound reasons that would have deterred Anson from trying to effect a suspension of the labour supply to Alma. The British were striving to establish a strong foothold in Province Wellesley with a view to doing the same in the Malayan Peninsula;[32] and, as shown previously, there was a great need for labourers, especially from India, to develop the dormant resources of the country. The Commission's report on Alma was not so unfavourable as to warrant a cutting off of the estate's labour supply from India. Knaggs had told Anson he had given "express orders" that no labourers, sick or otherwise, should be forced to work, and that he had forbidden flogging or any other form of ill-treatment on his estate. Knaggs had voluntarily permitted an untrammelled examination of his estate by government officers with the expressed view of benefitting the labourers by any advice that they might give; he had expressed his willingness and anxiety to carry out any practicable suggestions for the amelioration of the conditions of the labourers; he had invited the Magistrate of Province Wellesley to visit Alma and examine the labourers at any time he might think proper; and above all, he had given the assurance that the result of any future enquiry would prove that his labourers were much better treated.[33] This was confirmed in 1888. In that year, when there were 529 indentured Indians at Alma, 202 of them deserted in one night because of a rumour that the estate was to be sold to a Chinese proprietor, and the labourers imagined they would all be handed over to him.[34] The deserters returned to Alma as soon as they learnt the rumour was false.

Scandal at Malakoff
The Tassek and Alma incidents had scarcely subsided when the fear of prosecution spread further and uncovered what had probably been going on for a long time. From the Malakoff estate, large numbers of labourers began arriving at the Butterworth Hospital from 11:00 P.M. on 8 December 1873. A few days later, Acting Colonial Surgeon Coghill reported as requested to Gottlieb thus:

> All or nearly all, of the coolies received in the course of a few days – about 100 in number from Malakoff Estate – were in such a state of extreme debility from diarrhea [sic], gangrene, and open wounds from flogging, that large and frequent doses of wine or spirits had to be administered to keep them alive. Many were unable to take food.[35]

The sending of so many labourers to Butterworth in such awful condition shortly after the Alma affair suggests that the manager, J.T. Thompson, had realized the implications of the Alma proceedings. It seems that he had become fearful of being penalized by the Straits authorities for neglecting the labourers' health, and had tried to forestall repercussions to his own estate. Since Knaggs had failed in what appears to have been an attempt to suppress evidence even though only five labourers were principally involved, where such numerous sick labourers were dispatched to Butterworth within such a short space of time, Thompson could not have succeeded in avoiding attention.

A few days before 13 December 1873, it was rumoured in Province Wellesley that a number of labourers were in the Butterworth Hospital in such miserable condition that there were strong suspicions some harsh treatment brought these men to the hospital.[36] A journalist investigating the rumour went to Malakoff, and from what he described as the "scene of griefs", he reported thus:

> Some of these coolies, were in the Convict Lines [an apparent sarcasm for "labour lines" as the labourers' dwellings were commonly called], making their statements, and shewing their backs, with the clear marks not of Dr. Birch's[37] impressions, but the 'rattong' [rattan][38] layings, on. Some were lying down, looking forward, for that resting bourn, where the wicked cease from troubling, and the weary are at rest, to lodge their complaints before the Judge of all the earth. Some were just picking up flesh, and lisping, not their porridge, but some sago; others looked, as the Klings [i.e. Tamils] say of a poor penniless na-ada ponungal – or walking corpses, or in Medical language, unfit subjects even for the demonstrator of anatomy, unless you used the blow-pipe, and injected fresh blood into their frizzled up veins, and muscles, and galvanized the walking skeletons. One man said, when he saw food, he was more inclined to throw out, than take in nonrishment [sic], and he doubted, whether he could retain any thing, when he took any food. At the [estate] Hospital,

there were some cases, who were recovering flesh, and could become themselves again. There were other buildings in which many were found, who were in different stages of suffering …. There was one woman lying down, … a frail cooly girl, leaving her skeleton behind, and appealing to heaven, to forgive her Tindal tyrants. There was a man, with a sore leg, was paralyzed, who said, how can I live sir, unless you amputate this limb, of what use is it to me? There was another, whose foot was bandaged, but the Apothecary took the large patch of cloth off to shew how flesh, and bones were thrown off, by his skill; the gangrene was setting in, and a mortification was taking place.[39]

As soon as Sir Andrew Clarke, Governor Ord's successor, read this report he immediately visited Malakoff. Reporting shortly afterwards to the Colonial Secretary, he stated that the labourers who had been flogged had suffered "abominable cruelty" and had been kept at the estate hospital in a "wretched condition".[40] Shortly after visiting Malakoff, Clarke appointed a three-man commission to enquire into various aspects of the management of the estate.

When the commission arrived, the manager of Malakoff, Thompson, used his best endeavours to thwart their investigation. "The system of espionage was so complete," the Commission reported, "that we found it impossible to avoid the Tindals and Malay watchmen who followed us by direction."[41] But a number of labourers who voluntarily showed evidence of their own flogging impassionedly told the Commission of a house in which some "severely flogged" labourers were locked up.[42] Thompson then intensified his efforts to suppress incriminating evidence. The Commission saw him surreptitiously whispering in the ear of his overseer, I.I. Durnford, who immediately dispatched a tindal, as it was soon discovered, to remove from the house all those whose floggings were severe and apparent.[43] The Commission prevented this by circumventing the tindal.

Once the sequestered labourers were released they spontaneously exposed their bodies to reveal the evidence of flogging which the Commission unanimously described as "cruel in its nature and severely affecting the health of the labourers." Among the eleven more serious cases reported by the Commission were the following six.[44]

Attynal Cavenden had one scar each on his neck and arm, and two on his back; his buttocks were "quite covered with abrasions equal in severity to two dozen lashes inflicted by a cat of nine tails." The flogging had been inflicted by the tindals Udumansa and Ponnen because they had found Cavenden resting in the field during the hours of work. Cavenden later said that he had told the tindals he took a rest because he was not feeling well. At this, he added, Udumansa told him "he might die for all they cared."

Sitha suffered blows on his arms, back, buttocks, and cheek because he had rested when he became tired. In addition to doing this, Ponnen had severely kicked him and then "pricked his ulcers with a stick until he fainted."

Gooroosami, who had complained of having a headache and wanted to sit down for a while, was dealt two blows on the right arm, four on the back, four on the thighs, and several on the buttocks.

Nellapan exhibited twenty-six scars on the neck and shoulders, and twenty-two on the buttocks and legs. He had been flogged for being the last to leave for work. At the time, he said he had diarrhoea.

Vaylaiden had been dealt several blows for lagging behind on the way to the field. He later accused Udumansa of stealing his earrings.

Ramalingam had been flogged because he did not turn out to work although he said he had told Udumansa he was sick. The tindal, he added, ignored his excuse and took him to the place where the labourers defecated and threatened to cover him with filth if he did not go to work. When he pleaded to be exempted for the day, Udumansa "made him take a basket and fill it with ordure (which trickled down his face) and place it on his head and made the rest of the Coolies spit in his mouth – was covered with filth. Udumansa also made the Women come and spit on him."

A seventh labourer, Ramsamy, had been so badly beaten that he died eight days after the day of flogging. Of the several witnesses[45] testifying at the inquest held into his death on 9 December 1873, five were labourers, each of whose testimony was basically consistent.[46] The translated evidence of one such witness, Mootoosamy, reads:

> I am a Cooly on the Malakoff Estate at present an inmate of the General Hospital at Butterworth. I knew deceased Ramsamy. I assisted to bury him. His age was about 45 years …. Eight days before his death deceased and myself were flogged for running away. We had run away two days when we were arrested by the Tindal and taken before the little master [i.e. the overseer, Durnford] …. The deceased Ramsamy was seized by two men one on each side and placed against a pillar with his face towards it. The little master gave the orders for Ramsamy to be held in this position and then ordered a man, whose name I do not know,[47] to flog him with a rattan. The deceased received eight cuts when the rattan split and the rest of the twelve strokes ordered to be given were delivered with the split rattan. The little master was standing by at the time. Ramsamy cried out during his flogging and fainted. The little master ordered Brandy to be poured on the cuts, this was done and deceased was lifted up and a Chunkol [changkol] placed in his hand and because he could not walk a Tindal gave him two more cuts with a rattan and deceased was sent to work. On the day following deceased had fever accompanied by shivering, he was made to work, and on the third day had Diarrhoea, he was made to work, on the 8th day he was so ill and could not work, he was taken to [the estate] hospital and died the same night. The next morning I was called to bury him …. When Ramsamy was flogged he was not ill.[48]

Also testifying at the inquest was the Acting Colonial Surgeon, Coghill, who had been requested by the coroner of Province Wellesley to perform an autopsy on Ramsamy's body which they found buried in a two-feet deep grave at Malakoff estate. Coghill's post mortem revealed the following state of the body:

1st A large patch of ecchymoses (i.e. effused blood) about ten inches long by five or six inches in breadth, over the right side of the chest at the angles of the ribs extending beyond the lower ribs. This was inflicted on the deceased during life by a blunt stick or similar weapon.

2nd The buttocks were covered with the remains of recent wounds caused by a rattan, fourteen were very distinct, but owing to their running together many others could not be counted, especially about the folds of the nates. There were the marks of five very severe rattan cuts on the left buttock as deep as an ordinary lead pencil cutting through the true skin and as close as possible together running obliquely downwards and outwards from which I gathered that the deceased had been tied or held so that he could not move and that the person administering the punishment was more elevated than his patient who was rather short in stature.

3rd There were also nine cuts with a rattan over the Kidneys (more particularly the right one) and the loins generally. The body appeared to have been buried seven or eight days.

> I am of opinion that the deceased Ramsamy died of "shock" consequent upon the administration of a severe flogging with a rattan and stick, equal in severity to one hundred lashes with a cat o' nine tails and which at his time of life and feeble state of body he was not able to undergo.[49]

The verdict reached at the inquest found Durnford and the tindals, Udumansa and Ponnen, guilty of culpable homicide.[50] During the inquest, a warrant was issued by the Police Magistrate of Province Wellesley, Gottlieb, for the arrest of Thompson, who, it was alleged, had caused the death of one of his labourers, Pakiri, "a very emaciated boy of about 16 years old, almost skin and bone". Pakiri, Governor Clarke reported, had suffered "severe abrasions occasioned by flogging" by Thompson for drinking curds which, allegedly, he had stolen, but which the boy claimed he had purchased from a shop.[51] Other details of this case were not available.

The brutal flogging of the Malakoff labourers represented only one aspect of the flagrant failure of the commitment Governor Ord had given to the government of India on the planters' behalf. Although Thompson had tried to frustrate the progress of the enquiry ordered by Governor Clarke, the Commissioners were still able to discover that the majority of the labourers were half-starved; that they were neglected when sick; and that there was neither proper food nor water nor facilities for cooking nor clothing in the hospital, which they described as a "large attap hut dimly lighted by a lamp – having no means of ventilation – the temperature high with a feeling of great closeness." At the time of the enquiry, there were 88 men in this hut, and in a smaller one of similar construction 10 women were "shut up" in an apartment measuring 12 feet by 8 feet.[52]

The Straits Governments' Apparent Indifference
The Straits government must be held partly culpable for the gross neglect and ill-treatment of the labourers at Alma and Malakoff estates. It will be recalled that in 1872, the government of India was induced to allow emigration to the Straits before all the regular measures for the protection of the labourers were finally settled. This was in consequence of Governor Ord's distinct promise that "the government of India may rely on the watchful care of this government over any men who may thus be sent over previous to final arrangements being concluded". Notwithstanding, there seems to have been a total absence of supervision on the part of officials of the Straits government. The reasons why the government was so

slow to legislate and so ineffectual in protecting the interest of the labourers cannot be ascertained because there are no indications that any explanations had been offered. It may be surmised that once the labour traffic had been resuscitated and the labourers began arriving in the colony, Indian indentured immigration was allowed to relapse into a semi-regulated status and things were taken for granted.

It will also be recalled that after the Indian authorities had lifted the ban on emigration to the Straits in 1872, Ord had committed the Straits government to "do all that the Indian Government could ask for the health and safety of the coolie and were perfectly prepared to do it". This paternalistic pledge had apparently not been accompanied by adequate or effectual provisions. The Chief Executive Officer of Butterworth and Police Magistrate of Province Wellesley, Gottlieb, pointed out the absence of and the urgent need for an elaborate medical system in the Province.[53] It was not until 1880, eight years after Ord had given his commitment, that the Protector of Immigrants was able to report: "Each estate ... has now got its own hospital ... and each is supervised by a Medical subordinate under the general superintendence of the Assistant Colonial Surgeon, Province Wellesley, who visits them not less than once a week."[54]

The Solicitor-General of the Straits Settlements observed that there was "no law in the Colony to oblige proprietors to make provision for their sick Coolies".[55] How far the general law of the colony, if put into operation, would have protected the labourers is difficult to say. But that it had not done so is quite evident. It was, therefore, more incumbent upon Governor Clarke to intercede for the protection of the labourers.

Clarke's appointment of the Commission to enquire into the Malakoff scandal and his "making arrangements" to provide better medical attendance for the labourers were mere patchwork expedients quite insufficient to meet the requirements of the case. Where the labourers were half-starved and cruelly beaten, medical care, which would come in only at the end, would be a poor protection. What seemed wanted was a law that would compel the employers by adequate penalties to supply proper and sufficient food and lodging for their labourers, to abstain from violence towards them, and to provide proper hospital accommodation and medical care.

It will also be recalled that before the resumption of the indenture traffic to the Straits in 1872, Ord had promised the Madras government to appoint, *inter alia*, a Protector of Immigrants.[56] This was not done until 1876 when the Indian immigration labour Ordinance I of that year was promulgated.[57] A Protector of sufficient firmness and honesty of purpose invested with full powers to inspect estates would, in all likelihood, have effectively prevented such occurrences as had taken place at Alma and Malakoff.

The *Penang Gazette* criticized the Lieutenant-Governor of Penang, Colonel Anson, for not taking an active interest in the affairs of immigrants in Province Wellesley; for not being easily accessible to them; and for not visiting the estates even periodically.[58] Where such apparent official indifference existed, it was no surprise that abuses had been perpetuated. In an artificial labour system of this kind, dealing with men's lives and liberties, the "watchful care" of the government of the Settlement of Penang, under whose administration Province Wellesley directly fell, was indispensable.

The Indian Authorities' Inaction

The events of October and December 1873 depicted a more disgraceful situation than had been revealed just before 1870. At that time, it will be recalled, Tamil males were being kidnapped in the Tanjore District for the Province Wellesley labour market, and females were sold to a life of prostitution.[59] As soon as the Indian authorities discovered the existence of these abuses, they unhesitatingly prohibited any further indentured emigration to the Straits. Why then did they not do so in 1873? It was not as if they were unaware of what had transpired at Alma and Malakoff. The Governor-General of India expressed indignant consternation over what he described as the "inhumane treatment" of the labourers.[60] Beyond this there was no indication that the government of India did anything tangible that would tend to compel the Straits authorities to honour their promise. The Governor-General of India merely threatened to terminate emigration to the Straits if a sufficient remedy was not immediately applied to prevent a repetition of the abuses.[61] This inaction created a precedent.

In the 1830s, when Indian labourers were cruelly ill-treated and inhumanely neglected in British Guiana[62] and in Mauritius[63] mainly because their immigration had not been accompanied by the provision of efficient protection against tyranny and oppression on the part of the planters, and by a proper system of inspection and medical attendance on the estates, the government of India in conjunction with the Colonial Office swiftly suspended emigration to these colonies. The traffic was only re-permitted when the government of India was satisfied with the various protective measures adopted. As far as the labourers in the Straits were concerned, the government of India appeared to have compromised, if not abandoned, their hitherto consistent policy of "benevolent neutrality", and could not claim with justification as they had done previously to be the "protector of the weak."[64]

Several reasons may be adduced why the Indian authorities refrained from ordering the immediate cessation of emigration to the Straits. They considered that as the major atrocities had been confined to only two estates and as the cane-reaping season had been in progress, a discontinuance of fresh supplies of Indian labourers would have been injurious to the pecuniary interest of the general body of planters.[65] The first of these is indisputable, but the last is somewhat doubtful. Unless a large number of labourers deserted or had fulfilled their contracts and had taken employment elsewhere during the cane-grinding season, an embargo on emigration to the Straits could not have so immediate an effect as to impede harvesting of the current crop. Another reason why the government of India did not stop the labour traffic was because the Acting Solicitor-General of the Straits Settlements had given the assurance that the large majority of planters had "on the whole well treated and cared for [their labourers]".[66] Furthermore, Governor Clarke had signified his intention to the government of India that he would enact a short ordinance,[67] (pending final agreement on the more comprehensive labour ordinance still being negotiated) that would authorize him to appoint a Protector of Immigrants and all necessary officers with full powers to enter upon the estates and deal summarily with all complaints, and to prohibit the employment of Indian labourers where it was proved they were neglected or ill-treated.[68] This assurance must have convinced the Indian authorities that a recurrence of any systematic cruelty towards the labourers would be unlikely. Finally, the speedy prosecution of the offenders in the Malakoff case must have so placated the Indian authorities as to dissuade them from imposing another embargo.

The Malakoff Trial

A major redeeming factor for the Straits government under Governor Sir Andrew Clarke was the prosecution without any apparent fear or favour of those who were principally responsible for the atrocities at Malakoff. At the trial at the Supreme Court, the overseer, Durnford, was acquitted on the charge of culpable homicide but he was found guilty on the lesser count of assault, and was fined $200.00 with three months' imprisonment; the two tindals, Udumansa and Ponnen, were each sentenced to one month imprisonment with hard labour.[69] Thompson, the manager of Malakoff, was sentenced to two months' imprisonment, having been found guilty of assaulting Pakiri.[70] The details of the trial itself were not available.

For perpetrating what the Secretary of State for the Colonies, Lord Carnarvon, called "a system of brutal cruelty and ill treatment" of the Malakoff labourers,[71] and what the *Penang Guardian* described as "supercilious [*sic*] brutalities",[72] the sentences imposed on the four defendants were quite lenient. This might have been caused by several major factors operating against the testifying labourers. Before the trial commenced, the senior staff members of the Malakoff estate tried to dissuade the Commission enquiring into the Malakoff scandal from relying on statements made by labourers on the estate. The labourers, they told the Commission, concocted grievances if asked whether they had any complaints to make.[73] Similarly, other planters (apparently out of solidarity with their colleagues) described those labourers who had recounted their ill-treatment at Malakoff to the *Penang Guardian* reporter as "perjurers who would lie in any court of law."[74] The apparent intention of the Malakoff and other planters was to prejudice the judiciary against those labourers who would testify for the prosecution. This seemed to have been already established.

In a dispatch to Clarke, Carnarvon observed that because summary jurisdiction had since 1867 fallen from the hands of police magistrates into those of merchant and planter magistrates there had been a "much advanced deterioration in the impartiality of the judiciary towards Indian Coolies."[75] In support, Lord Stanley,[76] former Secretary of State for the Colonies (1858), observed in Parliament that there had been a "diminution of protection given to Coolies in the Straits, owing to the falling off in the quality and independence both of Judges and magistrates" since the transfer of the Straits Settlements from the India Office to the Colonial Office (in 1867).[77] Although Clarke pointed out that there was "an overwhelming weight of testimony" in the defendants' favour,⁷⁸ apart from the autopsy report, the labourers' case rested almost entirely on their own testimony. Even this seemed to have been ineffectual. The Chief Justice, who tried the case, said he had found the labourers' evidence "in many cases ... most untrustworthy."⁷⁹

During the trial, when Thompson and Durnford realized that some labourers were determined to testify, they began "to tamper" with them.⁸⁰ It was not until the presiding judge repeatedly requested the two defendants not to interfere with the labourers that they desisted. What would have been a charged and intimidating court atmosphere for the rest of the testifying labourers was apparently a terrifying ordeal for one key witness. A pregnant labourer, herself a flogged victim who had been also "rough handled" by the tindals, Udumansa and Ponnen,⁸¹ was initially intent on testifying. As she was about to be interrogated, she became "so terribly frightened that she fell into two or three fits", and had to be taken to hospital where she died a few days later.⁸² Although there was a "proficient" Tamil interpreter,⁸³ and since most indentured Indians were described as illiterate,⁸⁴ the testifying labourers could not have been able to follow systematically the proceedings of the trial. One Madras government official believed they would have been incapable of "preconception and a logical mental organization" during the course of the cross-examination.⁸⁵

Remission of the Planters' Sentences

The two tindals served their full one-month sentence; but about half way through Thompson's two-month term of imprisonment, Governor Clarke remitted the sentence on a representation that the prisoner's brother had died after falling from a horse, and that there was no one else to manage his estate.⁸⁶ Clarke also remitted half of Durnford's three-month sentence⁸⁷ on the ground that as the charge against him was for abetting Thompson "it was not right to keep the subordinate in prison when the principal was released."⁸⁸ In remitting these sentences, Clarke had acted with the concurrence of the Chief Justice who justified the remission of both sentences by claiming that "justice had been fully vindicated."⁸⁹

The Colonial Office disagreed with the remissions. Lord Carnarvon remarked to Clarke: "It was unfortunate that in so atrocious a case it became necessary to remit any part of what appears to have been a very lenient punishment – but if it was so necessary it would I think have been better to mark by retaining Durnford's punishment, that the remission in Thomson's [*sic*] case was the result only of necessity not of relenting towards him."⁹⁰ Lord Stanley rightly observed: "If the Governor had made his remission of the sentence conditional on the payment of some compensation to the families of the Coolies whose deaths they had caused, he would have shown more regard for justice and for those safeguards which the ... Secretary of State for the Colonies desired to establish for the protection of Coolie immigrants."⁹¹

The Alma-Malakoff events having appeared to subside, Clarke visited these estates to acquaint himself with the state of affairs. In April 1874, he wrote to the Colonial Office thus: "I am gradually getting all we want for the Indian coolies without making a fuss about it".⁹² But in May 1874, Clarke disappointedly informed the Secretary of State for the Colonies that he had been obliged to dispatch Dr Coghill, the newly-appointed Acting Principal Civil Medical Officer of the Straits Settlements, to Tassek estate where he found eighteen labourers bearing "occasional marks of the rattan."[93] The circumstances of this further violence towards the labourers had not been found in the sources available; and from all indications, no enquiry had been made. Apparently because Coghill had described the flogging as "very trifling in most instances and of old standing among many", and as the Acting Solicitor-General had not found anyone criminally responsible, no one was prosecuted.[94]

In June 1874, Clarke again visited the estates, and on that occasion he reported to the Colonial Office thus: "I have just returned from a visit to the sugar estates in Province Wellesley, and have examined carefully into the treatment by the planters of their Indian coolies. From all I could gather, any ill usage must have been exceptional, and in all I saw there was every appearance of the coolies being well cared for and contented."[95] Clarke also assured the Madras government that the previous malpractices against the immigrants had ceased, there being no fresh complaints to this effect.[96]

The scandalous ill-treatment of the labourers of Alma and Malakoff estates emphasized the imperative need for a labour law that would have the power to compel the employers to fulfill the obligations it would impose on them, and to abstain from violence to their labourers. Immediate control of the indenture system through local legislation and local official supervision, both of which were long overdue, would tend to afford the planter and the labourer the most effective protection. Such legislation would render both employer and employee liable to a penalty for improper acts of commission or omission. It could prevent occurrences which might lead to the prohibition of emigration to the Straits Settlements, which would be disastrous to the further development and agricultural interests of the colony. Mainly because of the protracted negotiations between the Straits government and the government of India over the terms on which indenture would be regulated, the labour ordinance took four years to perfect.[97] Eventually, it emerged on 1 March 1876 as Ordinance I of that year. This Ordinance and its successor, Ordinance V of 1884, could each be seen as an extended formalization of the Straits government's original promise given to the government of India in May 1872. It would be informative to test how far the terms of these Ordinances were upheld in practice.

The Tindals' Chastisement

On the Province Wellesley sugar estates, Indian indentured labourers generally worked on a 'piece' or task rather than on a 'time' basis. A day's work usually entailed the completion of two tasks. How hard the tasks or how long they would take to complete often depended on the labourers' relationship with their tindal. It was in the tindal's power to set one man a difficult task, and another an easy task; he could given a favourite a strong partner, and to a rival or disagreeable labourer a weak one; he could choose to be either strict or indulgent, and could recommend cutting of pay.

A common abuse practised by some tindals was to discriminate in their allocation of tasks.⁹⁸ Some labourers complained of tindals compelling them to hand over a part of their wages because they had been given easy and light tasks. It was usual for certain labourers to complete their first task by 10:00 A.M. and the second by 5:00 P.M. or even earlier.⁹⁹ The planters (who were either unaware of or indifferent to the tindals' discriminating practices) contended that the two daily tasks could be accomplished by a steady worker within the statutory hours of work,¹⁰⁰ i.e. from 6:00 A.M. to 11:00 A.M. and from 1:00 P.M. to 6:00 P.M. as prescribed by the labour ordinances. The planters maintained that those labourers who failed to complete their daily tasks were "idle malingerers indisposed to work".¹⁰¹ This may have been true in some cases, but on the basis of the testimony of many labourers, the Commission of 1881 rejected the planters' view. Those who could not finish their tasks, the Commission reported, included those who had refused to be induced by their tindal to pay them sums of money on promises of lighter work, or who had refused to cut grass for their tindal's cows or to attend upon him in his house.¹⁰²

The testimony to the Protector of Emigrants at Negapatam of one returning labourer, Irulandy, revealed some aspects of the character of a tindal whom he referred to as a *maistry* most likely because this headman had also been a recruiter. The translated testimony reads:–

> The maistry, Negappen, used to beat me. Wages were not paid to me fully and regularly. Only if the maistry was bribed we used to draw our full wages. If he was not he would enter in the pay list a smaller number of days than actually worked. With the amount thus due, but not defrayed he would pay those who worked in his own house. If a labourer worked for half a day and failed to report on the other half on account of inability or otherwise, the maistry would misrepresent the matter to the employers informing them that the particular labourer had deserted, whereupon he would be arrested and subsequently thrown into custody.¹⁰³

Another returning labourer, Nadarasa Pillay, spoke of the tindals thus (in translation): "My wages was not fully and regularly paid to me. If I worked for twenty-days they would enter into the accounts only as if I worked ten days. As soon as we received this reduced wages and come out the *maistries* used to snatch it away from us. They never used to return it to us."¹⁰⁴

Although article 56 of Ordinance I of 1876 forbade the personal ill-usage of labourers, those who failed to finish their tasks on the day they were allocated, or who resisted the tindals' extortion were sometimes severely beaten. For instance, on the Golden Grove estate in 1879, the tindal Sivasami struck Karpen and the "blow drew blood."¹⁰⁵ On another estate in 1881, Apparoo told the Protector of Immigrants at the Butterworth Hospital where he was admitted, that he had been repeatedly beaten by his tindal.¹⁰⁶ In the same year, three labourers from Batu Kawan estate, who were also hospitalized at Butterworth, told the Commission of 1881 that their tindal had compelled them to do extraordinary tasks. When they did not finish their second task at 6 P.M., the tindal severely flogged them.¹⁰⁷ During the flogging, the labourers said they cried out; upon this, the tindal told them that if they died, the estate would immediately get another supply of labourers, and that "their death was no matter of consequence to them." Complaints of this nature, the Commission of 1881 added, were most prevalent at Batu Kawan estate,[108] the largest employer of indentured Indians in Province Wellesley.

Prosecutions initiated by the Immigration Department against tindals for inflicting corporal punishment on labourers were often dismissed because they could not produce witnesses who could substantiate their accusations. For instance, in 1879 the tindal Mardamutu was prosecuted by the Inspector of Immigrants[109] for flogging Abai and Vellasami; but because the witnesses to the incident could not be induced to go to court and testify, the tindal was acquitted.[110] For the same reason, the case against the tindal Sivasami of Golden Grove estate, who had assaulted Karpen, was dismissed, although, as the Commission of 1881 remarked, "there appeared to have been *prima facie* evidence" against the tindal.[111]

In 1881 when twelve tindals were prosecuted and four were convicted and fined sums varying from two to twelve dollars for flogging labourers, the Protector of Immigrants reported: "One Tindal, I am sorry to say, escaped condign punishment, though the evidence [tendered by the assaulted labourers] against him seems to have been very clear."[112] Commenting on this case, the Commission of 1881 observed: "Allowing even for the disadvantage at which an Immigrant stands in making complaints, it will be seen that little reliance can be placed on such unsupported statements."[113] Many labourers, therefore, would have assumed that bringing charges against tindals for flogging them would be futile. This is suggested by the small number of tindals prosecuted for this offence as shown in the following table:–

TABLE XIII
NUMBER OF TINDALS PROSECUTED FOR FLOGGING
LABOURERS, 1880-85

YEAR	PROSECUTED
1880	5
1881	12
1882	2
1883	7
1884	2
1885	N/A

N/A = Not Available. After 1885, the column in the ARII dealing with this subject was removed; no explanation was given.
Source: ARII 1880-85.

There are strong indications that the small number of tindals prosecuted for flogging labourers sprang from some fear of retribution among the labourers. This was because flogging for refusing to work was generally accepted as the norm. The Commission of 1881 reported that the planters had recommended flogging for all those labourers who refused to work, since they claimed that "gaol had no deterrent effect whatever" upon them.[114] Although the tindals carried a rattan nominally as a "badge of office", it was often used to intimidate and punish labourers.[115] Consequently, "the dread of the Tindals by the coolies" was an ever present factor.

Another reason why so few tindals were prosecuted was that some planters apparently suppressed evidence by withholding from the Protector of Immigrants' quarterly inspection those labourers whom they believed would tell him about their grievances. This is suggested by the sizeable number of labourers absent from the estates whenever the Protector paid his scheduled visits of inspection. The following table shows the number of labourers who were absent on seven successive occasions. The "No [of labourers] on Estates" excludes those in hospital and gaol.

TABLE XIV
NUMBER OF LABOURERS PRESENTED FOR AND ABSENT FROM INSPECTIONS, 1884-85

1884	April	July	October	December
No. on Estates	N/A	3,648	3,679	3,636
Presented for Inspection	"	3,364	3,235	3,322
Absent from Inspection	"	284	444	314
% " " "	"	8	12	9
1885				
No. on Estates	3,484	3,476	3,215	3,070
Presented for Inspection	3,043	2,718	2,683	2,551
Absent from Inspection	441	758	532	519
% " " "	13	22	17	17

N/A = Not Available
Source: Compiled from ARII 1884-85.

There is hardly any reason to doubt that labourers who were absent from the Protector's inspections were deliberately withheld so as to prevent them from communicating with the Protector. After visiting seven estates, the Labour Commission of 1890 remarked that a "large body of labourers on these estates was deliberately held from making complaints."[116] On one of these estates, as number of labourers who, it was later learnt, had been flogged by the tindals, were locked up in a building. Somehow they learned of the Commission's visit and managing to break out, they prostrated themselves on the ground before the Commission "making loud complaints" against the tindals.[117]

On Batu Kawan estate, the manager, Vermont, disliked frequent inspections. In 1888, he wrote:

> The frequent inspections that took place ... did little or no good: they caused groundless suspicious [sic] in the mind of the labourers, which led indirectly to great insubordination, undermined the authority of the manager, and caused great inconvenience and anxiety to the employer. No reasonable objection can be raised against inspections as prescribed by the Ordinance, for if carried out in a proper system, they are unquestionably beneficial, but at the same time, great circumspection should be used, and they ought not to be frequent.[118]

In 1900, the Acting Superintendent of Immigrants,[119] H.W. Firmstone, reported from the Batu Kawan estate thus: "It is a remarkable fact that on any occasion when this estate is inspected the number of coolies at muster is invariably about thirty per cent less than the number on the books."[120] Firmstone's enquiries elicited the explanation from Vermont that the labourers preferred to hide in the canes. Firmstone retorted: "There is obviously something radically wrong here." The fact that he urged Vermont to "make a clean sweep of his native assistants [i.e. the tindals]," whom he declared had "from time immemorial been regarded with suspicion by this [Immigration] Department",[121] suggests that potential complainants against the tindals had been customarily and deliberately held incommunicado. This was a violation of the labour law. According to articles 66 and 69 of Ordinance V of 1884, any employer or other person who wilfully failed to produce before the Protector of Immigrants "all or any of the Statute Immigrants then under contract with him" was liable to be prosecuted. There is no evidence of anyone being prosecuted for committing this offence.

Preventing labourers from complaining to the Protector of being ill-treated was to the advantage of the employers and their subordinates. According to Ordinance I of 1876, if any employer or any person placed in authority over any immigrant by such employer was convicted of any offence of causing injury to the person of any immigrant, or had subjected him to ill-usage, the magistrate was empowered to cancel that immigrant's contract and to award him compensation not exceeding $15.00.[122] When this ordinance was superseded by Ordinance V of 1884, the penalty was increased to a fine not exceeding two hundred dollars or imprisonment not exceeding six months.[123]

The fact that there were so few prosecutions of tindals was also due to the labourer's difficulty in reaching the Protector's office situated at Penang. There was the long distance from the estates to Butterworth from where there was a ferry to Penang. Of much greater importance, any labourer who was found beyond the precincts of the estate on which he was employed could be apprehended by his employer, by one of his overseers or tindals, or by an estate constable.[124] Were the labourer found without a "pass" (issued by the manager), he was liable to be taken before a magistrate. If the labourer could convince the court of his intention *not* to desert, he would be ordered to return to his estate. If he was found guilty, the offence was punishable on the first occasion by imprisonment, sometimes with hard labour, for a period not exceeding one month; and on the second and subsequent occasions, for a period not exceeding two and three months respectively.[125] The "pass" system, therefore, was an effective device to impede the labourer's access to the Immigration Department.

In the sources available, there is no further evidence of any systematic physical ill-treatment of labourers by their employers or tindals. The vigilance exercised by the Straits government after the Malakoff scandal, the determination of the Police Magistracy of Province Wellesley to prosecute any oppressor, and the fear by the employers of a possible cessation of a labour supply from India determined the labourers' better treatment. Since the relative strength of the parties to the labour contract was such that the intervention of the Straits legislature was necessary to protect the weaker party, the Straits government embodied in Ordinance V of 1884 wider protective measures for the labourers' safety, and prescribed stiffer penalties for delinquent planters and tindals.

References

1 A Malayan coffee planter in 1902. See Turner, "Tamil Labourer", p. 21.
2 See Chapter IV.
3 Ord was succeeded by Sir Andrew Clarke on 4 November 1873. For a list of the Governors of the S.S., 1867-1911, see Appendix A.
4 C.O. 273/57. Enclosure in Ord to Kimberley, no. 45, 16 May 1872.
5 PSSLC, 4 July 1872, p. C40.
6 C.O. 273/71. Enclosure in Clarke to Carnarvon, no. 397, 25 December 1873.
7 The headquarters of the North District of Province Wellesley, situated on the coast opposite Penang.
8 C.O. 273/71. Enclosure in Clarke to Carnarvon, no. 397, 25 December 1873.
9 *Singapore Daily Times*, 23 December 1873.
10 C.O. 273/71. Enclosure in Clarke to Carnarvon, no. 397, 25 December 1873.
11 *Ibid*.
12 See *Ibid*.
13 *Ibid*.
14 *Ibid*.
15 *Ibid*.
16 Knaggs claimed that he had in his employ "three hands to attend to [sick labourers] night and day and the expenses amount to ten or twelve cents each per day." *Ibid*.
17 *Ibid*.
18 *Ibid*.
19 *Ibid*.
20 *Ibid*.
21 *Ibid*.
22 The surgeon's assistant during hospital operations.
23 C.O. 273/71. Enclosure in Clarke to Carnarvon, no. 397, 25 December 1873.
24 *Ibid*.
25 *Ibid*.
26 *Ibid*.

27 *Ibid*.
28 See Chapter V.
29 *Ibid*.
30 *Ibid*.
31 ARII 1879, p. 3.
32 For a detailed discussion on this subject, see, for example, Cowan, *Nineteenth Century Malaya,* especially Chapters 5-7; Khoo Kay Kim, "The Origin of British Administration in Malaya," *JMBRAS*, XXXIX, I (1966), 52-91; C.N. Parkinson, *British Intervention in Malaya, 1867-77* (Singapore, 1960).
33 C.O. 273/71. Enclosure in Clarke to Carnarvon, no. 397, 25 December 1873.
34 ARII 1888, pp. 12, 1.
35 C.O. 273/71. Enclosure in Clarke to Carnarvon, no. 397, 25 December 1873.
36 *Penang Guardian*, 13 December 1873.
37 A reference to the birch rod used in England for flogging.
38 The cane from the palm of this name.
39 *Penang Guardian*, 13 December 1873.
40 C.O. 273/71. Enclosure in Clarke to Carnarvon, no. 397, 25 December 1873.
41 Enclosure in *Ibid*.
42 Writing later to the Police Magistrate, Province Wellesley, Thompson explained that a few days before the enquiry took place he had removed these men to a "comfortable house" situated in another part of the estate, where they would have "no manner of work to do," and which he considered a "much healthier situation than the Butterworth Hospital." See *Ibid*.
43 C.O. 273/71. Enclosure in Clarke to Carnarvon, no. 397, 25 December 1873.
44 See *Ibid*.
45 The evidence of Thompson, Durnford, and the tindals, if taken, was not available.
46 C.O. 273/71. Enclosure in Clarke to Carnarvon, no. 397, 25 December 1873.
47 In the sworn statement made by Wohmandie, one of the other labourers present at Ramsamy's flogging, it was revealed that the man referred to was the tindal, Ponnen. *Ibid*.
48 MPP, vol. 275, 2 July 1874.
49 *Ibid*.
50 C.O. 273/71. Enclosure in Clarke to Carnarvon, no. 397, 25 December 1873.
51 *Ibid*.
52 *Ibid*.
53 *Ibid*.
54 ARII 1880, p. 5.
55 C.O. 273/71. Enclosure in Clarke to Carnarvon, no. 397, 25 December 1873.
56 C.O. 273/57. Ord to Kimberley, no. 45, 16 May 1872.
57 ARII 1879, p. 12.
58 *Penang Gazette*, 18 December 1873.
59 See Chapter III.
60 MPP, vol. 275, 2 July 1874.

61 *Ibid.*
62 See Nath, *Indians in British Guiana*, pp. 14-20.
63 See Mookherji, *Indenture in Mauritius*, pp. 22-32.
64 Sanderson, *Report on Emigration*, C5192, p. 9.
65 C.O. 273/71. Enclosure in Clarke to Carnarvon, no. 397, 25 December 1873.
66 C.O. 273/76. Enclosure in Clarke to Carnarvon, no. 259, 4 September 1874.
67 i.e. Ordinance IX of 1875, "The Indian Immigrants' Protection Ordinance." It was passed on 6 May 1875, but it was never brought into operation, for the government of India had raised several relatively minor objections which were, however, not connected with the major issues affecting the labourers' protection.
68 C.O. 273/75. Clarke to Carnarvon, no. 12, 6 March 1874.
69 *Madras Standard*, 9 January 1874.
70 *Ibid.*
71 C.O. 273/75. Carnarvon to Clarke, no. 12, 6 March 1874.
72 *Penang Guardian*, 13 December 1873.
73 C.O. 273/71. Enclosure in Clarke to Carnarvon, no. 397, 25 December 1873.
74 *Ibid.*
75 C.O. 273/75. Carnarvon to Clarke, no. 12, 6 March 1874.
76 Lord Edward Henry Stanley, created Earl of Derby in 1869, was again Secretary of State for the Colonies in 1882-85.
77 Great Britain, Parliament, *Parliamentary Debates* (House of Lords), 3rd ser., Vol. CCXXV (16 June - 23 July 1875), p. 1636.
78 C.O. 273/71. Enclosure in Clarke to Carnarvon, no. 397, 25 December 1873.
79 *Ibid.*
80 *Ibid.*
81 *Penang Guardian*, 13 December 1873.
82 *Singapore Daily Times*, 23 December 1873.
83 C.O. 273/71. Enclosure in Clarke to Carnarvon, no. 397, 25 December 1873.
84 Some officials of the government of India rather uncharitably described Indian indentured labourers in the Straits as being "ignorant as dirt". See PDARC, no. 39, February 1874. In less derogatory terms, the P.C.M.O., S.S., said they were of "very inferior intellect". See PSSLC, 12 December 1879, p. C335.
85 PDARC, no. 39, February 1874.
86 Great Britain, Parliament, *Parliamentary Debates* (House of Lords), 3rd ser., Vol. CCXXV (June - 23 July 1875), p. 1635.
87 *Ibid.*
88 C.O. 273/71. Enclosure in Clarke to Carnarvon, no. 397, 25 December 1873.
89 *Ibid.*
90 C.O. 386/113. Colonial Office Letter Book, no. 1204, 9 February 1874.
91 Great Britain, Parliament, *Parliamentary Debates* (House of Lords), 3rd ser., Vol. CCXXV (16 June - 23 July 1875), p. 1635.
92 R.H. Vetch, ed., *The Life of General Sir Andrew Clarke* (London, 1905), p. 126.
93 C.O. 273/75. Enclosure in Clarke to Carnarvon, no. 151, 12 May 1874.
94 *Ibid.*

95 Vetch, *Sir Andrew Clarke*, p. 126.
96 MPP, vol. 275, 19 August 1874.
97 RLC 1890, p. 37.
98 PHRAD, no. 54, September 1884.
99 ARII 1879, p. 5.
100 *Report of the 1881 Commission*, p. 3.
101 *Ibid.*
102 *Ibid.*
103 MPP, no. 1508, 11 October 1880.
104 *Ibid.*
105 *SSGG*, 24 October 1879, p. 974.
106 *Report of the 1881 Commission*, p. 2.
107 *Ibid.*, p. 3.
108 *Ibid.*
109 In 1879, the Protector of Immigrants, F.H. Gottlieb, former Magistrate of Police and Chief Executive Officer, Butterworth, was suspended for a while on suspicion of taking bribes from certain planters. In February 1880, he was dismissed. During Gottlieb's suspension, his functions were performed by the Inspector of Immigrants. On 15 February 1880, A.M. McGregor, a Deputy Collector from India was appointed Protector. See C.O. 273/99. A.E.H. Anson to Hicks-Beach, no. 223 (Confidential), 8 July 1879; Heussler, *British Rule in Malaya*, p. 33.
110 *SSGG*, 24 October 1879, p. 974.
111 *Report of the 1881 Commission*, p. 4.
112 ARII 1181, p. 3.
113 *Report of the 1881 Commission*, p. 2.
114 *Ibid.*, p. 3.
115 *Ibid.*, pp. 2-3.
116 RLC 1890, Inspection no. 7, n.p.
117 *Ibid.*
118 Vermont, *Immigration from India*, p. 31.
119 Following the Federation of four of the Native States of Malaya (Perak, Selangor, Pahang and Negri Sembilan) in 1895, and the expanding employment of Indian immigrants there, the Immigration Department was enlarged, and the designation Protector of Immigrants was changed to Superintendent of Immigrants.
120 ARII 1900, p. 7.
121 *Ibid.*
122 See Ordinance I of 1876, article 60.
123 See Ordinance V of 1884, article 89.
124 See Ordinance I of 1876, article 46.
125 See *Ibid.*, articles 46 and 48.

VIII

WAGES

The whole of these, without a solitary exception, when asked, why they came to Penang; said: we were told, we would get high wages, some 16 or 18 rupees [about $7.20 or $8.10 (monthly)], that we could live well, save money to be sent to our country, and make ourselves very comfortable; in short sir, poyaka vunthom, we came to get a living.[1]

Previous to the enforcement of Ordinance I of 1876, what was known as a 'joint and several' contract had been in operation on the Province Wellesley sugar estates. Under this system, all the indentured Indians in a gang would sign a common document rendering themselves jointly liable for any default of any of their number. In a case arising under such a contract, a Straits judge criticized the planter-imposed arrangement as being "capable of a very inhuman application, even to the making one man in a hundred work out the defaults of ninety-nine absconders."[2] This system ceased when Ordinance I of 1876 came into effect on 3 March but some of its component features were carried over. One – formation of first and second class gangs – continued until the end of 1884.

First and Second Class Gangs

Since 1872, all indentured recruits were required by the Emigration Agent stationed at Negapatam to sign a "joint and several" contract. This arrangement was discontinued in March 1876. Between then and 1884 the emigrants were required to sign individual contracts. When the adult male immigrants arrived on the estates, the planters allocated them either to first or second class gangs, and then required them to sign another contract which stipulated daily wage rates of twelve and ten cents to labourers in the respective categories mentioned above.[3]

Commenting on this system the Lieutenant-Governor of Penang, Colonel Anson, believed the wage clause in the new contracts was contrary to the wage clause in the original agreements signed in India.[4] The original contracts were not available for scrutiny but Anson claimed that in the original contracts there was "not a word about first and second class gangs, and the rate of daily wages of almost every full grown male coolie" was clearly expressed as twelve cents.[5]

There is further evidence of violation of the original agreement. Article 15 of the Straits Settlements Emigration Act V of 1877, which was enacted by the Governor-General of India in Council following negotiations and final agreement with the Straits government in 1876, reads in part: "Every contract shall ... specify the... rate of wages (not less than twelve cents a day for an able-bodied male adult)." On the other hand, the Straits complement of this Act, that is, Ordinance I of 1876, which had also been negotiated and agreed upon by both governments, does not mention any wage rate in the text. Appended to the Ordinance is a "Form of Contract between Immigrant and Employer" which the immigrant was made to sign shortly after arriving on the estate to which he was consigned. It was this contract that caused him to be placed in either a first or second class gang and to be paid accordingly. Reviewing the history of labour contracts in the colony, the Labour Commission of 1890 noted that the apportionment into first and second class gangs was dependent on the will of the employer.[6] This, Anson feared, was open to serious abuse as an employer could make very small first and very large second class gangs.[7]

In 1880, Governor Sir Frederick Weld assured the Colonial Office that "no pains shall be spared to see that the [Indian] Immigrants after their arrival are properly treated during the period of their engagements to labour."[8] In the sources available, there is no indication of the Straits government taking any action that would compel the employers to comply with the wage clause in the original contracts. Since the government of India had no jurisdiction over the immigrants' terms of employment in the colony (but only over the recruiting process), there was a moral responsibility on the Straits government to ensure that the original contracts were honoured. The employers' formation of first and second class gangs and the payment to the labourers in the latter of two cents less for every day's work having continued until the end of 1884,[9] the Straits government had failed to protect these labourers against exploitation.

Denying the labourers relegated to second class gangs the originally agreed wage rate of twelve cents a day was unjust. Upon the arrival of the immigrants on the estates, the planters asserted that in some cases their physique was such that it left much to be desired.[10] The P.C.M.O. described some of them as being utterly unfit for the work they would be required to do.[11] But in many cases, he added, the labourers' health improved after the effects of the voyage from Negapatam to Penang had worn off. The Commission of 1881 discovered that once the new arrivals became acclimatized, many of them were quite able to work daily regularly.[12] The planters' policy, therefore, of classifying the immigrants shortly after they arrived on the estates would have deprived some second class labourers of payment at the twelve cents a day rate (of the first class gangs) when they recovered their capacity to work more efficiently.

Victualling the Labourers
When regulated indenture began in 1872, the employers were supplying each labourer with food for which they charged and deducted $1.20 from the labourer's monthly-paid wages.[13] There were widespread complaints about the discriminatory manner in which the tindals distributed the food. On Malakoff estate, for instance, while some labourers (most likely the tindals' favourites) were served an adequate amount of rice with salt-fish and *bringall* (egg-plant) curry, the rest received

"two hands full of boiled rice in the morning, and the same at six in the evening, with a little salt." [14]

When the Commissioners appointed by Governor Sir Andrew Clarke to enquire into the Malakoff scandal visited the estate in December 1873 (having previously notified the manager to the effect), they were shown "several boilers filled with rice of good quality, well cooked curry stuffs, and two kinds of fish." [15] In their report, the Commissioners found it "peculiarly significant" that in their presence each labourer was served a quantity of food, especially of fish and soup, enough for two.[16] They concluded: "The occasion of such distribution of good is exceptional and ... the Tindal who served it out was unused to the distribution of food of that kind."

On the other estates, the usual fare consisted of an insufficient amount of boiled rice and salt with only occasional servings of *bringall* curry.[17] In a report on the existing condition of the indentured Indians in Province Wellesley, Colonel Anson wrote on the subject of food thus: "My attention was particularly attracted to it by the complaints made to me that 'I not get rice enough to fill my belly;' which complaints were sufficiently numerous on different estates to make me believe there must be some foundation for them; and this notwithstanding the assurances of the managers to the contrary." [18]

The existing system of providing food for the labourers on most estates was discontinued in 1879 when the Colonial Surgeon, Dr J.T. Veitch, objected to it because, as he said, "it formed the basis on which the mortality of the coolies has been founded."[19] So as to keep them in good health and vigour, Veitch prescribed a basic daily requirement for an adult labourer not less than as shown in the following table:-

TABLE XV
RECOMMENDED DIET FOR ADULT INDENTURED INDIANS

Cooked rice	...28 ozs. daily
Fresh meat such as pork or fish	... 6 ozs. four times weekly
Salt-fish	... 4 ozs. thrice weekly
Vegetables	...6 ozs. daily
Condiments: salt, curry staff, coconut-oil	...1 oz. daily

Source: *SSGG*, 24 October 1879, p. 961.

Veitch calculated the cost of this diet at six cents a day or about $1.80 per month.[20] The diet was not provided by the employers. Because of the labourers' dissatisfaction with the previous system, it was decided by the Colonial Surgeon and the P.C.M.O. in conjunction with the employers that the latter would supply each labourer with uncooked rice equivalent to twenty-five ounces per day. For this, they charged and deducted the wholesale price of $1.00 per month from the labourer's wages.[21]

An immediate advantage of this system to the labourer was that he received his rice in advance of his pay (which, in accordance to article 59 of Ordinance I of 1876, was usually paid two weeks in arrears), and would thus be certain of his supply. From the planters' point of view, by providing this facility they effectually prevented the labourer from going off the estate to buy rice. This would tend to reduce the opportunities for the crimps in the villages to induce him to desert. As far as accessories to the labourer's rice were concerned, Veitch calculated that they would cost a minimum of eighty cents per month.[22]

The labourer who worked 30 days a month at either 10 or 12 cents per day could easily afford the recommended diet out of his net wages. In a second class gang, he would earn $3.00. From this, his employer was entitled under article 59 of Ordinance I of 1876 to deduct not more than $1.00 per month towards recovering the cost of his importation, which added to the cost of rice supplied, the employer would deduct $2.00. The labourer would then receive a net wage of $1.00. Out of this, he could buy the supplements to his rice, and would have a surplus of about 20 cents.

The average labourer did not work every day. One of the main reasons was provided by the manager of Batu Kawan estate, Vermont, who wrote: "The coolies do not refuse to turn out in the fields; many have not been accustomed to work daily, but off and on as their needs required: They come here and find they must do daily work, hence when they do not wish to work they either plead sickness or absent themselves."[23] Frequent rainfall, averaging between 80 and 130 inches annually,[24] also prevented regular work.[25] According to T.H. Hill, a planter in the Straits Settlements since 1878 and Protector of Labour, 1901-5, the general complaint of the labourer was this: "'I was told I was to get so much a task; and if it takes me two days to finish a task, I only get one day's wage for two days.'"[26]

The combined effect of these factors, as calculated by the Labour Commission of 1890 from the pay-lists (which are not available), was that on the average, the newly-arrived labourer earned pay for only 20.5 days per month, and (without giving any explanation), the second and third year labourer, only 22.5 days per month.[27] Too much weight cannot be put on the difference between the average number of days worked in a first year and in subsequent years. This difference was, after all, only estimated averages. Thus, it could not be expected that as soon as any labourer had completed his first year he would automatically begin to work the higher number of days per month. In fact, while some second-year labourers may well have worked more than 22.5 days per month, it would follow that, in order to arrive at an average of 22.5, other labourers must have worked less than that number. Similarly, some first-year labourers must have worked more and others less than 20.5 days per month. Nevertheless, an analysis of the existing wage rates will reveal whether the average labourer could afford to pay $1.00 per month towards liquidating his original debt, and $1.00 per month for rice received, and to purchase the recommended accessories to his rice, which cost about 80 cents. In other words, for him to survive he needed to earn at least $2.80 per month.

The 1876-84 Wage Rates
The newly-arrived labourer working in a first class gang and earning pay for 20.5 days per month at 12 cents per day would earn $2.46. From this, his employer would deduct $2.00, leaving him with 46 cents. Thus, he would be 34 cents

monthly short of the cost of the accessories to his rice. If he worked in a second class gang, he would be earning pay for 20.5 days per month at the daily rate of 10 cents. Thus, his gross wage would be $2.05. After his employer deducted $2.00, he would receive 5 cents. This would be 75 cents short of the cost of supplements to his rice. The wages of the average newly-arrived labourer working either in a first or second class gang were, therefore, quite inadequate.

During his second year, the first class labourer would be earning pay for 22.5 (instead of 20.5) days per month at the daily rate of 12 cents. Thus, his gross wages would be $2.70. After $2.00 were deducted, he would receive 70 cents. This would be 10 cents short of the cost of the accessories to his rice. Assuming he had repaid the cost of his importation, that is, $20.00, in his twentieth month, thereafter from his gross earnings of $2.70, the only deduction would be $1.00 for rice supplied. From his net wages of $1.70, he could buy the other food items costing 80 cents, and would have a surplus of 90- cents. The financial position of the average first class labourer, therefore, would be greatly enhanced from his twenty-first month of employment, provided ill-health and other misfortunes had not curtailed his work.

The second class labourer also could not afford to buy adequate food until after the first eight months of his second year. As he would now be earning 10 cents per day for 22.5 days per month, his gross wages would be $2.25, of which, after $2.00 were deducted, he would receive 25 cents. This would be 55 cents short of the required total. From the twenty-first month onwards, only $1.00 for rice would be deducted. Thus, he would have on hand $1.25 with which to buy the other food items that went to make up his meals. He would then have a surplus of 45 cents. The assertion made by the Commission of 1881 that "many coolies, no doubt, do save a little,"[28] would be applicable only to those labourers who had liquidated the cost of their importation or those who deliberately kept themselves on a diet below that recommended by Veitch.

Deductions from Wages
Apart from the cost of passage, a few other deductions were quite likely to be made. The labourer who broke or lost tools or caused crops to be damaged through his failure or his negligence to look after draught cattle or got drunk and created a disturbance in the labourers' quarters was liable to be fined by his employer.[29] The imposition of fines for these offences, not being controlled by the labour ordinance, was left to the discretion of the employer. In judging such cases, the employer would be an interested party. If he was liberal and kindly disposed, the offending labourer would probably be fairly dealt with. Where his profits were affected and his business undermined, not every employer could be expected to assess damages and impose penalties in an equitable manner.

A second type of deduction was frequently made. Every time a tindal declared a labourer's work unsatisfactory, he was liable to be fined ten cents.[30] On the Batu Kawan, Caledonia, and Golden Grove estates, for instance, the employers admitted to the Commission of 1881 that they had authorized wages to be cut in this way without reference to the magistrates,[31] who sat at Butterworth. As the magistrates did not usually try these cases at once, resulting in the labourer having to "hang around the courts for several days",[32] the employers had in effect prevented a further loss of wages to the labourer and also loss of labour-service to themselves. But by usurping legal authority and imposing this type of fine, the employers had violated the labour ordinance. According to article 55 of Ordinance I of 1876, the labourer whose work was deemed unsatisfactory was liable to be taken before a magistrate who would adjudicate upon such charge. If the labourer was found guilty, the fact would be endorsed on his contract and the deduction would be authorized. Only then could the deduction be legally made. According to the Lieutenant-Governor Anson, the illegal practice of cutting ten cents for work declared unsatisfactory was of "common occurrence".[33] No evidence was found of any employer being prosecuted for infringing this article of the labour ordinance.

Some Consequences of Inadequate Wages
In 1879, the P.C.M.O. found that especially among the newly-arrived labourers there was a "feeling of wretchedness".[34] This feeling, he asserted, led some of them to sell or barter a great portion of their rice for the worst description of spirits. Of these, arrack (spirits obtained by distilling a fermented mixture of rice and molasses) was described by an ex-planter, Hill, as a "most arrant poison."[35] When drunk immoderately, the consumer would become "absolutely killed".[36]

The plight of those labourers who had deprived themselves of their rice and could not afford to buy another supply was described by the P.C.M.O. as follows:-

> Thus starving, they eat all the rubbish they can lay their hands on, living the remainder of the time on unripe fruit, sugar cane, garbage and offal of all descriptions and if they do happen to get any rice, their physical condition makes them too lazy to cook it, and they eat it in its raw state, soon bringing themselves into a condition of poverty which, if death does not supervene, requires months to recover from; added to which they lie skulking in the ditches at night; get wet, lose all interest in life, contracting bowel complaints, which soon terminate their existence.[37]

The P.C.M.O. attached some blame for this predicament to what he described as the "ill-advised and iniquitous system of dealing out in advance, monthly or fortnightly rations of rice, in place of giving it out day by day."[38] He added: "The India coolly who is engaged to work in the Province is, as a rule, a man of very inferior intellect and to give him, who knows not how to take care of himself and who has no thought for the tomorrow, a month's supply of rice ahead, is … utterly absurd". On his suggestion, the planters then began to supply their labourers with a daily ration of twenty-five ounces of uncooked rice at the same monthly cost of $1.00. This system was a more effectual check against the improvident labourer disposing of his rice for arrack.

The labourer whose wages did not enable him to purchase an adequate amount of accessories to his rice was compelled to borrow money at high interest rates from an older hand or a tindal.[39] This further worsened his financial position. On pay-day, the P.C.M.O. noted, the labourer's pay "is not in his possession for five minutes before it is pounced upon by his creditors, and openly so, before the very eyes of the paymaster himself."[40] The labourer's consequent penury and low living, the P.C.M.O. added, contributed strongly to diseases, nostalgia, and to his inability and unwillingness to work.

When the labourer's gross earnings could not sustain full deductions towards repayment of the cost of his importation and for rice supplied, some employers continued to supply rice and confined their deductions to the payment for this commodity.[41] While this was the case, deductions towards liquidating the original debt were suspended. At superficial observation, this practice might be interpreted only as an expression of the employers' care for the labourer. At closer scrutiny, it was disadvantageous to the labourer as it would prolong his indebtedness and dependence on the estate. Where this continued until the end of the third year, the labourer would be legally compelled to continue working until he liquidated his debt.

On the Batu Kawan estate, the Commission of 1881 discovered two distinct problems regarding the supply of rice. The employer withheld a supply of rice to those labourers who were absent from work without prior permission being obtained.[42] The general rule, the Commission added, was "no work no rice". Furthermore, when the labourers returned late from work, they often found the rice godown closed.[43] Both situations led to indigent labourers eating certain unripe fruits, fish caught in stagnant drains, raw sweet potatoes, and the flesh of animals that had died from disease.[44]

The consequences of inadequate food for the constitution of some labourers on the Province Wellesley estates had been so harmful that when medical officers of the Straits government discovered their condition, they returned many of them to India on compassionate grounds. It must be emphasized that because there was no organized system of repatriation from the Straits Settlements (as in most of the other colonies), Madras emigration officials admitted being seldom able to identify indentured labourers among the South Indians returning from the colony.[45] Nevertheless, a few cases were reported.

In June 1880, eighteen labourers were returned on the steamship *C.T. Hook*.[46] When they landed, their condition rendered immediate hospitalization imperative. Nine of them insisted on proceeding at once to their villages, preferring as they told emigration officials, to die among their relatives and friends. The officials were doubtful whether the immigrants' weak state would have enabled them to reach their destination alive.

The other nine in hospital told the Protector of Emigrants and the District Surgeon of Negapatam that their existing condition was due to "bad, unwholesome food and want of care and attention." [47] Observing their condition, the Surgeon declared that in all his experience with famine-stricken Tamils, he had not seen such "woe-begone specimens of humanity." [48] "Neglect and want of proper nourishment," he added, "had materially assisted in producing their wretched state". He found one man "stone-blind" from the destructive inflammation of the corneas of both eyes which, he declared, was a most common result of starvation. Five others, he added, were suffering from debility and emaciation. The other four whom the Surgeon had declared beyond all hope of recovery died in hospital. Some details given are shown in the following table:-

TABLE XVI
DETAILS OF FOUR RETURNED IMMIGRANTS WHO DIED IN HOSPITAL IN INDIA
IN 1880

DATE ADMITTED	NAME	AGE	DATE OF DEATH
29.6.1880	Thanen	29	2.7.1880
"	Samigadoo	40	"
"	M. Karuppan	50	18.7.1880
"	Andee	30	20.7.1880

Source: MPP, no. 1328, 3 September 1880.

In September 1880, a batch of sixteen labourers was returned to Negapatam on board the *S.S. Decima*. The District Surgeon reported that all were in a weakened condition.[49] When questioned by the Protector of Emigrants, they all attributed their condition to the inadequate quantity and quality of the rice supplied by their employers on the different estates. Some said it was insufficient only on account of the waste in it; others said they had received less than they believed they had been paying for, and asserted that, the waste inclusive, the quantity was still short.[50]

Two of the repatriated labourers made other complaints. In his translated testimony, Nadarasa Pillay said in part:

> The rice which is supplied to us there is of a bitter taste and consists partly of paddy and partly of rice. No sufficient quantity of even this was given to me. We are not supplied with mortars and pounders so as to enable us to cleanse the rice supplied to us. If we ask for them we used to be told to get them from our native places. No sufficient time is allowed to us for cooking. Before we finish our cooking we used to be taken to the [sugar] garden and to resume our work. We are made to work both in the day and night.[51]

Pillay died seven days after his repatriation. The other labourer, Irulandy, said (in translation): "As for the nature of the rice itself, it consists partly of paddy and partly of rice. We are not supplied with mortar and pounder for pounding it. No sufficient time is allowed for cooking. We used to be conveyed to the labor [*sic*] before we finished our cooking." [52] Several other labourers complained to the Protector of Emigrants of being forced out of their quarters at irregular hours in the morning so that they were compelled to either abandon their preparation or swallow their food imperfectly cooked.[53]

In April 1881, seven labourers were returned to India. Their physical condition was as shown in the following table:–

TABLE XVII
STATEMENT SHOWING THE PHYSICAL CONDITION OF
SEVEN IMMIGRANTS RETURNED FROM THE STRAITS
SETTLEMENTS PER *S.S. ELGIN* ON 21 APRIL 1881

Name	State of health	Protector's remarks
Mootoosawmy	Fair	Weak, poorly and trembling
Ramasawmy	Dying	A perfect living skeleton
Allagan	Weak and debilitated	Very emaciated; bag of bones
Solay	" " "	Emaciated and very poorly
Anoomanthan	" " "	Emaciated and sickly
Curpen	" " "	Weak and sickly
Anga Pillay	Very low and weak	A living skeleton

Source: MPP, no. 697, 25 May 1881.

When these labourers were questioned by the Protector they complained that their wages were irregularly paid; that the tindals had often misappropriated their wages; that they were dealt a scanty supply of coarse rice; and that their wages did not enable them to buy enough food.[54]

Comparative Standards of Diet
Indentured Indians on the estates fared worse than their countrymen in prison or hospital. Indians imprisoned in the colony were provisioned in accordance with the following table:-

TABLE XVIII
SCALE OF DIET IN THE CRIMINAL PRISON, 1883

Item	Long sentence		Short sentence		Remarks
	lbs	ozs	lbs	ozs	
Rice	1	8	1	6	Daily
Fish, fresh	0	7	0	7	Four times wkly.
Mutton	0	7	0	7	Twice weekly
Daal	0	2	0	2	Daily
Beans	0	5	0	5	"
Vegetables	0	7	0	7	"
Tea	0	1/8	0	1/8	"
Salt	0	1	0	1	"
Curry-Stuff	0	1	0	1	"
Oil or Lard	0	1	0	1	"

Source: PSSLC, 19 June 1881, p. 224.

Labourers who were imprisoned admitted liking this diet not only because it was considerably more ample than the estate diets, but because in many respects it was similar to what they had been accustomed in Madras Presidency.[55] This scale of diet was served in return for a small amount of stone-breaking. Indian prisoners who could not work in prison were not penalized by a reduced diet.[56]

Details of the diet served at the estate hospitals in the 1880s were not available, but at the Government General Hospital, Butterworth, the daily diet was as follows:-

TABLE IXX
DAILY DIET SERVED AT THE BUTTERWORTH HOSPITAL

7:00 A.M.	Wheat flour *congee* (or *kanji*, Tamil for the residual semi-liquid after rice has been boiled) with sugar
10:30 A.M.	Hot meal of rice with curry-stuff, vegetables, *daal* or green peas, one egg or fresh or salt-fish
4:30 P.M	Hot meal similar to above

Source: Turner, "Tamil Labourer", p. 28.

In order to gain admission into the Butterworth Hospital, it was said that some labourers deliberately injured themselves or aggravated their ulcers.[57] Gaining admission was not as easy as it might appear. From the estate hospital, only the more serious cases were referred to Butterworth, and only on the recommendation of the District Medical Officer or the P.C.M.O., or on the initiative of the planters. Once a labourer was admitted into this "lap of luxury", he was reluctant to be discharged even if he was cured.[58]

In Madras Presidency, the Tamil peasant who earned not less than three rupees monthly (about $1.35 in Straits currency) would normally have a *chota-haziri* (literally, little breakfast); at noon and for dinner, his meals usually consisted of (sometimes goat) curry and rice, or rice with some dried fish and *daal* or other pulse.[59]

In the Straits, most indentured Indians could not afford adequate food and were compelled to live on a comparatively smaller quantity and poorer quality of diet. Cecil Clementi Smith, the Administrator of the Straits Settlements (1884-85), wrote that in the morning, the labourers usually went to work with no food except what rice they might have saved from the meal of the night before.[60] At eleven o'clock and in the evening, they returned to their quarters to prepare a meal which usually consisted of rice and salt-fish. After evening meal, Clementi Smith added, most of them would pour water on any rice that remained, which they would keep for their breakfast.

The diet of the average Chinese immigrant in the Straits between 1876-84 could not be ascertained. Nevertheless, around 1899, the highest daily wage rate for an indentured Indian was 14 cents,[61] whereas the Chinese miner earned between 70 and 80 cents a day.[62] Compared with what the average Chinese miner bought with his earnings, the indentured Indian ate "poorly." "The Chinese eat to live and work hard", observed an Indian writer, adding that like the Indian immigrant, his fare also consisted basically of rice, but his accessories included pork, beef, fish, prawns, lobsters, crabs, chicken, duck, etc.[63]

Wage Increases Denied
The plight of those Indian indentured labourers who could not afford to buy adequate food began to engage the serious attention of the Colonial Office from at least 1881. To mitigate the labourers' difficulty in procuring adequate food and to encourage them to remain in the colony after their indentures expired, the Secretary of State for the Colonies, the Earl of Kimberley, suggested a new wage system. He asked Governor Weld whether the planters could not pay indentured labourers the same wage rate being paid to unindentured labourers on the same estate or on other estates in the same neighbourhood.[64] When the Straits government made this recommendation to the planters, they flatly rejected it.[65]

In 1882, the new Secretary of State for the Colonies, the Earl of Derby, reiterated the need for equal wage rates, and as an alternative, he advocated an ascending scale of wages. In the planters' interest, he suggested empowering the Protector of Immigrants to relieve them from the increases in cases where labourers proved inefficient and unworthy of the higher scale.[66] The planters would not accede to Derby's proposal. They contended that in 1876, the government of India and the Straits government had agreed to fix the minimum wage rate at twelve cents per day, and they would not pay more.[67] By making this statement, the planters implicitly admitted violating the agreement by paying some labourers ten cents per day after relegating them to second class gangs.

As far as equating wage rates for indentured labourers with those paid to unindentured labourers was concerned, the planters unanimously declared it would seriously hamper enterprise and would have a most deterrent effect upon the introduction of fresh capital into the Straits. They added it would introduce such an element of uncertainty among employers that it would have a most unfortunate effect. Significantly, they drew frequent attention to the fact that only they were legally required to provide free housing and medical facilities. The cost of providing these, they contended, was equivalent to the wage differential.[68]

The validity of this contention could be tested as far as it related to the provision of medical facilities in respect of the largest estate, Batu Kawan, the only one for which some reliable statistics were available. For 1873, the estate spent $1,500 on its medical services.[69] This amount divided among the 917 indentured Indians then employed there averaged $1.64 per labourer. Assume that each of these labourers was paid 11 cents per day, that is, the average between the first and second class rates. As the average daily wage rate in the open colonial market was 18 cents,[70] for every day an indentured labourer worked, the manager of Batu Kawan was paying 7 cents less. Taking the average number of days worked by first-year labourers and older hands at 21.5 per month, the manager would have been saving $1,380.09 a month (i.e. 917 x 21.5 x 7). By paying indentured wage rates the estate would have recovered its medical expenditure for that year in about five weeks.

A similar test could be made for a later year. For 1880, when 577 indentured Indians were employed at Batu Kawan,[71] the manager reported spending $2,584.71 on medical services.[72] The wage differential then being 9 cents (20 - 11), let us assume that the 577 labourers worked the average 21.5 days per month. The sum thus saved for the year would be $13,397.94. Discounting the $2,584.71 expended, the planter's gain by paying the indentured rate would be $10,813.23 for 1880 alone. Due consideration must be given to the cost of constructing the labourers' quarters and the hospital, details of which have not been provided. Normally, the manager would seek to amortise the initial capital outlay over a number of years, so that the initial cost should be so spread after it was incurred. In 1881, the Protector of Immigrants revealed: "It is known that the average [annual] net profits [sic] on Batu Kawan Estate is $35,000, and the other estates can scarcely make less, so a small increase of wages could easily be given, and the employer would be repaid by fewer desertions and more contentment."[73]

The New Wage Rates

In July 1883, a conference was held in the Straits Settlements between a two-man delegation from India and three local representatives appointed by Governor Weld. The main object of the meeting was to devise means to promote Indian indentured immigration into the Straits. Following the conference, a new ordinance, V of 1884, was promulgated on 1 January 1885. Among the new terms of Ordinance V of 1884, article 42 required the employers to deduct from the labourer's wages not more than $1.00 per month towards recovery of the cost of importing the immigrant, but only to a maximum of $12.00. It has not been ascertained whether the planters reduced the amount of the cash advance so that when it was added to the cost of the passage the total came up to $12.00. This was hardly likely at least before 1887. In that year, the Straits government introduced subsidized steamer fares reducing the cost of the passage from the earlier rate of $6.75 to $3.60.[74]

Another important change effected by Ordinance V of 1884 was related to wages. From 1 January 1885, the new daily wage rate prescribed by article 47 was a minimum of 12 cents for all adult males during their first year of employment, and 14 cents during their second and subsequent years. For males under 21 years of age and for females, the rate was 8 cents during their first year and 10 cents thereafter. In each case the higher rate would not be paid to labourers who were still financially indebted to their employer.

One of the most compelling considerations that gave rise to the new wage structure was a rise in the cost of living. In the early 1880s, certain officials of the Straits government petitioned the Colonial Office requesting an increase to their salaries on the ground that provisions were dear.[75] One item which became more expensive was rice, the labourers' staple food. Consequently, the employers increased the price they charged for uncooked rice from $1.00 to $1.20 per month.[76]

Following the promulgation of the new wage rates, the Administrator of the Straits Settlements, Clementi Smith, observed in December 1884: "Those who had prescribed the new wages were ignorant of the high cost of living of the labourer, or must have hardened their hearts against the dictation of all humanity and justice."[77] Since the enactment of Ordinance I of 1876, Clementi Smith added, the cost of basic foodstuff had steadily continued to rise, in consequence of which, "the Indian labourer working on the Straits plantation was reduced to semi-starvation". He concluded: "So the Straits government who had proclaimed that through this Ordinance they had provided for the comfort and protection of the Indian labourer had in reality, by means of this Ordinance adopted measures for his perpetual servitude, or for his extinction by scanty living, hardship and misery."

The employers believed otherwise. In 1888, the manager of Batu Kawan, Vermont, the planters' chief spokesman, wrote: "It is a well known fact that with care a cooly on an estate can live on five cents a day; his wants are but few, he gets rice at wholesale prices, he pays no interest on his advances, his house is free, he pays no taxes, water supply is generally at his door, and fuel maybe be [sic] had for the picking up of it; consequently he can save a good half of his wages." [78]

As will be seen in the following Chapter, the quality of housing and water-supply on several estates, especially at Batu Kawan, was not in accordance with the requirements of the labour ordinance. The planters' provision of interest-free cash advances, the availability of freely obtainable fuel, and the labourer's freedom from taxes were undeniable. But that the labourer could subsist on five cents a day and at the same time maintain himself in vigorous physical condition is tenuous, and deserves examination.

It will be recalled that in 1879, the cost of the diet recommended by Veitch, the Colonial Surgeon, for one adult labourer was 6 cents per day or $1.80 per month. The Labour Commission of 1890 discovered that around 1890, the labourer required 8 cents a day or $2.40 a month.[79] Of this, $1.20 would be deducted from his wages for rice supplied by his employer and $1.20 would be required to purchase accessories that went to make up his meal.[80] The Commission added: "This would be a bare minimum, just sufficient to procure daily food and necessaries, and make no provision for other occasional unavoidable expenses."

While the estimated average number of days on which the labourer earned wages remained at 20.5 and 22.5 per month in his first and subsequent years respectively, there was one significant change for which there is no information as to when and why it was made. Instead of deducting $1.00 per month towards recovering the cost of importing the labourer, the Labour Commission of 1890 discovered that the employers of the Prye and the Batu Kawan estates deducted 55 cents.[81] In the absence of evidence to the contrary, one must presume the other employers asserted their right conferred by article 42 of Ordinance V of 1884 and deducted $1.00. The following calculations test whether Clementi Smith's diagnosis was accurate or whether Vermont's assertions were correct.

The wages of the newly-arrived labourer earning pay for 20.5 days per month at 12 cents per day would be $2.46. If he was employed at Prye or Batu Kawan, his employer would deduct $1.75 ($1.20 for rice + 55 cents towards recovering the cost of the labourer's importation). His nett wage of 71 cents would thus be 49 cents short of the cost of the basic supplements to his rice.

For most of his second year, a labourer employed at either Prye or Batu Kawan would be in a more favourable position. Assuming 55 cents were deducted every month during his first year of employment, the labourer would have repaid only $6.60 out of the maximum recoverable $12.00. Thus, from the beginning of his second year, he would not be eligible for the higher wage rate of 14 cents per day. But, according to the estimated average, he would now earn wages for 22.5 days per month; thus, his gross wages would be $2.70. From this, the employer would deduct $1.75 until the ninth month. During this time, his nett wages would be 95 cents per month. On this he could not afford the other foodstuff by 25 cents. In his tenth month, only 45 cents would remain to be deducted to pay off his original debt. For this month, his nett wages would be $1.05 ($2.70 - [$1.20 + 45 = $1.65]). In this case, he would be short of 15 cents of the required $1.20 to buy supplements to his rice.

If the labourer had liquidated his original debt in the tenth month of his second year, from then onwards, his daily wage rate would rise to 14 cents. Monthly, his gross earnings would be $3.15 (22.5 x 14). From this, his employer would deduct $1.20 for rice supplied; his nett wages would be $1.95 per month. He could spend $1.20 on the other food items; and he would have a surplus of 75 cents.

It may be observed that by deducting 55 cents instead of $1.00 monthly towards liquidating the labourer's original debt, the employers of Prye and Batu Kawan had effectively delayed the labourer's eligibility for the increase from 12 to 14 cents until the eleventh month of his second year. This would be a substantial saving for those employers. For every 100 labourers so delayed, they would be saving $2.00 every day for 22.5 days per month for 10 months.

A newly-arrived labourer employed at an estate other than Prye or Batu Kawan would be even less able to afford adequate food. During his first year, he would be earning wages for 20.5 days per month at 12 cents per day: a gross of $2.46. From this, his employer would deduct $1.00 towards recovering the cost of importing him, and $1.20 for rice supplied, a total of $2.20. His nett wages would be 26 cents, or 94 cents short of the $1.20 required to purchase accessories to his rice.

If at the end of his first year, this labourer had liquidated the maximum recoverable twelve-dollar debt, his financial position would then be greatly improved. In his second year, instead of earning pay for 20.5 days per month, he would be earning for 22.5 days per month. Furthermore, his wage rate would rise from 12 to 14 cents a day. His monthly gross earnings, therefore, would be $3.15. From this, his employer would deduct $1.20 for rice supplied, which would leave him with $1.95. He could afford to buy an adequate amount of basic supplements to his rice, and would then have a surplus of 75 cents.

On the basis of all the calculations made above, the average newly-arrived labourer could not afford an adequate amount of accessories to his rice throughout his first year of employment, no matter which estate employed him. After scrutinizing the wages earned by a large number of newly-arrived men on three large estates, the Labour Commission of 1890 concluded: "We think it incontestable that the Ordinance [V of 1884] minimum wages for the colony are too low if advances are deducted, and that the contract terms must be so modified as to improve the financial position of the coolly."[82]

The physical condition of some labourers who managed to return to Negapatam around 1890 was commented upon by S. Patrao, the Acting Civil Surgeon, Negapatam, thus:

> I had occasion to see some of the returned emigrants who sought admission into the municipal hospital during the last one year I had been in medical charge and found many of them suffering from chronic diarrhoea and dropsy, which clearly show that among the coolies who returned from the Straits, most of them, with a very few exceptions, are subject to some disease or other contracted during their sojourn there, and as these men are found quite helpless and destitute with regard to their means and health, it is a question open to answer whether those who go there with the hopes of earning their fortunes or at least bettering their prospects, do really obtain their object in view.[83]

Redemption of Contracts

It has been shown above that before the average labourer could save any money, he had to overcome the obstacle of repaying his employer the cost of importing him. Between 1876 and 1884, the employer was legally entitled under article 59 of Ordinance I of 1876 to deduct not more than $1.00 per month until the original debt (which averaged $20.00) was recovered. But according to article 65 of the Ordinance, the labourer could abrogate his contract at any time by repaying his employer the aggregate amount of $2.50 for every remaining month of the three-year indenture. That amount was termed "smart money".

From the calculations in the preceding sections, it is clear that the average labourer could not afford to redeem his contract by purchase. It has also been shown that before 1884 it was only from the twenty-first month of his employment that the average first class labourer would have a surplus, and then only of ninety cents a month. The second class labourer would only have a surplus of forty-five cents a month, also commencing only from the twenty-first month.

The apparent intention in imposing the payment of "smart money" was to make cancellation of the contract difficult and to anchor the labourer to his place of employment until his original term of indenture expired. If the labourer could not procure the required "smart money", the only alternative means of early release from his contract was to desert. According to Governor Sir Frank Swettenham, of the Straits Settlements, 1901-3, desertion to the Malay States was quite prevalent among Indian indentured labourers, especially among the newly-arrived.[84]

When Ordinance V of 1884 came into force on 1 January 1885, the terms for redeeming contracts were changed. The immigrant was not required to sign a contract in India. But according to article 51 of the ordinance, he could not be compelled to enter into a contract in the Straits either if he could pay at once $12.00 to the employer who had imported him. Once he entered into a contract it was more expensive for him to redeem it by purchase.

Article 51 of Ordinance V of 1884 provided that a labourer could redeem his contract by paying his employer the aggregate amount of (a) the remaining portion of the cost of his importation (b) $1.00 for every remaining month of his first year of employment and (c) $2.00 for every remaining month of the second and third years. The average labourer certainly could not afford any of these from his surplus earnings, at least until just before his contract was due to expire. As has been shown earlier, the average labourer who was employed on estates other than Prye or Batu Kawan could only have a monthly surplus of 75 cents from the beginning of his second year of employment; and the labourer who was employed either at Prye or Batu Kawan could only have the same monthly surplus beginning from his twenty-third month of employment.

Since the average labourer could not save enough money to redeem his contract by purchase, why was paying "smart money" introduced? Swettenham provided the answer: "A good many of them redeem themselves very shortly after their arrival. That is quite easy to be explained, because they find that the rate of wages is so much higher outside that it will pay them to borrow the money from somebody and to immediately go somewhere else and get much higher wages." [85]

It was not always possible for a labourer to ascertain the state of his indebtedness. According to Anson, the Lieutenant-Governor of Penang, the labourer was simply handed his wages without any explanation.[86] It is true that the labourer could make enquiries regarding the state of his accounts. But as Anson added, he was too timid to do so. There was at least one exceptional occasion. A Madras government official visiting the Province Wellesley estates recorded this incident which occurred at Malakoff in 1883: "One man, for instance, the lawyer, apparently, of his gang, who had been but a few weeks in the colony, said that he had asked Mr. Charles deMornay how much of his advance he had yet to repay, and that that gentleman merely smiled at him; and, as this complaint induced a laugh, several other coolies of the same batch, following his lead, made a similar statement." [87]

When a labourer wanted to rid himself of his contract, because his wages were less adequate than he had been led by his recruiter to expect, and was in a position to borrow the "smart money", but was frustrated by his employer in his attempt to redeem his contract, the natural inclination would be to desert. Commenting on this disposition, the Protector of Immigrants remarked: "The wages given here are, I believe, considerably lower than in any other Colony, and the employer recovers a considerable sum from the coolie of the expenses incurred in bringing him here, which is not done elsewhere, so the employer has advantages here which he could not get in other Colonies, while the coolie is far less liberally treated. Are then desertions from the estates to be wondered at?" [88]

Desertion

A very common feature of Indian indenture in the Straits Settlements was desertion from the Province Wellesley estates mainly to the Malay States. The labour ordinances defined desertion as the continuous absence of a labourer from his employer's estate for more than twenty-four hours, exclusive of any Sunday or authorized holiday, without leave from his employer or without reasonable excuse, or being absent from the estate under such circumstances as showed that he did not intend to return to honour his contract. He would also be deemed a deserter if he was found either on or off the estate under circumstances from which it might be reasonably inferred by a magistrate that he had intended to desert.[89] The penalty prescribed for a deserter was one month's imprisonment for the first offence, two months for the second, and three months for the third and any subsequent desertion.[90]

Desertion to the Malay States, especially neighbouring Kedah and Perak, could be interpreted not only as an expression of the labourers' protest against ill-treatment and corruption perpetrated by the tindals but more especially against their inadequate wages. This is suggested by the steady rise in wages in the Malay States and, with the unexplainable exception of 1882, a corresponding increase in desertion as shown in the following table:

TABLE XX
DAILY WAGES IN THE MALAY STATES AND DESERTION
FROM PROVINCE WELLESLEY, 1879 - 84

YEAR	AVERAGE WAGE RATES IN		LABS. ON ROLL	DESERTIONS	%
	PROVINCE	STATES			
1879	11¢	18¢	3,677	186	5
1880	11¢	20¢	2,801	319	11
1881	11¢	20¢	3,366	415	12
1882	11¢	20¢	3,733	352	9
1883	11¢	24¢	4,369	567	13
1884	11¢	24¢	4,655	586	13

Source: Compiled from ARII 1879-84.

Commenting in 1880 on the incidence of desertion, Governor Weld observed: "As long as employers seek to engage labourers at $3 per mensem and deduct $2 monthly from that sum for rice and ... passage money, it is not astonishing that the Coolies should abscond to other employers or to the Native States [of Malaya] where free labour commands as much as $6 and $7 per mensem." [91]

Between 1885 and 1888, the average annual percentage of desertion from Province Wellesley rose to 18 per cent.[92] Explaining this rise, the Protector of Immigrants wrote: "There has, doubtless, been a greater demand for labourers [in Malaya], owing to the falling off in Chinese Immigration, and I cannot help thinking that crimps have been at work." [93] He added: "Again, when the high pay given to coolies on public works is considered, it is surprising more coolies do not desert, for the chances of detection are not great, and they have everything to gain if they can get away."

Between 1889 and 1902, the average percentage of indentured labourers deserting fell to 10 per cent.[94] This decrease was due to the difficulty of procuring fresh supplies of labour, which had led the employers to exercise increased vigilance in preventing their labourers from deserting. Some employers erected fences around the labourers' quarters and placed watchmen at strategic points to prevent unauthorized egress.[95]

At the end of 1903, desertion fell to 5 per cent.[96] The restraining measures aside, two other reasons could be offered for this drastic drop. The sugar planters of Province Wellesley offered various bonuses (see below) to all labourers willing to enter into a second three-year term of indenture.[97] In the decade 1891-1900, the annual average number of labourers recruited in Madras Presidency for the Province Wellesley estates was 1,565.[98] For 1901-3, recruitment fell to 1,023, 830, and 364 respectively.[99] With the diminished supply of indentured recruits in 1903, the renewal of contracts by time-expired labourers was one of the chief sources of supply to the employers. They, however, found it necessary to increase very greatly the daily rate of wages on three occasions as follows:-[100]

	RATE OF WAGES	
	Men	Women
1 Jan. to 27 Apr. 1903	25¢	18¢ with $15.00 bonus
28 Apr. to 7 May 1903	30¢	20¢ " " "
8 May to 31 Dec. 1903	35¢	25¢ " " "

From the beginning of 1903 also, the daily rate of wages at which male and female immigrants were recruited in Madras Presidency was increased to 25 and 20 cents respectively.[101]

If the planters had any expectation that from 1903 onwards the significant increase in the daily wage rates would continue to discourage desertion, they would have been disappointed. In 1904, the desertion rate rose to 8 per cent.[102] The Protector of Immigrants could not suggest any satisfactory reason.[103] The average annual desertion for 1905-8 continued at 8 per cent, and in 1909, it rose to 10 per cent.[104] This time an explanation was provided by Sir Frank Swettenham who said: "… but today the number of desertions is enormous; and it is simply … because in the rush for rubber planting the [rubber planters] … are prepared to offer absurd wages [sometimes as high as forty cents a day], and so the new estates take away the labour from the old estates."[105]

In 1910, the daily wage paid by rubber estates in the Malay States was anything up to 50 cents a day.[106] Consequently, desertion from Province Wellesley rose to 11 per cent.[107] The temptation to the labourers to free themselves from their contracts by deserting and to earn higher wages as free labourers on estates that provided house accommodation, water supply, sanitary arrangements, and medical services free of cost, would have been very strong.

References

1 This was told by indentured Indians on the Malakoff estate to a Straits journalist. See *Penang Guardian*, 13 December 1873.
2 RLC 1890, p. 52.
3 MPP, vol. 276, Appendix A, November 1875.
4 MPP, vol. 275, 1 July 1875.
5 *Ibid.*
6 RLC 1890, p. 52.
7 MPP, vol. 276, 1 July 1875.
8 C.O. 273/105. Weld to Kimberley, no. 259, 7 December 1880.
9 RLC 1890, p. 52.
10 Vermont, *Immigration from India*, p. 51.
11 C.O. 273/834. Enclosure in Jervois to Carnarvon, no. 5, 3 January 1876.
12 *Report of the 1881 Commission*, p. 10.
13 C.O. 273/71. Enclosure in Clarke to Carnarvon, no. 397, 25 December 1873.
14 *Ibid.*
15 *Ibid.*
16 *Ibid.*
17 *Ibid.*
18 MPP, vol. 276, Appendix A, November 1875.
19 PSSLC, 12 December 1879, p. C338.
20 *SSGG*, 24 October 1879, p. 961.
21 *Report of the 1881 Commission*, p. 6.
22 *SSGG*, 24 October 1879, p. 961.
23 Vermont, *Immigration from India*, p. 47.
24 Frederick A. Weld, "The Straits Settlements and British Malaya, "*Proceedings of the Royal Colonial Institute,* vol. XV (1883-84), p. 269.
25 *Report of the 1881 Commission*, p. 9.
26 Evidence of T.H. Hill, in Sanderson, *Report on Emigration,* C5193, p. 433.
27 RLC 1890, p. 52.
28 *Report of the 1881 Commission*, p. 5.
29 MPP, no. 292, 1 November 1875.
30 PSSLC, 12 December 1879, p. C336.
31 *Report of the 1881 Commission*, p. 3.
32 C.O. 384/133. Enclosure in Weld to Kimberley, no. 171, 5 May 1881.
33 *Ibid.*
34 *SSGG*, 24 October 1879, p. 962.
35 Evidence of T.H. Hill, in Sanderson, *Report on Emigration,* C5193, p. 431.
36 *Ibid.*
37 PSSLC, 12 December 1879, p. C335.
38 *Ibid.*
39 *Ibid.*
40 *SSGG*, 24 October 1879, p. 962.

41 C.O. 384/133. Enclosure in Weld to Kimberley, no. 171, 5 May 1881.
42 *Report of the 1881 Commission*, p. 2.
43 *Ibid.*, p. 3.
44 C.O. 384/133. Enclosure in Weld to Kimberley, no. 171, 5 May 1881.
45 MPP, vol. 372, 14 June 1882.
46 MPP, no. 1328, 3 September 1880.
47 *Ibid.*
48 *Ibid.*
49 MPP, no. 1508, 11 October 1880.
50 *Ibid.*
51 *Ibid.*
52 *Ibid.*
53 *Ibid.*
54 MPP, no. 697, 25 May 1881.
55 PSSLC, 19 June 1883, p. C226.
56 *Ibid.*
57 ARII 1881, p. 3.
58 Turner, "Tamil Labourer", p. 28.
59 C.O. 273/130. Smith to Derby, no. 541, 29 December 1884.
60 *Ibid.*
61 Ordinance V of 1884, article 47.
62 Blythe, "Chinese Labour in Malaya", p. 66.
63 Ambikapath Rai, "The Indian Cooly in British Malaya," *The Indian Review* (June, 1914), 454.
64 MPP, no. 276, 25 May 1882.
65 *Ibid.*
66 *Ibid.*
67 *Ibid.*
68 See *Penang Guardian*, 9 January 1874; Vermont, *Immigration from India*, p. 54; *Singapore Free Press*, 29 September 1897.
69 *Singapore Daily Times*, 6 January 1874.
70 C.O. 273/71. Enclosure in Clarke to Carnarvon, no. 397, 25 December 1873.
71 ARII 1880, p. 8.
72 C.O. 384/133. Vermont to Colonial Secretary, S.S., 25 March 1881.
73 ARII 1881, p. 2.
74 Sandhu, *Indians in Malaya*, p. 61.
75 C.O. 273/130. Enclosure in Smith to Derby, no. 541, 29 December 1884.
76 *Ibid.*
77 *Ibid.*
78 Vermont, *Immigration from India*, p. 54;
79 RLC 1890, p. 56.
80 *Ibid.*
81 *Ibid.*
82 *Ibid.*

83 PSSLC, 15 November 1890, p. C249.
84 Evidence of Sir Frank Swettenham, in Sanderson, *Report on Emigration*, C5193, p. 403.
85 *Ibid.*
86 MPP, vol. 275, Appendix A, November 1875.
87 MPP, no. 25 August 1884.
88 ARII 1881, p. 2.
89 See Ordinance I of 1876, article 45; Ordinance V of 1884, article 75.
90 See *Ibid.*
91 C.O. 273/105. Weld to Kimberley, no. 171, 18 December 1880.
92 See ARII 1885-88.
93 ARII 1888, p. 1.
94 See ARII 1889-1902.
95 ARII 1896, p. 3.
96 ARII 1903, p. 22.
97 *Ibid., p. 5.*
98 See ARII 1891-1900.
99 See ARII 1901-3.
100 ARII 1903, p. 5.
101 *Ibid.*
102 ARII 1904, p. 10.
103 *Ibid.*, p. 5.
104 ARII 1909, p. 4.
105 Evidence of Sir Frank Swettenham, in Sanderson, *Report on Emigration*, C5193, p. 403.
106 Parr, *Report of the Commission of 1910*, p. 5.
107 ARII 1910, p. 8.

IX

HOUSING AND HEALTH

> [The planters can] encourage ... our immigrant population to remain here instead of being birds of passage .... If we are to induce labourers to come here in large numbers and to remain as settlers, employers must make their service such as first to attract and then to retain the labour they desire.
>
> RLC 1890

All employers of Indian indentured labourers in Province Wellesley were required by the various labour ordinances to provide their employees with sufficient and proper house accommodation and sanitary arrangements, a sufficient supply of wholesome water, hospital accommodation, medical attendance, and a sufficient quantity of medicines of good quality.[1]

House Accommodation

The labourers' dwellings on only two estates could be described as sufficient and proper. At Prye, the manager, Eddie Brown, a "shrewd, sensible, steady young Scotchman" took quite an "enthusiastic interest in his work, and appeared ... to be very decidedly popular with his coolies, whom he seemed to treat with great kindness and consideration."[2] A visiting Madras government official who made this observation after paying a surprise call at the estate in 1883 went on to describe the labour lines, that is, the labourers' quarters and the surroundings, thus:

> The lines ... were models ... and were infinitely superior to anything of the same kind that any coolie there had ever inhabited in his own country. The streets were spacious and well-laid out, so that the air circulated freely throughout the lines; and the huts ... afforded ample accommodation for an ordinary native family. They were ... solidly constructed of attap [the dried branch of the neepa palm] ... which affords a much more comfortable and durable dwelling house .... In front of, and forming part of, each block was a broad commodious verandah; and within it, and opposite each hut, was the cooking place of each separate family. The whole lines, in fact, bore unmistakable evidence of quiet content and comfort.[3]

The same official visited the Krian estate where he observed: "The lines consist of one long, broad, and very cleanly kept street with houses *a la* Prye, and the inevitable *gopurum* (temple) in the centre; and I was glad to find that, unlike the Alma and Golden Grove Estates, each married couple had a whole house to themselves." [4]

In striking contrast, a common feature of housing on the other estates was overcrowding. The labour lines were constructed as one-storey buildings flat on the ground with the bare earth forming the floor, and with a verandah serving as a kitchen. In most cases, they were divided into rooms ten feet by ten in which six persons usually lived.[5] On some estates, stealing of milk directly from cows compelled the owners to pen their animals in the verandah during the night.[6] This arrangement confined the occupants to their rooms, which added to the congestion and lack of privacy, and to the already poor ventilation.[7] To relieve the congestion, some employers increased sleeping accommodation by erecting temporary floors overhead inside the rooms.[8] Those in this sort of attic complained of the smoke from the hearths.[9]

With the exception of Prye and Krian, the estates had no special housing for married couples. On some of these estates, in rooms measuring twenty feet by fourteen, eighteen married persons usually lived, "men and women indiscriminately."[10] At Caledonia estate, the Labour Commission of 1890 found three married couples sharing one room with several single men.[11]

One of the major causes of overcrowding on at least two estates was managerial lack of forethought. In 1884 at Batu Kawan, for instance, there was an accession of 366 immigrants without any proportionate provision having been previously made for their accommodation.[12] The new arrivals brought the total number of indentured Indians to an unprecedented 1,037.[13] Consequently, some of the blocks became so overcrowded that in several rooms separate "families were living in a promiscuous manner."[14] Similarly, on the Malakoff estate where there were 506 labourers already resident in 1900, an additional 331 arrived within two months, making a total of 837.[15] As the existing buildings were not extensive enough, and the accommodation at the estate hospital was quite inadequate, and as the immigrants were a particularly unhealthy and emaciated lot, a large number of them overflowed into the government hospitals.[16]

It was not until the Protector of Immigrants reported this matter to the Straits government and an order consequently given for the immediate erection of additional dwellings, that some time later in the year the labourers were properly housed without overcrowding. In his report for 1900, the Protector wrote: "It was known that a large number of coolies were to arrive during the year and ample time should have been allowed for the provision of the necessary additions."[17] Either the manager or the directors of the Penang Sugar Estates Company (the proprietors of Malakoff), the Protector added, were "much to blame for what was little short of a scandal. The fact that the coolies arrived sooner than expected is no sufficient excuse."

The Surroundings
In contrast to Prye and Krian estates, the wretchedness of the living quarters on some estates was surpassed only by the sordid squalor of their surroundings. At Golden Grove, for instance, in 1879, the lines were not clean by any means - the verandah was blocked up and the drains were uncleared and obstructed.[18] In the

same year, the P.C.M.O. and the Colonial Surgeon paid a surprise visit and the former afterwards reported thus:

> We next proceeded to the Caledonia lines, which the Protector told me were at the last visit [of his] amongst the cleanest. I regret they were not so on this occasion; at our visit they were dirty decidedly – the drains were choked up, smelt badly, the verandahs were obstructed with the belongings of the coolies, and altogether there was a want of supervision on this important matter which was most apparent.[19]

In 1883, the visiting official of the Madras government mentioned earlier found similar insanitary conditions on a number of estates. At Caledonia, he observed: "The blocks ... tenanted by the old or re-engaged coolies seemed to me especially shabby and comfortless".[20] At Alma, the lines "looked everywhere as if they were left a good deal to the will of those who inhabited them, and were not, consequently, so neatly kept as those at Prye".[21] At Victoria and Caledonia, where he was joined by a visiting colleague, he noted: "It was noticeable that there was more rubbish lying around about ... than we had hitherto seen ... on any other estates".[22]

At Alma, the latrines were situated too far from the labour lines.[23] As dysentery and diarrhoea were endemic among a large number of labourers, some of them became so weak that they were seldom able to reach the latrines.[24] Consequently, the ground around the labour lines was "evidently saturated with faecal matter which gave forth a most penetrating odour".[25] On the Malakoff estate in 1881, the open ground in front of the dwellings was "thoroughly permeated with filth which gave forth a most putrescent stink ... In short, all the neighbourhood was pervaded by foul smelling odours."[26] Latrines had not been provided for the labourers.[27]

The faecal pollution of the ground in the precincts of the labour lines became a permanent menace to the labourers' health. The soil in this vicinity being sandy and, therefore, permeable, it could not be easily disinfected. Consequently, for a considerable radius round the dwellings and within the lines as well, the ground became infected and gave rise to ankylostomiasis,[28] commonly known as hookworm.

In 1915, the conception of the nature and effects of this disease was given thus:

> The mouth of this small creature (i.e., the hookworm or ankylostoma duodenale) is provided with a fringe of hooks by means of which it attaches itself to the inner lining of that portion of the small intestine .... It lives on the blood which it sucks from the bowels .... Once deposited in damp soil, the eggs ... hatch out little larvae which grow for a while, and then develop a protective capsule in which they lie dormant, until swallowed by men, in food or water, or through the medium of soiled hands. The disease set up by the worms is apt to run a chronic course, owing to constant reinfection .... When trodden upon by bare feet the larvae sometimes burrow into the skin and produce the form of irritation known as ground itch.[29]

A report made in 1881 showed that large numbers of labourers had been infected and re-infected with hook-worm and had to be hospitalized.[30] The attempt to cure the afflicted labourers was more of a palliative than a remedy so long as they had to return to the source of the infection. It was mainly because of re-infection that between 1886 and 1896, 405 labourers died as a direct consequence of the disease.[31]

This was largely avoidable. On the Prye estate, which stood out prominently as a commendable exception to the prevalence of the disease, and where certain simple, well-understood, and inexpensive measures were adopted, the effects of hookworm were negligible.[32] This was mainly due to the employer's provision of excellent latrines.[33] Furthermore, he exercised a strong-arm compulsion to ensure that his labourers used them properly; and, moreover, he liberally applied permanganate of potash on the mud-floor huts, which effectively destroyed the faecal dust germs that had previously been settling on open plates of food.

Another method of minimizing or preventing hook-worm suggested by the Secretary of State for the Colonies (1908-10), the Earl of Crewe, was ignored by the majority of planters, although it involved no elaborate sanitary appliances. If the latrines, Crewe advised, were built over a hole in the ground and the contents of which were occasionally covered with earth, re-infection would certainly be prevented.[34] Since in many cases the planters' own residences were in close proximity to the labour lines, their disregard of this exhortation was very much to their personal disadvantage as well.

Various reasons explained why the planters adopted a negative attitude towards the suppression or eradication of ankylostomiasis. Generally, they were inclined to exaggerate the difficulties of dealing with the prevalence of the disease. Specifically, they maintained that the complete eradication of the disease was impracticable because the labourers abhorred the use of latrines and were addicted to insanitary habits; and, furthermore, they claimed that the cost of preventive measures was prohibitive.[35]

On the basis of the evidence of Hill, the Protector of Labour (1901-5) in Malaya, before the Sanderson Committee in 1909, the prevalence of the hook-worm disease continued until about 1896 or 1897.[36] Describing how the disease was suppressed afterwards, Hill said that the planters ensured that the labourers kept their dwellings in an absolutely healthy condition by using large quantities of permanganate of potash and destroying those dust germs which used to be blown upon the occupants' rice.[37] He added that after 1896 or 1897, "certain managers who had ... taken preventive measures, not according to ordinances, but according to intelligences," had effectively decreased the prevalence of the disease.

Water Supply
Before Ordinance I of 1876 came into effect on 1 March, labourers were not supplied with water in the fields. They usually drank from the canals, but permission to do so during the hours of work was refused by the tindals.[38] Even after the Ordinance was promulgated, the water supply on some estates was still either insufficient or contaminated.

Labourers on the Batu Kawan estate suffered the most in obtaining potable water. Since they were not supplied with water in the fields, they continued to drink from the canals.[39] Owing to the low-lying position of the cane-fields and their consequent occasional subjection to tidal influence, the water in the canals sometimes became brackish.[40] In 1881, the water-supply problem of the Batu Kawan labourers was worsened by drought. From March to May, the rainfall was only 17.67 inches; the previous average for those months had been 30.4 inches.[41] To facilitate the transportation of cane to the mills, water was channelled from the nearby sea; but, as the Colonial Surgeon discovered, this water was unwholesome for drinking purposes.[42] Notwithstanding, the labourers were compelled to drink it, and an unusual number of cases of diarrhoea and dysentery were traced to that cause.[43] Commenting on the labourers' water-supply problem in the fields, Vermont, the manager of Batu Kawan, claimed that he had furnished the labourers with water-bottles which he had told them to fill at the pipes on the estate[44] but that the labourers were too lazy to do so. Having investigated the matter, the Commission of 1881 did not dispute the provision of water-bottles, but they were not convinced that effective precautions had been taken to enforce the order.[45]

In 1882, the labourers at Batu Kawan suffered another problem relating to obtaining a sufficient and wholesome supply of water. Owing to the great drought prevailing since 1881 and the want of the usual rainfall in June and July 1882, the Colonial Surgeon, J.H. McClosky, recorded that the labourers were compelled to drink water from "foul water wells" situated in the vicinity of the labour lines.[46] Very soon after, this source also disappeared, and "there was not a drop of wholesome drinking water whatever in the Island of Batu Kawan."[47] The labourers were then reduced to drinking impure water wherever obtainable, and those newly arrived, being less acclimatized, became more susceptible to the influence of fever.

The Colonial Surgeon declared that the labourers' drinking unwholesome water at Batu Kawan caused "Remittent and Intermittent" fever which, in turn, resulted in a number of deaths. In 1880, there were 39 attacks of fever and 5 deaths; in 1881, 54 labourers suffered from fever and 3 died; in 1882, there were 61 cases of fever and 9 deaths.[48] There appeared to be no doubt in McClosky's mind that the deficiency of the water supply in July 1882 was the important factor in the causation of the disease.[49] On a suggestion from McClosky in 1882, Vermont arranged for an artesian well to be sunk. In 1883, the water problem was still largely unsolved. The visiting official of the Madras government found one filter at the well useless, another under repair, and a third out of repair.[50] This made it necessary for the labourers to use water from surface wells. Since these were near to the labour lines, the water was contaminated by impurities passing through the easily permeable soil.[51] The effects were not reported. The question of water-supply on the Batu Kawan estate was not mentioned again in the sources available until 1909 when the Protector of Immigrants wrote that as there was some suspicion that the water supply was not quite satisfactory a system of filtration was started at the end of the year.[52]

The water-supply on some other estates was also defective. In 1900, at Caledonia, the pressure in the pipe conducting water to the estate was not high enough to keep the labourers sufficiently supplied.[53] This made it necessary for them to drink water from the canal that ran in front of the labour lines. Consequently, diseases of the digestive tract and gastro-intestinal disorders became widespread, and between June 1900 and January 1901, according to the Protector of Immigrants, they caused the death of twenty-four labourers.[54] On the Golden Grove estate in 1900, the employer reported it was difficult to induce his "careless and lazy labourers to drink good water instead of that which was unwholesome and more easily accessible."[55] Following his investigation, the Colonial Surgeon discovered that most of the labourers referred to had been ill, and being unable to reach the source of the potable water, had resorted to a nearby stagnant pool.[56]

Sexual Disproportion
For every batch of labourers emigrating to the West Indian colonies and Fiji, the government of India required a minimum sexual proportion of 40 females (ten years and over) to every 100 males.[57] No such stipulation was made in the Indian Emigration Act V of 1877 which regulated indentured emigration to the Straits Settlements. The government of India gave no reasons.

The percentage of female to male indentured immigrants in the Straits was very small. Between 1877-79, the annual average was 15 per cent.[58] Between 1880-1903, it averaged 16 per cent.[59] Since the Straits government always wanted more Indian labourers to emigrate to the colony, they were particularly anxious for a large number of married as well as respectable single females. Since the presence of these would tend to encourage permanent settlement, a reservoir of labour would be built up; agricultural enterprise could be expanded; any competition for employment would tend towards lower wages; and since Indians generally preferred European to Chinese employers, this would tend toward British economic supremacy in the colony. Presumably, with these likely advantages in mind, the Straits government requested the Madras authorities through the Colonial Office to promote actively the recruitment of females.[60] But the Madras government declined on the ground that the easy and frequent communication between the Straits and Madras Presidency particularly favoured those male labourers who wanted to return to India to marry.[61]

This response was merely evasion tactics. Madras government officials had often referred to the low wages earned by indentured Indians in the Straits, and their consequent inability to save substantially.[62] They were also quite aware that many male labourers could hardly afford to return to India, marry and re-migrate under indenture to the Straits. The real reason, it seems, was that they were required to comply with the general emigration policy of the government of India. This policy was expressed by the government of India to the Secretary of State for India in 1871 thus: "Our policy may be described as one of seeing fair play between the parties to a commercial transaction, while the Government altogether abstains from mixing itself in the bargain."[63]

Another reason may be advanced. Following reports of Tamil women becoming prostitutes in the Straits in 1873,[64] and again in 1880,[65] the Madras government seemed apprehensive that if they were to promote the emigration of females to the Straits, they would be held originally responsible for any social degradation that the immigrants might suffer. Like the entire indentured traffic to the Straits, female recruitment continued unaffected by the judicious neutrality of the Madras government.

Several factors prevented a larger number of females from emigrating to the Straits. The planters had limited the number of female recruits to between 15 and 20 per cent of the males, which they said was sufficient for all practical purposes.[66] Female labourers were generally required for light tasks such as gathering and storing truncated pieces of cane for replanting; digging up old cane stumps as part of the preparation for replanting; and moulding young canes.[67] For some of these tasks, some planters preferred to employ male minors (between 16 and 21 years) because they were less difficult to recruit, and their wage rates were the same as for females. Thus, the nature of sugar cultivation directed the pattern of employment which in its turn dictated the formula for recruitment.

For moral reasons it was difficult to induce the average Tamil female to emigrate. A Madras government official observed that because the polygamous tendencies of the Tamil male were well known, in most cases the married woman would not accompany her husband for fear of losing her reputation through being enticed by other males.[68]

The low wage rates paid to indentured labourers, also made it difficult for many Tamils to emigrate with their wives. A few examples will illustrate what their financial position would be. Between 1876-84, the daily wage rate for a female labourer was 8 cents, and for an adult male labourer working in a first class gang, it was 12 cents. In their first year, as calculated by the Labour Commission of 1890, unless they were above-average labourers, a married couple would earn wages for 20.5 days per month.[69] Thus, they would earn a total of $4.10 (20.5 x 20). From this amount, under the authority of article 59 of Ordinance I of 1876, their employer would deduct $1.00 each to recover the cost of their importation. For rice supplied by the estate, $1.00 each would also be deducted. Their total deductions would be $4.00, and their net wages 10 cents. As an adequate amount of accessories to their rice would cost 80 cents each, as calculated by the Colonial Surgeon, Veitch,[70] or $1.60 for both, they could not afford the necessary commodities by $1.50 a month.

If the husband worked in a second class gang, he and his wife would together earn $3.69 ($2.05 + $1.64) per month in their first year. As deductions for both would be $4.00, their gross wages would be in a deficit of 31 cents.

If they immigrated after 1885, according to article 47 of Ordinance V of 1884, there being no second class gangs, a husband and wife would respectively earn 12 and 8 cents daily during their first year. As they would be earning wages for 20.5 days per month, their total gross wages would amount to $4.10. If they were employed at Prye or Batu Kawan, around 1890, their employer would deduct $1.20 each for rice supplied, and 55 cents towards recovering the cost of importing them, making a total of $3.50. Thus, their total net wages would be 60 cents. As accessories to their rice would cost each of them $1.20, as calculated by the Labour Commission of 1890,[71] they could not afford an adequate amount for the month by $1.80.

If they were employed on estates other than Prye and Batu Kawan, from their gross wages of $4.10, their employer would seek to deduct $1.00 each towards liquidating their original debts, and $1.20 each for rice supplied, making a total of $4.40. Instead of receiving any wages they would together be in a deficit of 30 cents. The likeliest outcome of such economic pressure was that the labourers would eat less than was sufficient to sustain health rather than sink further and further into debt to their employer (even supposing that he would let them do so). It must again be emphasized that the average number of days worked by the husband and wife in these hypothetical cases was not necessarily an actual but rather a statistical average.

The calculations above do not consider the possibility of fines, extortion by the tindals, or expenses of children. Commenting on the financial position of the average married labourer and his wife vis-à-vis the wage rates prescribed by Ordinance V of 1884, Clementi Smith, the Administrator of the Straits Settlements (1884-85), observed that these labourers could not afford to buy sufficient rice to feed themselves even with a "half stomach full of cooked rice and water."[72]

As for the respectable single female, apart from the general reluctance to emigrate abroad, betrothal at an early age frequently prevented her from being recruited.[73] Also it would have been impossible for her to subsist on the prevailing wage rates in the Straits. For instance, as an average labourer, between 1876-84, she would be earning pay for 20.5 days per month at 8 cents per day. Her gross wages would be $1.64. This sum could not sustain deductions for rice supplied and for repaying the cost of importing her – a total of $2.00. If she immigrated after 1885 and was employed at Prye or Batu Kawan, in her first year, she would be earning $1.64 (20.5 x 8). From this amount, her employer would deduct $1.55 ($1.00 + 55), which would leave her with the paltry net of 9 cents to buy supplements to her rice for the entire month. This she could not afford to do by $1.11 ($1.20 - 9).

Exogamous marriages which would have lessened the sexual disproportion in the Indian indentured community seemed to have been non-existent. Cultural and language differences and the social limitations imposed on the labourers by the legal framework of indenture tended to prevent Indians marrying Javanese women.[74] Between Indian men and Malays, instances of marriage were few, and these were between the (Muslim) Malays and the rich trading-class *Chulias* (Tamil Muslims resident in the Straits Settlements).[75] The majority of indentured Indians being Hindus,[76] it was almost impossible for them to marry Malays. Malay men preferred to keep their women to themselves.[77] Most importantly, indentured Indians would have lacked the necessary economic competence either to attract or retain Malay women.

Whilst there were, of course, considerable numbers of non-indentured Indians in Malaya, including a number of females, the possibility of these women becoming wives of indentured labourers under the conditions of poverty and deprivation common in the Province Wellesley estates was remote. In the context of the general shortage of Indian females, the higher wages earned by the free Indian males living and working under better conditions elsewhere gave the latter an overwhelming advantage over the indentured labourers in obtaining wives.

The P.C.M.O. condemned the existing sexual disproportion as the principal cause of the prevalence of venereal diseases among female labourers.[78] In 1879, gonorrhea seemed to be pretty prevalent throughout the Estates.[79] At Batu Kawan, for instance, of the 81 indentured women (among 526 men) employed, 7 carried venereal diseases – 4 with gonorrhea, 2 with syphilis, and 1 with syphilitic bubo.[80] In 1880, between January and June, 18 labourers of both sexes suffering from venereal diseases were sent to the Butterworth Hospital for admission; during the rest of the year, 12 more were sent.[81] During the years 1901-10 when the sexual ratio was 6 males to 1 female, among the female labourers admitted into the Butterworth Hospital, there was an annual average of twenty-three cases of venereal diseases.[82]

Illness Resulting from Injuries
A frequent cause of illness among the labourers was injury sustained while using the *changkol* (or hoe). This implement was foreign to most Indian indentured immigrants.[83] In South India, soil turning and digging was usually done by using the oxen-drawn plough.[84] For agricultural cutting and weeding, the cutlass was usually used.[85] In Malaya, the *changkol* was commonly used in many aspects of agriculture. The Malays had been using this "versatile" instrument at least since the end of the eighteenth century in tin-mining.[86] Among the newly-arrived indentured Indians at Batu Kawan in 1879, for instance, nine out of ten had been weavers previously and had never used the *changkol* before.[87]

The *changkol* the indentured Indians were required to use on the estates was a strong and heavy implement, weighing about five pounds; this included its short handle of only two and a half feet.[88] For it to be used effectively, it must be pulled swiftly towards the body. The P.C.M.O. had himself tried to use one as an experiment and he admitted how easy it was, especially for a novice, to injure himself with one of these "awkward instruments".[89]

Injuries resulting from using *changkols* were most prevalent among newcomers – convincing proof of their inexperience. In 1878, for instance, 463 newly-arrived labourers were treated for diseases among which the most common was ulcer of the lower extremities caused by *changkol* cuts.[90] Some of the wounds did not heal, and "dead tissue began dropping off from living flesh"; the result was blood poisoning and death in a number of cases.[91] The P.C.M.O. ascribed two major reasons for the injuries deteriorating into ulcers. Many of the injured labourers had arrived in a low state of physical health and suffered from poverty of blood and feebleness of circulation.[92] This was mainly due to the effects of the 1876-78 famine that had ravaged Madras presidency.[93] Also, their employers had put them to work immediately after their arrival on the estates, instead of allowing them to overcome the effects of the famine. "This sort of thing," the P.C.M.O. observed, "has been neglected on all the Estates, and many men were at work who were physically unfit and who only hang on to die."[94] Had these immigrants been allowed to recuperate and become acclimatized, he believed, they might have regained their vigour and resistance to disease.[95]

In 1879, the situation was worse. Between January and August, out of about 900 labourers on the Batu Kawan estate, 75 sustained *changkol* injuries which soon afterwards turned into ulcers.[96] These injured labourers had been compelled to work;[97] and in their ignorance of how to take care of their injuries, they had bandaged them up tightly, and by this means aggravated their ulcers.[98] Consequently, there was a "virulent" outbreak of gangrene. Between January and March 1879, no fewer than 14 of these labourers died.[99] During the rest of the year, 5 labourers with gangrene committed suicide, and 57 died as a direct consequence of the disease.[100] Regarding the other injured labourers, when the P.C.M.O. visited the estate hospital, he instructed the manager, Vermont, to wait till the cicatrices had thoroughly hardened before sending them back to work.[101]

Medical Facilities
In a despatch of 1880, Governor Weld represented to the Secretary of State for the Colonies, Lord Kimberley, that those labourers who had been patients in the estate hospitals had received, under the direction of the Colonial Surgeon, all the medical extras and comforts which were necessary in the treatment of their respective ailments.[102] He added: "There is no room to believe that these particular coolies receive any ill … treatment" while hospitalized. He assured the Colonial Office: "It is almost impossible that coolies can be either neglected or ill-treated without the Protector becoming cognizant of it." Weld did not say whether he had actually visited the estate hospitals and had seen the conditions for himself. From the tone of the despatch and from the rather general impressions he gave, it seemed that he did not have first-hand information.

There were two other contemporary accounts of the medical facilities on the estates. One was made in 1879 by the P.C.M.O. who wrote, as he said, from personal knowledge, and the other by an official of the Madras government who visited a number of estate hospitals in 1883. With two notable exceptions, the observations contained in both of these reports not only conflicted materially with the Governor's rather impressionistic account, but showed that the quality of the medical facilities on eight other estates was quite unsatisfactory.

Deserving compliment was the hospital at Batu Kawan estate which the P.C.M.O. described in part thus: "The wards were all clean, there was not the slightest smell perceptible, and there was nothing that the hardest critic could find, in any fairness, fault with. The patients were cheerful, there was not a single complaint amongst them, they were gaining flesh rapidly, and better example of what well directed medical treatment could effect was never witnessed."[103] The quality of the service provided was impressive. The P.C.M.O. added: "The first thing that struck me on entering, was the evident care that was being taken of the sick. They were remarkably well nourished and shewed it; they were almost all receiving extras in the shape of medical comforts, & c., and their appearance convinced you that they had swallowed them. Their sores were well attended to, [and] could not be better so." A great deal of the patients' care was attributed to the hospital staff. The cases were under the direct care of a Straits dresser, a Mr. Boudville, functioning under the direction of the Colonial Surgeon, McClosky, who, in a private capacity, visited the hospital regularly once a week and on other occasions when required.[104] An apothecary from Madras, a Mr. Hamilton, "with due qualifications and excellent testimonials," had joined the staff just before October 1879.

In 1879, the P.C.M.O. described the hospital at Prye estate as a mere makeshift; and he explained that a very good substantial upper storey building was being constructed to house a new hospital which, when completed, would accommodate about fifty patients, and that a kitchen and latrines would adjoin it.[105] Of the existing hospital, he reported:

"The patients seem pretty well attended to, ... the dispensary was clean; Hospital books were kept, a diet book was in use, and altogether one could see throughout that the Manager [James Lamb] looked to everything himself. The supply of medicines was good and ample ... A diet table is in force at the Hospital, which, if attended to by the Apothecary, is an excellent one." [106]

In 1883, when the Madras official paid an unexpected visit to Prye, he described the new hospital thus:

> The estate hospital, which is close to the lines, is a two-storied [sic] building of brick and mortar; on the ground floor of attap, and of wood above. The upper wards, which are large, cool, scrupulously clean, and admirably ventilated, were tenanted by Indian coolies .... Everything here, in the wards, in the dispensary, in the latrines, in the cooking ranges, bore witness of careful and constant supervision ....[107]

In direct contrast to the hospitals at Batu Kawan and Prye, the others presented a miserable picture. Describing the hospital at Krian estate, the P.C.M.O. wrote in 1879: "The Hospital on it is a low building, badly ventilated, ill-suited for the purpose, imperfectly lighted and is occupied by cases coming from the adjoining Estates of Krian, Victoria, and Caledonia. The patients are not separated one from the other as at Batu Kawan." [108] The manager, Morrison, explained that this building was soon to be abandoned and a new hospital on an improved and more sanitary plan and centrally located would be erected in its place.

In 1879, the P.C.M.O. discovered that most of the patients at the Krian estate hospital were "looking very emaciated and wretched. They were by no means receiving the attention they should have done".[109] On enquiry, he found that "men supposed to be in receipt of extras daily had not in fact got them for days together and the want of them was very evident." This he ascribed to the fault of the apothecary, whom he described as a "half qualified man, who evidently had not the interest in the cases he should have had".[110] Despite the critical comments on these aspects of the hospital, the dispensary was found to be an excellent one with a large supply of the best and requisite medicines in stock.

In 1883, the visiting Madras government official found a new hospital at Krian as the manager had said he would erect. Of this, the official wrote: "The hospital, which is, perhaps, one of the largest in the province, struck me as remarkably well suited to insure not only the comfort and well-being of ordinary patients, but their more effectual treatment in the event of epidemics; and the manner in which it is distributed evinces a most commendable care and fore-thought".[111]

The hospital at Golden Grove estate in 1879 was positively objectionable. In the company of the Colonial Surgeon, the P.C.M.O. observed:

> The Hospital here is a bad building, quite unfit for the treatment of the sick who are under the care of a good-for-nothing native [Indian] .... This man knows nothing of the treatment of disease, and some of the sick looked simply miserable. We found that up to 11 a.m., the hour of our visit, they had not even had a cup of conjee to drink, and such a thing as extras was unthought of. Besides, there were cases there which were of far too serious a nature to be treated by an ignorant native and should have been sent to the District Hospital at once, and though, I conclude, the Manager was not aware personally of these facts, yet it is a pity that such apparent neglect should have been permitted. There were twenty under treatment, five of whom were in a pitiable condition; these I picked out and sent to Butterworth Hospital. One of them was so ill that he only lingered three days after reaching there. A case like this had no right to be treated on the Estate at all; he had been ill for months .... The want of proper treatment of cases was more apparent here than on any other [estate hospital] .... The supply of medicines here was not good.[112]

The patients' miserable health may have been in part due to the disregard of the recommended diet. The Colonial Surgeon had prescribed for them chicken, tea, milk, bread, sago, eggs, wine or spirits; but instead, they were served chiefly rice and salt-fish.[113] Beds were not provided at this hospital; the patients had to lie on a raised platform made of split bamboos without mats.[114] There was an entire absence of blankets; the only covering supplied was a piece of thin skirting "very small in extent and universally in a very filthy condition."[115]

Except at Prye, in the estate hospitals, blankets and mosquito curtains were supplied only to fever patients.[116] Many of these were unable to go to the latrines, which were usually situated at a considerable distance away, or to the buckets, which were provided only at night. On the occasion of the Madras official's visit, the patients were found to have used either the blankets or the curtains to clean their persons.[117]

In 1879, the P.C.M.O. reported on the Alma estate hospital thus:

> The Hospital is a miserable building, quite unsuited for the purpose and should be condemned, and a proper one on the plan of our District Hospitals be built. There are six [patients] under treatment, two of whom I had returned to their country as incurable and who would otherwise soon have died. They were under the charge of a Mr. Dickson, who is not strongminded enough and not sufficiently experienced for the post. He was formerly a Dresser under this Government and holds no qualification .... If this estate continues to employ Immigration coolies, the Hospital and management will have to be reformed. The stock of medicines was insufficient.[118]

In 1883, there was no perceptible improvement. The hospital remained a "rather low-built but airy arrangement in attap"; and as the Madras official added, it was inadequate to meet the needs of the patients; there was no separate ward for women; the management was "rather of the masterly inactive kind"; and the apothecary he described as a "dull and surly Madrassee leech".[119] In a concluding comment, the official said: "On the whole ... the general impression left on my mind by my visits to Alma and Golden Grove was not exhilarating".[120]

Mortality

The gradual supplanting of sugar cultivation by the rubber industry, the inadequate supply of Indian indentured labourers, the growing competition from other sugar-producing countries, the diminishing supply of firewood for the sugar-mills, and the mounting criticism of the Indian indenture system in the other colonies combined to bring about the end of Indian indentured recruitment for the Straits in 1910. According to E.S. Montagu, the Under-Secretary of State, India Office, the decision taken by the Colonial Office to discontinue the system was rendered imperative by the high mortality rate among the labourers.[121]

The mortality in the last decade of the indenture system, calculated on the average Indian indentured population in Province Wellesley, was according to the following table:-

TABLE XXI
MORTALITY AMONG INDENTURED INDIANS IN
PROVINCE WELLESLEY, 1901-10

YEAR	AVERAGE POPULATION	DEATHS	PERCENTAGE
1901	4,180	254	6.08
1902	3,082	179	5.80
1903	1,948	88	4.52
1904	1,572	50	3.18
1905	1,782	206	11.56
1906	1,912	86	4.50
1907	1,916	104	5.43
1908	2,639	96	3.64
1909	2,602	119	4.57
1910	2,173	122	5.61
AVE.	2,381	130	5.46

Source: ARII 1910-10.

Between 1904 and 1908 the average annual mortality-rate for the rest of the population in the Straits was 4 per cent, for indentured Indians in Province Wellesley it was 5.6 per cent.[122] In order of importance, the main causes given in the Annual Reports on Indian Immigration were diarrhoea, dysentery, and anemia. Commenting on the high mortality-rate among indentured Indians, the Sanderson Committee observed: "This is not satisfactory, as the majority of the immigrant labourers being in the prime of life, the death-rate among them should be constantly lower, not higher, than that of the general population."[123]

In April 1910, a private member of the House of Commons exposed the high death-rate prevailing amongst the Indian indentured labourers in the Federated Malay States, and called upon the Colonial office for an explanation for the deplorable conditions.[124] This caused a furore in the house, in the midst of which, the Colonial Office made a reply to the effect that the issue was being investigated – an apparent reference to the Sanderson Committee enquiry. Their report was circulated in the House of Commons in mid-June 1910.

During the uproar in Parliament, no specific mention was made regarding the end of indenture in the Straits Settlements. But in his last Annual Report on Indian Immigration, that is, for 1910, the Superintendent of Indian Immigrants wrote: "… at the end of the year the recruiting of statute immigrants was stopped altogether."[125] The indentured Indians on the Province Wellesley estates continued to serve their existing contracts until 1913.[126]

References

1 See Ordinance I of 1876, articles 36-37; Ordinance V of 1884, article 52.
2 PRAD, no. 25, August 1884.
3 *Ibid*.
4 *Ibid*.
5 RLC 1890, pp. 47-48.
6 *Ibid*., Appendix B, Inspection no. 4.
7 RLC 1890, pp. 48.
8 *Ibid*.
9 RLC 1890, Appendix B, Inspection no. 6.
10 RLC 1890, pp. 48.
11 *Ibid*.
12 PRAD, no. 25, August 1884.
13 ARII, 1884, p. 10.
14 PRAD, no. 25, August 1884.
15 ARII, 1900, p. 16.
16 *Ibid*., p. 5.
17 *Ibid*.
18 *SSGG*, 24 October 1879, p. 967.
19 PSSLC, 12 December 1879, p. C340.
20 PRAD, no. 25, August 1884.
21 *Ibid*.
22 *Ibid*.
23 RLC 1890, Appendix B, Inspection no. 3.
24 *SSGG*, 24 October 1879, pp. 959-68; PSSLC, 19 June 1883, pp. C217-20; RLC 1890, Appendix B, Inspection no. 3.
25 RLC 1890, Appendix B, Inspection no. 7.
26 C.O. 384/133. Enclosure in Weld to Kimberley, no. 171, 5 May 1881.
27 *Ibid*.

28 Evidence of Sir Frank Swettenham, in Sanderson, *Report on Emigration*, C5193, p. 404.
29 McNeill and Lal, *Report to the Government of India,* Pt. I, p. 12.
30 C.O. 284/133. Enclosure in Weld to Kimberley, no. 171, 5 May 1881.
31 C.O. 273/254. Enclosure in Sir John Anderson to Earl Crewe, Secretary of State for the Colonies (1908-10), no. 184, 6 May 1909.
32 *Ibid.*
33 *Ibid.*
34 C.O. 273/254. Enclosure in Crewe to Anderson, no. 1396, 4 February 1909.
35 Sanderson, *Report on Emigration*, C5193, pp. 35, 42.
36 Evidence of T.H. Hill, in Sanderson, *Report on Emigration*, C5193, p. 432.
37 *Ibid.*
38 MPP, vol. 275, November 1874.
39 *Report of the 1881 Commission*, p. 2.
40 *Ibid.*
41 MPP, no. 799, 19 August 1882.
42 *Ibid.*
43 *Ibid.*
44 *Report of the 1881 Commission*, p. 2.
45 *Ibid.*
46 ARII, 1882, p. 5.
47 *Ibid.*
48 *Ibid.*
49 *Ibid.*
50 PRAD, no. 25, August 1884.
51 *Ibid.*
52 ARII, 1909, p. 15.
53 ARII, 1900, pp. 5-6.
54 *Ibid.*, p. 5.
55 C.O. 273/256. Enclosure in Sir James Alexander Swettenham, Administrator, S.S., to Chamberlain, no. 6, 2 January 1900.
56 C.O. 273/257. Enclosure in James Swettenham to Chamberlain, no. 161, 4 June 1900.
57 K.L. Gillion, "The Sources of Indian Emigration to Fiji," *Population Studies*, IX, Pt. 2 (November, 1956), 150; C.O. 884/9. (West Indies, 152). Memorandum on East Indian Emigration.
58 ARII, 1879, p. 4.
59 See ARII 1880-1903.
60 C.O. 273/102. Enclosure in Major-General Sir Archibald Edward Anson, Administrator, S.S., to Kimberley, no. 2, 2 January 1880.
61 PHRAD, no. 24, February 1880.
62 *Ibid.*; MPP, no. 658, 14 May 1881.
63 PHRAD, no. 24, February 1880.
64 MPP, no. 17, 13 September 1873.

65 PHRAD, no. 24, February 1880.
66 C.O. 384/133. Enclosure in Weld to Kimberley, no. 171, 5 May 1881.
67 Campen, "Cane Cultivation", pp. 102-5.
68 PDCI, no. 4, July 1908.
69 RLC 1890, p. 56.
70 *SSGG*, 24 October 1879, p. 961.
71 RLC 1890, p. 56.
72 C.O. 273/130. Smith to Derby, no. 541, 29 December 1884.
73 C.O. 273/45. Ord to Kimberley, no. 39, 24 February 1871.
74 Evidence of Dugald Ritchie, in Sanderson, *Report on Emigration*, C5193, p. 432.
75 Evidence of T.H. Hill, in Sanderson, *Report on Emigration*, C5193, p. 432.
76 *Ibid*.
77 Bird, *Golden Chersonese*, p. 31.
78 PSSLC, 12 December 1879, p. C333.
79 *SSGG*, 24 October 1879, p. 959.
80 C.O. 273/105. Enclosure in Weld to Kimberley, no. 259, 7 December 1880.
81 *Ibid*.
82 See Annual Medical Report of the S.S. for 1901-10.
83 *Report of the 1881 Commission*, p. 4.
84 Dharma Kumar, *Land and Caste in South India* (Cambridge, 1965), pp. 26, 108.
85 MPP, Appendix B, November 1880.
86 J.M. Gullick, "Yap Ah Loy," *JMBRAS*, XXIV, Pt. 2 (July, 1951), 9.
87 PSSLC, 12 December 1879, p. C339.
88 Campen, "Cane Cultivation", p. 94.
89 *SSGG*, 24 October 1879, p. 965.
90 C.O. 273/98. Enclosure in Anson to Hicks-Beach, no. 64, 23 February 1879.
91 PSSLC, 12 December 1879, p. C333.
92 C.O. 273/98. Enclosure in Anson to Hicks-Beach, no. 64, 23 February 1879.
93 *Ibid*.
94 PSSLC, 12 December 1879, p. C340.
95 *Ibid*.
96 *SSGG*, 24 October 1879, p. 959.
97 *Ibid*., p. 961.
98 PP, Colonies (General), vol. XIX, 5 July 1879, pp. 333-34.
99 ARII 1879, p. 3.
100 *SSGG*, 24 October 1879, p. 972.
101 *Ibid*., p. 959.
102 C.O. 273/105. Enclosure in Weld to Kimberley, no. 271, 18 December 1880.
103 *SSGG*, 24 October 1879, p. 959.
104 *Ibid*., p. 960.
105 *Ibid*., p. 967.
106 *Ibid*.
107 PRAD, no. 25, August 1884.

108 *SSGG*, 24 October 1879, p. 965.
109 *Ibid*.
110 *Ibid*., p. 966.
111 PRAD, no. 25, August 1884.
112 *SSGG*, 24 October 1879, p. 967.
113 C.O. 273/102. Enclosure in Anson to Kimberley, no. 2, 2 January 1880.
114 *Ibid*.
115 *Ibid*.
116 C.O. 273/102. Enclosure in Anson to Kimberley, no. 85, 15 March 1880.
117 *Ibid*.
118 *SSGG*, 24 October 1879, pp. 966-67.
119 PRAD, no. 25, August 1884.
120 *Ibid*.
121 Great Britain, Parliament, *Parliamentary Debates* (House of Commons), 5th ser., XVI (4 April - 22 April 1910), p. 567.
122 Sanderson, *Report on Emigration*, C5193, p. 35.
123 *Ibid*.
124 Great Britain, Parliament, *Parliamentary Debates* (House of Commons), 5th ser., XVI (4 April - 22 April 1910), p. 567.
125 ARII 1910, p. 5.
126 SSAR 1913, p. 189.

CONCLUSION

> I condemn the present system of indenture in toto. I believe it is the source of all our troubles. It is a standing abuse of law. It makes it possible for a few to induce ignorant coolies to pledge themselves to work below the market value of labour. That abuse, I think, is the main cause of their insufficiency in quantity and quality of our labour supply. The indenture system has given the Straits ... a bad name.
>
> A. Huttenbach[1]

One of the most noteworthy features revealed in this account of indentured labour in Province Wellesley is the notable discrepancy between the intentions of the Indian and the Straits Settlements governments regarding the conditions of labour for the indentured immigrants, and the actual conditions to which most of the labourers were subjected in reality. The expressed intention of the governments throughout the indenture period is amply documented, not only in the enactments and regulations cited throughout this account, but also in communications from the Secretary of State for the Colonies, and in the correspondence and public statements of the Governors and senior administrators concerned.

On the other hand, equally well documented throughout this account is incontrovertible evidence that a large proportion of the indentured labour force were grossly exploited, mistreated and subjected to conditions which were entirely contrary not only to what they had been led to expect, but to the expressed intentions of the legislatures of India and the Straits Settlements, and to the expressed views and assurances of the Governors and their senior staff.

It might be suggested that this is simply a case of cynical posturing, and that neither the intentions expressed in the legislation nor the views of the Governors were sincere in this matter. However, the evidence does not seem to support this facile explanation, and on a number of occasions the Straits government and the Indian government and their officials did take action to enforce, and at times to strengthen, the regulations; and they did on occasion openly criticize and deplore the conduct of the *maistries*, tindals and planters delinquent in these respects. The prosecution and imprisonment of the tindals and of the manager and his overseer of the remote Malakoff estate, inadequate though it may have been in terms of natural justice, clearly had an effect which extended considerably beyond the estate concerned. It also brought some improvement in the general situation far beyond the boundaries of the estate concerned by convincing the estate managers that there were limits to their disregard for their labourers' health and safety, although still falling far short of what had been intended. Similarly, the various Commissions of enquiry, ineffective though they were in the short run, and disappointing as they were to the Governor and the Colonial Office, nevertheless brought about a very gradual improvement.

It must be remembered that the government and administration of the Straits Settlements were inexperienced in these matters throughout most of the time the indenture system was operating. Plantation agriculture on a substantial scale was only just beginning at this time, and did not really get under way until rubber planting began to take over at the very end of the period. Moreover, the indenture system was introduced to encourage an industry that was not at any time particularly strong economically, and which was to die out completely within a few years of the termination of the system. Without this artificial labour system, the combination of capitalist investment, European technology and free market competition was not deemed economically sufficient to attract the labour required to produce sugar on a large scale in Province Wellesley. The indenture system in effect reduced the freedom of the labour market for the immigrants so recruited, and gave the estate management an effective monopoly over their employment, thus reducing the cost of the labour below what it would otherwise have been, or (which is merely the other side of the coin) providing the estates with considerably more labour than they could have afforded to attract on the free market.

This restriction of the rights and options of the indentured labourers, and the enhancement of the power of the employers under (or even despite) the law, provided an opportunity for exploitation and mistreatment on a scale that would not otherwise have existed. What the Governors and their senior administrators did not realize, and had to learn over the years, was just how elaborate and strong the protective mechanism would have to be to make up for this imbalance of opportunity and bargaining power, and how large were the resources necessary to make the mechanism effective.

This lesson was learnt, but not until the end of the indenture period. By this time the economic and political conditions of the Straits Settlements and the Malay States had changed. Sugar planting had become uneconomical and was dying out. Rubber planting was expanding on a very large scale, and was transforming not only the labour market, but the economic base of the whole country. The labour requirements of the plantation sector were growing very rapidly, but in industries which could afford better facilities and considerably higher wages than sugar had ever been able to pay. The special indenture conditions restricting the bargaining position of the labourers were no longer necessary to ensure an adequate supply of labour, and the government was in a position to afford a much improved level of protection and supervision. On this base, working from the bitter lessons of the quite small indenture experience, was built up a large and considerably effective Labour Department, and a system of regulation of employment on estates that produced greatly improved labour conditions for many decades after the indenture system was phased out.

Thus the sorry history of Indian indentured labour in Province Wellesley shows that the reasonably good intentions of the British Governors were largely ineffective, because they were initially dependent on the assumption that the British managers of the sugar estates and their junior staff would be similarly humane and well intentioned, even when it was contrary to their immediate commercial advantage. This was, perhaps, implicit in the British assumption, common at the time, of racial and moral superiority. In a few cases where the managers tried to live up to their moral obligations, the system was free from the worst abuses. However, in the majority of cases, despite the benevolent intentions of the Indian authorities and the Straits governments, and despite the positive efforts of a number of enlightened individual public officials and even some employers, the importation of indentured labour was, after all, designed to produce profit for sugar planters. Hence whenever considerations of humanity, pity or moral or legal duty conflicted with the drive for profitability, it was hardly surprising that the latter repeatedly prevailed. The gradual development of an effective government machinery to deal with this problem, and the allocation to it of the necessary powers and resources, were too slow to benefit many of the indentured labourers, but were of benefit to a much larger Indian labour force in Malaya in a later and happier age.

Reference

1 Businessman of Penang connected with the steamer line engaged in conveying emigrants from South India to the Straits. See evidence of A. Huttenbach, in RCII 1896, p. xxviii.

LIST OF APPENDICES

A. Governors and Administrators of the Straits Settlements, 1867-1910
B. Flow of Indian Indentured Labourers into Province Wellesley, 1872-1910
C. Indian Indentured Immigration into Selected Countries
D. Sugar Estates and their Average Labour Force
E. Labourers under Indenture on the Sugar Estates in Province Wellesley, 1872-1910
F. Summary Statistics on Indian Indenture in the Straits Settlements, 1872-1910
G. Translated Sample of Questions Asked of Emigrants at the Ports of Departure in India
H. Sample Emigration Contract (Copy)
I. Mrs. Sarojini Naidu's Speech Against the Indenture System

APPENDIX A

GOVERNORS AND ADMINISTRATORS OF THE STRAITS SETTLEMENTS, 1867-1911

Colonel HARRY ST GEORGE ORD, R.E., C.B., 1 April 1867 to 3 March 1871.

Lieutenant-Colonel ARCHIBALD EDWARD HARBORD ANSON, R.A., Administrator, 4 March 1871 to 22 March 1872.

Major-General Sir HARRY ST GEORGE ORD, C.B. (G.C.M.G.), 23 March 1872 to 2 November 1873.

Lieutenant-Colonel ARCHIBALD EDWARD HARBORD ANSON, R.A., Administrator, 3 November 1873 to 4 November 1873.

Colonel Sir ANDREW CLARKE, R.E., K.C.M.G., C.B., 4 November 1873 to 10 May 1875.

Colonel Sir WILLIAM FRANCIS DRUMMOND JERVOIS, R.E., K.C.M.G., C.B. (Major-General, G.C.M.G.), 10 May 1875 to 3 April 1877.

Colonel ARCHIBALD EDWARD HARBORD ANSON, R.A., C.M.G., Administrator, 3 April 1877 to 29 October 1877.

Sir WILLIAM CLEAVER FRANCIS ROBINSON, K.C.M.G., 29 October 1877 to 10 February 1879.

Major-General Sir ARCHIBALD EDWARD HARBORD ANSON, R.A., K.C.M.G., Administrator, 10 February 1879 to 6 May 1880.

FREDERICK ALOYSIUS WELD, C.M.G., Administrator, 6 May 1880 to 28 March 1884.

CECIL CLEMENTI SMITH, C.M.G., Administrator, 29 March 1884 to 12 November 1885.

Sir FREDERICK ALOYSIUS WELD, K.C.M.G., 13 November 1885 to 13 May 1887.

JOHN FREDERICK DICKSON, C.M.G., Administrator, 14 May 1887 to 19 June 1887.

Sir FREDERICK ALOYSIUS WELD, G.C.M.G., 20 June 1887 to 17 October 1887.

Sir CECIL CLEMENTI SMITH, K.C.M.G., 20 October 1887 to 8 April 1890.

Sir JOHN FREDERICK DICKSON, K.C.M.G., Administrator, 8 April 1890 to 11 November 1890.

Sir CECIL CLEMENTI SMITH, K.C.M.G. (G.C.M.G.), 12 November 1890 to 30 August 1893.

WILLIAM EDWARD MAXWELL, C.M.G. (K.C.M.G.), Administrator, 30 August 1893 to 31 January 1894.

Lieutenant-Colonel Sir CHARLES BULLEN HUGH MITCHELL, K.C.M.G. (G.C.M.G.), 1 February 1894 to 27 March 1898.

Sir JAMES ALEXANDER SWETTENHAM, K.C.M.G., Administrator, 28 March 1898 to 29 December 1898.

Lieutenant-Colonel Sir CHARLES BULLEN HUGH MITCHELL, G.C.M.G., 30 December 1898 to 7 December 1899.

Sir JAMES ALEXANDER SWETTENHAM, K.C.M.G., Administrator, 8 December 1899 to 18 February 1901.

Sir FRANK ATHELSTANE SWETTENHAM, K.C.M.G., 26 September 1901 to 12 October 1903.

WILLIAM THOMAS TAYLOR, C.M.G., Administrator, 13 October 1903 to 15 April 1904.

Sir JOHN ANDERSON, K.C.M.G., 15 April 1904 to 1 March 1906.

Sir WILLIAM TAYLOR, K.C.M.G., Administrator, 2 March 1906.

Sir JOHN ANDERSON, K.C.M.G., 3 March 1906 to 1911.

Source: Wright and Cartwright, *Impressions*, p. 120.

APPENDIX B

FLOW OF INDIAN INDENTURED LABOURERS INTO PROVINCE WELLESLEY, 1872-1910

YEAR	No.	YEAR	No.
1872	N/A	1891	2,644
1873	"	1892	1,192
1874	"	1893	1,189
1875	"	1894	1,053
1876	"	1895	719
1877	"	1896	1,784
1878	1,175	1897	1,766
1879	853	1898	1,792
1880	1,191	1899	1,347
1881	879	1900	2,160
1882	1,452	1901	1,023
1883	1,448	1902	830
1884	1,539	1903	364
1885	1,025	1904	784
1886	1,915	1905	1,087
1887	2,666	1906	857
1888	2,567	1907	1,397
1889	1,965	1908	1,229
1890	1,529	1909	1,117
		1910	1,432

N/A = No reliable figures available.
Source: ARII 1879-1910.

APPENDIX C

INDIAN INDENTURED IMMIGRATION INTO SELECTED COUNTRIES[1]

Country	Dates	Number	Indian Pop. in 1969
Mauritius	1834-1910	453,063	520,000
British Guiana	1838-1916	238,909	357,000
Trinidad	1845-1916	143,939	360,000
Jamaica	1845-1915	36,412	27,951
Grenada	1856-1885	3,200	9,500
St. Lucia	1858-1895	4,350	N/A
Natal	1860-1911	152,184	614,000
St. Kitts	1860-1861	337	N/A
St. Vincent	1861-1880	2,472	3,703
Reunion	1861-1883	26,507	N/A
Surinam	1873-1916	34,000	101,715
Fiji	1879-1916	60,000	241,000
Seychelles	1899-1916	6,319	N/A

1 Sources: G.W. Roberts and J. Byrne, "Summary Statistics on Indenture and Associated Migration Affecting the West Indies, 1834-1948"; Geoghegan, *Coolie Emigration*; PP. vol. LVII (1900), pp. 467-68; Hugh Tinker, "Indians Abroad: Emigration, Restriction and Rejection" in Michael Twaddle (ed.), *Expulsion of a Minority: Essays on Ugandan Asians*, (London, 1975), p. 15.

APPENDIX D

SUGAR ESTATES AND THEIR AVERAGE LABOUR FORCE

1	Alma	....	154
2	Bertam	....	54
3	Byram	....	671
4	Batu Kawan	....	1,290
5	Caledonia	....	1,505
6	Golden Grove	....	470
7	Malakoff	....	639
8	Prye	....	1,055
9	Tassek	....	298
10	Krian	....	226
11	Val D'or	....	229
12	Victoria	....	251

APPENDIX E

LABOURERS UNDER INDENTURE ON THE SUGAR ESTATES IN PROVINCE WELLESLEY, 1872-1910

Year	Number	Year	Number
1872	N/A	1892	1,628
1873	"	1893	2,106
1874	"	1894	3,209
1875	"	1895	2,615
1876	"	1896	3,160
1877	"	1897	3,751
1878	2,824	1898	4,178
1879	1,655	1899	1,742
1880	2,221	1900	4,354
1881	2,314	1901	3,537
1882	2,921	1902	2,446
1883	3,130	1903	1,636
1884	3,582	1904	1,652
1885	3,265	1905	1,854
1886	N/A	1906	1,992
1887	4,584	1907	2,410
1888	5,006	1908	2,625
1889	4,118	1909	2,544
1890	3,878	1910	2,173
1891	3,443		

APPENDIX F

SUMMARY STATISTICS ON INDIAN INDENTURE IN THE STRAITS SETTLEMENTS, 1872 - 1910

	Population	Births	Deaths	Deserters	Deserters Arrested
1872	N/A	N/A	N/A	N/A	N/A
1873	"	"	"	"	"
1874	"	"	"	"	"
1875	"	"	"	"	"
1876	"	"	"	"	"
1877	"	"	"	"	"
1878	"	"	"	"	"
1879	3,677	"	173	186	"
1880	2,801	"	65	319	174
1881	3,366	"	121	415	252
1882	3,733	"	104	352	164
1883	4,369	"	92	567	213
1884	4,655	"	84	586	275
1885	4,636	"	70	543	175
1886	N/A	"	N/A	N/A	N/A
1887	"	"	"	"	"
1888	7,234	115	210	1,944	832
1889	N/A	N/A	N/A	N/A	N/A
1890	5,615	118	180	1,017	486
1891	N/A	N/A	N/A	N/A	N/A
1892	"	"	"	"	"
1893	5,382	160	134	760	311
1894	4,953	N/A	134	621	304
1895	4,146	115	92	489	243
1896	4,572	140	98	409	159
1897	5,103	164	242	784	379
1898	5,534	168	172	765	326
1899	5,571	191	158	664	269
1900	4,409	207	276	728	335
1901	5,344	230	254	474	197
1902	4,947	252	179	343	130
1903	1,948	259	88	N/A	N/A
1904	2,884	195	50	238	80
1905	2,903	216	206	305	150
1906	1,912	172	86	246	50
1907	3,520	88	104	231	46
1908	3,697	110	96	281	102
1909	3,740	131	119	326	64
1910	3,720	160	122	407	101

Source: ARII

APPENDIX G

TRANSLATED SAMPLE OF QUESTIONS ASKED OF EMIGRANTS AT THE PORTS OF DEPARTURE IN INDIA

1. "Do you know to what country you are about to emigrate?"

2. "By what conveyance are you to be sent there?"

3. "How long will you be on board ship?"

4. "What sort of food are you to be supplied with during the voyage?"

5. "Are you aware that anyone who objects to eat rice and doll [*sic*] on board ship must not go, because uncooked food, such as gram and *choorah*, is prohibited from being served out, except in stormy weather when it is impossible to cook?"

6. "Are you aware that there are no more than two cooking places on board ship, one for Hindus, the other for Muslims, and that you must eat all your food cooked in these cabooses; also, that anyone found with opium or ganga or other intoxicating drugs in his possession will be severely punished?"

APPENDIX H

SAMPLE EMIGRATION CONTRACT (COPY)

This contract made under the Straits Settlements Act, 1877, at Negapatam, the 5th day of March 1880, between Meenachee an emigrant labourer, hereafter called the emigrant of the one part, and Recruiter Thurmalingum duly authorized by the Emigration Agent of the Straits Settlements Government on behalf of A.G. Morrison, Esq., of Penang, Landed Proprietors, hereinafter called the employers of the other part. Whereas the said employers have advanced all necessary funds for the passage and other expenses of the said emigrant from India to Penang upon the promise of the said emigrant that upon arrival at Penang he will work for the said employers, their successors, representatives or assigns as a labourer working extra hours and performing night work whenever called upon to do so, and doing any kind of work customary upon the Estates, either in Penang or Province Wellesley of the said employers at the daily wages hereinafter mentioned.

Now this agreement witnesseth, that the said emigrant doth hereby, in consideration of the sums advanced as aforesaid by the said employers, and of the agreement by them hereinafter contained, agree with the said employers that the said emigrant will remain and labour as above specified on the Estates in Penang or Province Wellesley of the said employers, their successors, representatives or assigns as the said employers, their successors, representatives or assigns may from time to time direct for a period of three years from the date hereof, subject to the several provisions of the Straits Settlements Ordinance No. 1 of 1876, in that behalf made and enacted, and will repay to the said employers the sums advanced to him by the employers. And this contract further witnesseth, that the said employers do hereby for themselves, their successors, representatives and assigns, in consideration of the said agreement by the said emigrant, agree with the said emigrant that they the said employers will employ the said emigrant as a labourer for the period aforesaid, and will pay or cause to be paid to the said emigrant as wages for such labour at the rate of eight cents of a dollar for each day's work of ten hours, and two cents extra per day as is customary if the labourer is required to work more than ten hours and up to twelve hours a day any time; for the first two years and for the third year ten cents of a dollar per day of ten hours payable monthly as directed by the Straits Settlements Ordinance No. 1 of 1876, and will not deduct from the said wages in payment of advances made to the said emigrant more than the sum of one dollar each and every month, and will supply or cause to be supplied to the said emigrant, rice and all such other matters as are required to be supplied, according to the rules prescribed under the said Ordinance at such rates are by the said Ordinance or Rules directed, deducting the price of articles supplied from the wages of the said emigrant.

And the said employers hereby bind themselves, their successors, representatives and assigns generally to fulfill all the duties imposed on them by the said Ordinance.

Mark
MEENACHEE.
(Signed)

Source: MPP, no. 909, 16 June 1880.

APPENDIX I

MRS. SAROJINI NAIDU'S SPEECH AGAINST THE INDENTURE SYSTEM

Citizens of India, I think we represent almost every province, here to-night. The words that you have heard from the previous speakers must have made your hearts bleed. Let the blood of your hearts blot out the shame that your women have suffered abroad. The words that you have heard to-night must have kindled within you a raging fire. Men of India, let that be the funeral pyre of the indenture system. (Applause.) Words from me to-night. No, tears from me to-night. Because I am a woman, and though you may feel the dishonour that is offered to your mothers and sisters, I feel the dishonour offered to me in the dishonour to my sex. I have travelled far, gentlemen, to come to you to-night, only to raise my voice, not for the men, but for women, for those women whose proudest memory is that Sita would not stand the challenge to her honour, but called upon mother earth to avenge her and the earth opened up to avenge her. I come to speak on behalf of those women, whose proudest memory lies in this, that Padmini of Cluttoor preferred the funeral pyre to dishonour. I come to speak on behalf of those women, who like Savitri, have followed their men to the gates of death and have won them back by their indomitable love. I come to speak to you in the name of one woman who has summed up in her frail body all the physical sufferings the women of India have endured abroad — the broken body, the shattered health, of Mrs. Gandhi (Applause.) I ask you in the name of that murdered sister, that sister about whom Mr. Andrews told us, who found in death the only deliverance from dishonour. I ask you in the name of those two brothers, who preferred to save the honour of their family and their religion, in the blood of their sister, rather than let her chastity be polluted.

Do you think you who are clamouring for self-government to-day — do you think you are patriotic, if you cannot stop the agony that is sending its echoes to you night and day? Self-Government — for whom? And for what? For a dishonoured nation that does not know how to avenge the insult offered to its mothers? Self-Government — for whom? For men whose hands are folded while their women shriek, men whose voices are silent even in the face of the most terrible insult that can be offered to man? Wealth. What is wealth to us? Power. What is power to us? Glory. What is glory to us? How shall the wealth and power and glory of a nation be founded save on the immutable honour of its womanhood? Are we going to leave to posterity a wealth got with dishonour? Are we going to leave it to the unborn generations a sorrow and shame that we have not been able to wipe out? Men of India, rather the hour of doom struck than that after to-night you should live to say: 'We heard the cries and yet we were deaf. We heard the call for help, but we had not the courage. We felt in our hearts the challenge to our national honour and yet we were cowards.' If, after to-night, men of India, if after to-night I say, it is possible for the most selfish interest to use the humanity of

India to enrich, almost as a manure, the sugar plantations of the Colonies, if it is possible, I say, to let the forces of this greatest evil on earth daunt you, you are not only unworthy and degenerate sons of our mothers, whose name stood for glory in the past, but you are the murderers of national honour and national progress. You discount the future, nay, you slay the future. There can be no future for a nation when present men and women do not know how to avenge their dishonour.

I have come to-day to speak, but I think the fire within me is so strong that it bids me be silent, because words are so weak. I feel within me to-day the anguish that has been from year to year the lot of those women who had better be dead. I feel within me the shame, the inexpressible, the immeasurable, the inalienable shame, gentlemen, that has brought the curse of the indenture system to our women. And who is responsible, men of India, for this, that our men should have to go abroad for bread? Why is not your patriotism sufficient to have resources enough to give bread to them who go to seek bread abroad? Why is not your patriotism so vigilant, so strong, and so all comprehensive, that you are able to guard the ignorance of them, that go abroad, not merely to death — for death, gentlemen is tolerable — but to dishonour? Ours has been the shame, because ours has always been the responsibility. But we were asleep or we were dreaming of academic powers, we were discussing from platforms the possibilities in the future, we were not awake to the degradation of the present. Therefore the shame is ours in a measure that can never be wholly wiped out either by our tears or by our blood. So, to-night, if our patriotism means more than the curiosity to come by thousands, to hear a few speakers, if it means more than the hysteria of the moment, if it means more than the impulse to pity, then I charge you, men of India — I do not appeal to you, I lay upon you this trust, I entrust you with this burden, on behalf of those suffering women. I entrust you with this mission, to wipe out the dishonour that lies on our name. It is we who suffer, gentlemen, not those degraded people — it is the honour of the women in your homes who cannot show their faces. That mark of crime is written here on us, because we have no destiny apart from our sisters. Our honour is indivisible, so must be our dishonour. That is, our destiny is one, and whether for glory or for shame we share alike. And we women who give our sons to the country, we cannot endure our sons to think that their mothers belong to a generation part of whose motherhood was dishonoured.

Have I not said enough to stir your blood? Have I not said enough to kindle within you such a conflagration that must not merely annihilate the wrongs of the indenture system, but recreate in the crucible a new stirring, a new purpose, a new unity of self-respect, that will not sleep, that will not rest, that will be a sword to avenge, that will be a fire to burn. It will be the trumpet call to liberty that only comes when a nation grows bitter, that only comes when a nation says, 'the health within me has become rotten.' It is the bitterness that comes when we feel that we have let ourselves sleep.

Is national righteousness possible, when the chastity of your womanhood is assailed? Is national righteousness possible, till every man amongst you becomes a soldier of the cause, a devotee, a fanatic, everything and anything which means destruction of the wrong and triumph of the right? Gentlemen, it is a stormy sea that we have to cross, a storm-tossed sea in a crowded boat that may or may not stand the burden of our sorrow. But like Khusru of old shall we not say — even when the night is dark, when the waves are high, when there is a rush in the boat, when there is no pilot with us — shall we not say —

> Nakhuda dar kashteeay magar na bashad gu ma bash,
> Ma khuda dareem ma ra nakhuda, darkar nest.

"What though there be no pilot to our boat? Go, tell him, we need him not. God is with us, and we need no pilot."

Source: C.F. Andrews and W.W. Pearson, *Indian Indentured Labour in Fiji* (Calcutta, 1918), pp. 87-88.

SELECT BIBIOGRAPHY

A. PRIMARY SOURCES

i. Manuscript

C.O. 273 Series: Original Correspondence between the Governors, S.S., and the Colonial Office. (London).
C.O. 384//133 Series. Original (Emigration) Correspondence between the Governors, S.S., and the Colonial Office. (London).
C.O. 386/113. Colonial Office Letter Books. (London).

ii. Printed Material

Annual Report of the South Indian Labour Fund Board, 1959-64. (Kuala Lumpur).
British Guiana. An Indian Colony. Homes for Indians in South America. (Allahabad, 1919).
C.O. 884/9. (West Indies, 152). *Memorandum on East Indian Immigration.* (London).
C.O. 885/1. (West Indies, 21). *Memorandum on the Hill Coolie Papers*, 1839. (London).
General Report on the Administration of the Presidency of Madras, 1901-10 (London).
Government of India Acts: XXV of 1859; XIII of 1864; VII of 1871; XIV of 1872; V of 1877. (Canberra; Singapore).
Government of India: Emigration Proceedings, 1871-1910. (London).
Government of Madras: *Annual Report on Emigration and Immigration*, 1881-1910. (London).
Government of Madras: (Emigration) Proceedings in the Public Department, 1870-1910. (London).
Government of Madras: (Emigration) Proceedings in the Home, Revenue and Agriculture Department, 1870-1910. (London).
Government of Madras: (Emigration) Proceedings in the Revenue and Agriculture Department, 1870-1910. (London).
Government of Madras: (Emigration) Proceedings in the Department of Agriculture, Revenue and Commerce, 1871-1910. (London).
Government of Madras: (Emigration) Proceedings in the Department of Commerce and Industry, 1885-1910. (London).
Great Britain. Parliament. *Hansard's Parliamentary Debates*, House of Commons and House of Lords, 1873-75, 1909. (London).
Imperial Gazeteer of India. Provincial Series – Madras, Salem, Tanjore, 1880-1910 (various years). (London).
Indian Immigration Committee: Minutes of Meetings, 1907-10. (Kuala Lumpur).

Memorandum on the Census of British India, 1871-72. (London).
Moral and Material Progress and Condition of India during the Year 1898-99. Vol. LVII. (London).
Parliamentary Papers, Colonies (General), 1867-1910. (Canberra).
Report of the Commissioners Appointed for the Purpose of Enquiring into the Cases of Alleged Ill-Treatment of Indian Immigrants Employed on Certain Estates in Province Wellesley. (Singapore, 1881).
Report of the Commissioners Appointed to Enquire into the Question of Indian Immigration. (Singapore, 1896).
Report of the Commissioners Appointed to Enquire into the State of Labour in the Straits Settlements and Protected Native States. (Singapore, 1891).
Report of the Commissioners Appointed to Enquire into the Treatment of Immigrants in British Guiana. (London, 1871).
Review of the Madras Famine, 1876-78. (London, 1881).
Straits Settlements Annual Report, 1913. (Singapore).
Straits Settlements: Annual Report on Indian Immigration, 1879-1910. (Singapore).
Straits Settlements Blue Book, 1867-1910 (various years). (Singapore).
Straits Settlements: Ordinance I of 1876; V of 1884. (Singapore).
Straits Settlements: Proceedings of the Legislative Council, (1867-1910).
Straits Settlements Government Gazette, 1867-1910. (Singapore).

iii.   **Newspapers**

British Emancipator, The (London), 1839.
Friend of India, The (Madras), 1870-73.
Madras Standard, The (Madras), 1873-74.
Penang Gazette, The (Penang), 1870-1910.
Penang Guardian, The (Penang), 1870-73.
Singapore Daily Times, The (Singapore), 1841-1910 (various years).
Singapore Free Press, The (Singapore), 1835-1910 (various years).
Straits Times, The (Singapore), 1870-1910 (various years).
Tanjore Gazette, The (Tanjore), 1870.
The Times, (London), 1838-39.
Times of India, The (Madras), 1900.

B. **SECONDARY SOURCES**

i.   **Books (Contemporary)**

Anson, A.E.H. *About Others and Myself.* London, 1920.
A.W.S. *Rubber Estate Values.* Singapore, 1910.
Beaumont, Joseph. *The New Slavery: An Account of the Indian and Chinese Immigrants in British Guiana.* London, 1871.
Bird, Isabella L. *The Golden Chersonese and the Way Thither.* London, 1883.

Braddell, T. *Singapore and the Straits Settlements Described*. Penang, 1858.
Braddell, T. *Statistics of the British Possessions in the Straits of Malacca*. Penang, 1861.
Brett, W.N. *Indian Missions in Guiana*. London, 1851.
Bronkhurst, H.V.P. *The Colony of British Guiana and Its Labouring Population*. London, 1883.
Cameron, John. *Our Tropical Possessions in Malayan India*. 2nd ed. Kuala Lumpur, 1965.
Comins, D.W.D. *Note on Emigration from India to British Guiana in 1891*. Calcutta, 1893.
Comins, D.W.D. *Note on Emigration from the East Indies to Trinidad*. Calcutta, 1893.
Crawfurd, J. *History of the Indian Archipelago*. Vol. I. London, 1820.
Crawfurd, J. *Journal of an Embassy to the Courts of Siam and Indo-China*. London, 1828.
Dalton, Henry G. *History of British Guiana*. Vol. I. London, 1855.
Davidson, G.F. *Trade and Travel in the Far East*. London, 1846.
Doyle, P. *Tin Mining in Larut*. London, 1879.
Earl, G.W. *The Eastern Seas*. London, 1837.
Earl, G.W. *Topography and Itinerary of Province Wellesley*. Penang, 1861.
Gait, E.A. *Census of India, 1911*. Vol. I. Calcutta, 1913.
Garnham, Florence E. *A Report on the Social and Moral Conditions of Indians in Fiji*. Sydney, 1918.
Geerligs, H.C. Prinsen. *The World's Cane Sugar Industry: Past and Present*. Manchester, 1912.
Geoghegan, John. *Note on Emigration from India*. Calcutta, 1873.
Hamilton, Walter. *The East India Gazeteer*. London, 1815.
Harris, John H. *Coolie Labour in the British Crown Colonies and Protectorates*. London, 1910.
Holland, H.E. *Indentured Labour: Is it Slavery?* London, N.D.
Im Thurn, Everard F. *Among the Indians of Guiana*. London, 1883.
Innes, J.R. *Report on the Census of the Straits Settlements, 1901*. Singapore, 1901.
Jenkins, Edward John. *The Coolie, his Rights and Wrongs*, Vol. I. London, 1871.
Leith, G. *A Short Account of the Settlement, Produce and Commerce of Prince of Wales Island in the Straits*. London, 1804.
Lovat, Alice. *The Life of Sir Frederick Weld*. London, 1914.
Low, J. *A Dissertation on the Soil and Agriculture of the British Settlement of Penang or Prince of Wales Island in the Straits of Malacca; including Province Wellesley on the Malayan Peninsula. With Brief References to the Settlements of Singapore and Malacca, and Accompanied by Incidental Observations on various Subjects of Local Interest in the Straits*. 2nd ed. Singapore, 1972.
McNeill, J, and Lal, Chimman. *Report to the Government of India on the Conditions of Indian Immigrants in Four British Colonies and Surinam*. 2 Parts. London, 1915.

Marjoribanks, N.E., and Marakkayar, A.T. *Report on Indian Labour Emigration to Ceylon and Malaya.* Madras, 1917.
Merewether, E.M. *Report on the Census of the Straits Settlements, 1891.* Singapore, 1892.
Moor, J.H. *Notices of the Indian Archipelago and Adjacent Countries.* Singapore, 1837.
Newbold, T.J. *Political and Statistical Account of the British Settlements in the Straits of Malacca.* 2 vols. London, 1839.
Parr, C.W.C. *Report of the Commission Appointed to Enquire into the Conditions of Indentured Labour in the Federated Malay States.* Kuala Lumpur, 1910.
Premium, Barton. *Eight Years in British Guiana.* London, 1848.
Risley, H. H., and Gait, E.A. *Census of India, 1901.* Vol. I. Calcutta, 1903.
Scoble, John. *Hill Coolies: A Brief Exposure of the Deplorable Conditions of the Hill Coolies in British Guiana and Mauritius.* London, 1839.
Thoburn, J.M. *India and Malaysia.* New York, 1893.
Thomson, J. *The Straits of Malacca, Indo-China, and China.* London, 1875.
Tupper, C.L. *Note on Indian Emigration during the Year 1878-79.* Simla, 1879.
Vaughan, J.D. *The Manners and Customs of the Chinese of the Straits Settlements.* Kuala Lumpur, 1979.
Vermont, J.M. *Immigration from India to the Straits Settlements.* London, 1888.
Vetch, R.H. ed. *The Life of General Sir Andrew Clarke.* London, 1905.
"West Indian". *The Coolie in Demerara.* London, 1871.
Wray, Leonard. *The Practical Sugar Planter.* London, 1848.
Wright, Arnold, and Cartwright, H.A. eds. *Twentieth Century Impressions of British Malaya.* London, 1908.
Wright, Arnold, and Reid, Thomas H. *The Malay Peninsula.* London, 1912.

ii. **Books (Modern)**

Adamson, Alan H. *Sugar Without Slaves: The Political Economy of British Guiana, 1838-1904.* New Haven, 1972.
Ali, Ahmed. *Girmit: The Indenture Experience in Fiji.* Suva, 1979.
Andrews, C.F., and Pearson, W.W. *Indian Indentured Labour in Fiji.* Calcutta, 1918.
Arasaratnam, S. *Ceylon.* New Jersey, 1964.
Arasaratnam, S. *Indians in Malaysia and Singapore.* 2nd ed. Kuala Lumpur, 1979.
Ardizzone, Michael. *A Nation is Born.* London, 1946.
Beachey, R.W. *The British West Indies Sugar Industry in the Late 19th Century.* Oxford, 1957.
Bell, Kenneth N, and Morrell, W.P. *Select Documents on British Colonial Policy, 1830-1860.* Oxford, 1928.
Bolt, Christine. *The Anti-Slavery Movement and Reconstruction.* London, 1969.
Buckley, C.B. *An Anecdotal History of Old Times in Singapore.* Vol. I. Kuala Lumpur, 1965.
Burkill, I.H. *A Dictionary of the Economic Products of the Malay Peninsula.* Vol. 2. London, 1935.

Burn, W.L. *The British West Indies.* London, 1951.
Burton, J.W. *The Fiji of To-day,* London, 1910.
Campbell, P.C. *Chinese Coolie Emigration to Countries Within the British Empire.* London, 1923.
Chakravarti, N.R. *The Indian Minority in Burma: The Rise and Decline of an Immigrant Community.* London, 1971.
Clodd, H.P. *Malaya's First British Pioneer: The Life of Francis Light.* London, 1948.
Cowan, C.D. *Nineteenth Century Malaya: The Origins of British Political Control.* London, 1961.
Cumpston, I.M. *Indians Overseas in British Territories. 1834-1854.* London, 1969.
Deerr, Noel. *The History of Sugar.* 2 vols. London, 1949-50.
Devahuti, D. *India and Ancient Malaya*, Singapore, 1965.
Drabble, J.H. *Rubber in Malaya, 1876-1922*, Kuala Lumpur, 1973.
"Emigrant". *Indian Emigration.* London, 1924.
Gangulee, N. *Indians in the Empire Overseas: A Survey.* London, 1947.
Ganguli, Dwarkanath. *Slavery in British Dominion.* Calcutta, 1972.
German, R.L. Compiler. *Handbook to British Malaya.* London, 1937.
Gillion, K.L. *Fiji's Indian Migrants: A History to the End of Indenture in 1920.* Melbourne, 1962.
Gullick, J.M. *Indigenous Political Systems of Western Malaya.* London, 1958.
Hall, D.G.E. *A History of South-East Asia.* London, 1955.
Hazareesingh, K. *A History of Indians in Mauritius.* Phoenix, 1950.
Henderson, John W; Barth, Helen A; Heimann, Judith M; Moeller, Philip W; Soriano, Francisco S; and Weaver, John O. *Area Handbook for Malaysia.* Washington, 1970.
Heussler, Robert. *British Rule in Malaya: The Malayan Civil Service and Its Predecessors, 1867-1942.* Oxford, 1981.
Hitchins, Fred H. *The Colonial Land and Emigration Commission.* Philadelphia, 1931.
Jackson, J.C. *Planters and Speculators: Chinese and European Agriculture Enterprise in Malaya.* Kuala Lumpur, 1968.
Jackson, R.N. *Immigrant Labour and the Development of Malaya.* Kuala Lumpur, 1961.
Jain, Ravindra K. *South Indians on the Plantation Frontier in Malaya.* New Haven, 1970.
Jenks, J.W. *Report on Certain Economic Questions in the English and Dutch Colonies in the Orient.* Washington, 1920.
Kloosterboer, W. *Involuntary Labour Since the Abolition of Slavery*, London, 1960.
Knaplund, Paul. *The British Empire, 1815-1939.* London, 1942.
Kondapi C. *Indians Overseas, 1838-1949.* Bombay, 1951.
Kumar, Dharma. *Land and Caste in South India.* Cambridge, 1965.
Laurence, K.O. *Immigration into the West Indies in the Nineteenth Century.* Kingston, 1971.
Makepeace, W; Brooke, G.E.; and Braddell, R. *One Hundred Years of Singapore.* 2 vols. London, 1921.

Malefijt, Annemarie de Waal. *The Javanese of Surinam*. Assen, Netherlands, 1963.
Martin, Robert M. *History of the Colonies of the British Empire*. London, reprinted ed., 1967.
Mathieson, William Law. *British Slave Emancipation, 1838-1849*. London, 1967.
Mellor, George R. *British Imperial Trusteeship, 1783-1850*. London, 1951.
M.N. Menezes. *British Policy Towards the Amerindians in British Guiana, 1803-1873*. Oxford, 1977.
M.N. Menezes. *Scenes from the History of the Portuguese in Guyana*. London, 1986.
Merivale, Herman. *Lectures on Colonization and Colonies*. London. 1928.
Mills, L.A. *British Malaya, 1824-67*. Kuala Lumpur, 1966.
Mookherji, S.B. *The Indenture System in Mauritius, 1837-1915*. Calcutta, 1962.
Moorhead, F.J. *A History of Malaya*. Kuala Lumpur, 1963.
Nanjundan, S. *Indians in Malayan Economy*. New Delhi, 1950.
Nath, Dwarka. *A History of Indians in British Guiana*. London, 1950.
Neelakandha Aiyer, K.A. *Indian Problems in Malaya*. Kuala Lumpur, 1938.
Netto, George. *Indians in Malaya: Historical Facts and Figures*. Singapore, 1961.
Newell, William H. *Treacherous River: A Study of Rural Chinese in North Malaya*. Singapore, 1962.
North-Coombes, A. *The Evolution of Sugar Cane Culture in Mauritius*. Port Louis, 1937.
Ooi, Jin-Bee. *Land, People and Economy in Malaya*. London, 1963.
Parkinson, C.N. *British Intervention in Malaya, 1867-77*. Singapore, 1960.
Parmer, J. Norman. *Colonial Labour Policy and Administration*. New York, 1960.
Patwardhan, R.P., and Ambekar, D.V., ed. *Speeches and Writings of Gopal Krishna Gokhale*. Vol. I. London, 1962.
Prasad, Shiu. *Indian Indentured Workers in Fiji*. Suva, 1975.
Purcell, Victor. *The Chinese in Malaya*. Kuala Lumpur, 1967.
Rajkumar, N.V. *Indians Outside India*. New Delhi, 1951.
Ruhoman, Peter. *Centenary History of the East Indians in British Guiana, 1838-1938*. Georgetown, 1939.
Saha, Panchanan. *Emigration of Indian Labour, 1834-1900*. New Delhi, 1970.
Sandhu, K.S. *Indians in Malaya. Some Aspects of their Immigration and Settlement (1786-1957)*. Cambridge, 1969.
Song Ong Siang, *One Hundred Years of the Chinese in Singapore,* Singapore, 1967.
Swettenham, F.A. *An Account of the Origin and Progress of British Influence in Malaya*. Revised ed. London, 1948.
Tinker, Hugh. *A New System of Slavery: The Export of Indian Labourers Overseas, 1830-1920*. London, 1974.
Turnbull, C.M. *The Straits Settlements, 1826-67*. London, 1972.
Turnbull, C.M. *A History of Singapore, 1819-1975*. Kuala Lumpur, 1977.
Williams, Eric. *Capitalism and Slavery*. London, 1944.
Wood, Donald. *Trinidad in Transition: The Years after Slavery*. London, 1968.
Young, Allan. *Some Milestones in Village History, 1839-1956*. Georgetown, 1957.

iii. **Articles and Periodicals**

Alatas, Syed Hussain. "Occupational Prestige Amongst the Malays in Malaysia." *JMBRAS*, XLI, Pt. 1 (July, 1968), 146-56.

Andrews, C.F. "India's Emigration Problem." *Foreign Affairs*, VIII, No. 3 (April, 1930), 430-41.

Balestier, J. "View of the State of Agriculture in the British Possessions in the Straits of Malacca." *JIA*, II, No. 3 (March, 1848), 139-50.

Bastiampillai, Bertram. "Social Conditions of the Indian Immigrant Labourer in Ceylon in the 19th Century, with Special Reference to the Seventies, and some Comparisons with Conditions in other Colonies." *Proceedings of the First International Conference Seminar of Tamil Studies*, I (April, 1966), 678-725.

Blythe, W.L. "Historical Sketch of Chinese Labour in Malaya." *JMBRAS*, XX, Pt. 1 (June, 1947), 64-114.

Braddell, T. "Notices of Pinang." *JIA*, IV (1850), 629-44; V (1851), 1-14.

Brereton, Bridget. "The Experience of Indentureship: 1845-1917." *Calcutta to Caroni*. Edited by John Gaffar La Guerre. Port of Spain, 1974.

Campen, F. "Cane Cultivation in the Straits Settlements." *Timehri* (New Series), IX (1895), 91-106.

Carey, E.V. "Notes on a Trip to Negapatam." *Selangor Journal*, III (1895), 44-46.

Cheng Siok Hwa. "Indian Labour in the Rice Industry of Pre-War Burma." *Proceedings of the Second International Conference Seminar of Tamil Studies*. Edited by R.E. Asher, II (January, 1968), 341-52.

Crookewit, H. "The Tin Mines of Malacca." *JIA*, VIII (1854), 112-33.

Cruickshank, Graham. "African Immigrants after Freedom." *Timehri*, VI (1919), 74-85.

Darcy, Sir Lindsay. "Indians Overseas," in Sir John Comming, ed., *Political India, 1832-1932: A Cooperative Study of a Century*, Delhi, 1968.

Earl, G.W. "Industrial Pursuits, Sources of Labour and Markets for Produce." *JIA*, VII (1862), 170-87.

Erickson, E.L. "The Introduction of East Indian Coolies into the British West Indies." *The Journal of Modern History*, VI, No. 2 (June, 1934), 127-46.

Gillion, K.L. "The Sources of Indian Emigration to Fiji." *Population Studies*, IX, Pt. 2 (November, 1956), 139-57.

Gullick, J.M. "Yap Ah Loy." *JMRAS*, XXIV, Pt. 2 (July, 1951), 1-100.

Hill, Arthur A. "Emigration from India." *Timehri*, VI (September, 1919), 44-52.

Hunter, William. "Plants of Prince of Wales Island." *JSBRAS*, no. 53 (September, 1909), 49-127.

Jayawardena, Chandra. "Social Contours of an Indian Labour Force during the Indenture Period in Fiji." *Rama's Banishment: A Centenary Tribute to the Fiji Indians. 1879-1979*. Edited by Vijay Mishra. Auckland, 1979.

Khoo Kay Kim. "The Origin of British Administration in Malaya." *JMBRAS*, XXXIX, I (1966), 52-91.

Kruyt, J.A. "Address Delivered before the Indian Society on the Straits Settlements and the Malay Peninsula." *JSBRAS*, No. 28 (August, 1896), 19-51.

Lal, Brij V. "Fiji *Girmitiyas:* The Background to Banishment." *Rama's Banishment: A Centenary Tribute to the Fiji Indians, 1879-1979.* Edited by Vijay Mishra. Auckland, 1979.

Logan, J.L. "Journal of an Excursion from Singapur to Malacca and Pinang." *Miscellaneous Papers Relating to Indo-China and the Indian Archipelago,* 2nd Series, I (1887), 1-20.

Low, J. "An Account of the Origin and Progress of the British Colonies in the Straits of Malacca." *JIA*, IV, No. 2 (1850), 360-79.

Marriot, H. "Population of the Straits Settlements and Malay Peninsula during the last Century." *JSBRAS*, No. 62 (December, 1912), 31-42.

Maxwell, W.E. "The Malay Peninsula: Its Resources and prospects." *PRCI*, XXIII (1891-92), 3-46.

Nayagam, Xavier S. Thani. "Tamil Emigration to the Martinique." *Journal of Tamil Studies,* I, No. 2, Pt. 1 (October, 1969), 75-99.

Nayagam, Xavier S. Thani. "Tamil Migrations to Guadeloupe and Martinique, 1853-1883." *Proceedings of the Second International Conference Seminar of Tamil Studies.* Edited by R.E. Asher, II (January, 1968), 369-76.

Nilakanta Sastri, K.A. "The Beginnings of Intercourse between India and China." *Indian Historical Quarterly,* XIV (1938), 380-87.

O'Sullivan, A.W.S. "The Relations between South India and the Straits Settlements." Noctes Orientales: Being a Selection of Essays read before the Straits *Philosophical Society between the Years 1893 and 1910.* Singapore, 1913.

Rai, Ambikapath. "The Indian Coolie in British Malaya." *The Indian Review*, XV (June, 1914), 452-60.

Roberts, G.W. and Byrne, J. "Summary Statistics on Indenture and Associated Migration Affecting the West Indies, 1834-1948." *Population Studies*, Vol. XX, Pt. 1 (July, 1966), 125-34.

Rodway, J. "Labour and Colonization." *Timehri*, VI (September, 1919), 22-42.

Sandhu, K.S. "Some Preliminary Observations of the Origins and Characteristics of Indian Migration to Malaya, 1786-1957." *Papers in Malayan History*. Edited by K.G. Tregonning. Singapore, 1962.

Silcock, T.H. and Aziz, Ungku Abdul. "Nationalism in Malaya." *Asian Nationalism and the West.* Edited by William L. Holland. New York, 1953.

Sundaram, Lanka. "Indian Labour in Ceylon." *International Labour Review* (March, 1931), 369-87.

Tan Kim Hong. "Chinese Sugar Planting and Social Mobility in Nineteenth Century Province Wellesley." *Malaysia in History*, No. 24 (1981), 24-38.

Tayal, Maureen. "Indian Indentured Labour in Natal, 1890-1911." *IESHR*, XIV, No. 4 (1977), 519-46.

Thrower, D.A. "The Tamils and their Country." *Eastern World*, III (November, 1949), 8-9.

Tinker, Hugh. "Indians Abroad: Emigration, Restriction and Rejection." *Expulsion of a Minority: Essays on Ugandan Asians.* Edited by Michael Twaddle. London, 1975.

Turner, G.E. "Indian Immigration." *MHJ*, I, No. 2 (December, 1954), 80-84.

Turner, G.E. "A Perak Coffee Planter's Report on the Tamil Labourer in Malaya in 1902." *MHJ*, II, No. 1 (July, 1955), 20-28.

Vlieland, C.A. "The Population of the Malay Peninsula." *Geographical Review*, XXIV (1934), 61-78.

Weld, Frederick A. "The Straits Settlements and British Malaya." *PRCI*, XV (1883-84), 266-311.

Wheatley, Paul. "Land Use in the Vicinity of Singapore in the Eighteen-Thirties." *MJTG*, II (March, 1954), 63-66.

iv. **Unpublished Dissertations**

Chanderbali, David. "Sir Henry Light: A Study of Protection and Paternalism." (M.A. dissertation, University of Guyana, 1977).

Mangru, Basdeo. "Imperial Trusteeship in British Guiana with Special Reference to the East Indian Indentured Immigrants, 1838-1882. Myth or Reality?" (M.A. dissertation, University of Guyana, 1976).

v. **Pamphlets**

Ramphal, Shridath S. *Roots and Reminders: Reflections on Slavery, Indenture, Apartheid – and Some Personal Conjunctures*. Address to the Commonwealth Society of India, New Delhi, 20 January 1986.

INDEX

A New System of Slavery: The Export of Indian Labour Overseas, 1830-1920 (Tinker), 51-52
Aborigines Protection Society, 46
Advertisements for indentured labour (to Straits), 113-115
Ali, Ahmed, 51
Alma estate affair, 144-148
Anderson, Charles, 46
Anderson, Sir John, 63
Andrews, Rev. C.F., 49, on effects of sexual imbalance in colonies with indentured populations, 49-50
Ankylostomiasis (hookworm), prevalence of as result of insanitary conditions, 188-189; advice of officials ignored by planters, 189; low levels of incidence on two well-run estates, 189
Anson, A.E.H., 85, 137, 145, 146, 147; criticised in press for lack of protection of immigrants, 152-153; on violation of wages contracts, 165-166, on insufficiency of food provided, 167; on illegality of fines, 170; on temptation to desert, 180
Anti-Slavery Society (British), opposition to indenture, 23, 42, 44, 46-47
Arasatnam, Sinnappah, 16, 83
Argand, Joseph, 21
Arrack drinking, ill-effects on labourers, 170
Austin, W., 107

Bacon, N., 58
Balestier, Joseph, 57, 68
Beaumont, Joseph, 47-48
Birch, J.W.W. (Straits Colonial Secretary), 83, 88-89, 91
Bird, Isabella, 63
Boaz, Thomas, 22
Braddell, Thomas, 16
Brereton, Bridget, 48
British control of Straits region, 18
British East India Company, 17, 18
British Emancipator, 23

British Guiana, indentured migration to, 15, 22-23, 24
Brougham, Henry, 23
Brown, Eddie, 186
Burton, Rev. J.W., 48, 49

Carey, E.V., 129
Carnarvon, Lord, 154
Caste, loss of on emigration, 35; freedom to maintain culture, 35
Chasseriau, Leopold, 16
Chattopadhyay, K.L., 51
Chinese labourers in Straits Settlements, 64-66; regarded as superior labourers, 64-65; independence and reluctance to accept sugar estate day rates, 65; attraction to better wages rates in tin mining, 65-66
Chinese sugar planters, 16
Clarke, Sir Andrew, 149, 154-156, 167
Coghill, Dr J.D.M., 143-144, 145, 150, 155-156
Comins, D.W.D., 41
Commission of Enquiry 1871 (British Guiana), 27
Complaints about quality of recruits to Straits, 130-131; evidence of substitution of sickly for able-bodied emigrants, 131-133; recruitment of non-agricultural trades, 132; maintenance of illegal emigration (from Karikal), 133-136
Conditions on estates in Wellesley Province, 143-151; numbers on estates, 210; evidence of neglect and ill-health among labourers, 145; deaths from exhaustion, 145-146; workers compelled to work when ill, 146; low wages and undernourish-ment, 147; insanitary conditions, 147; evidence of floggings, 148-150, 156; death from flogging, 150-151; indifferent attitude of Straits government, 151-153; tardiness in appointing Protector of Immigrants, 152-153; inaction of

Indian Government to scandals in treatment of Tamil emigrants, 153-154; belated enaction of Ordinances (I, 1876, V, 1884) to protect immigrants from ill-treatment, 156
Contracts, sample of, 213
Crawford, John, 64, 68
Crewe, Earl (Secretary of State for Colonies), 189, advice to planters on sanitation ignored, 189
Cumpston, I.M., 17, 27

Darcy, Lindsay, 46
Davidson, G.F., 59
Debt bondage, 22
Deductions from wages (Straits Settlements), 169-170
Derby, Earl, (Secretary of State for Colonies), 175
Des Voeux, William, 20, 37
Desertion, prevalence of, 180-182; defined in labour ordinances, 180-181; rising levels and higher wage levels in non-indentured employment, 181; efforts of planters to combat desertion less than successful, 182
Doctor, Manilal Maganlall, 42
Donadieu, Joseph, 16
Durnford, (Overseer), 154-155

Earl, G.W., 68
"Emigrant", on indenture system, 50
Emigration Act (Government of India, XIII, 1864), 88
Emigration Acts, 18
Emigration depots as repressive institutions, 129-130; enforced embarkation, 130; food provided and grievances over, 130; improvements when run by Straits Government (1890), 138
Emigration process (to Straits Settlements), 127-138; medical inspection, 127-128; interviews, frequent unreliability of, 128-129;

Families, discouragement of by conditions for emigration and labour in Wellesley Province, 102-193
Fiji, 31-32
Fiji's Indian Migrants (Gillion), 48-49
Firmstone, H.W., 160
Fischer, Bowness, 70, 99, 133, 134

Gandhi, Mahatma, 42
Gangulee, N, 17, 50-51
Ganguli, Dwarkanath, 51
Garnham, Florence, 49-50
Geoghegan, John, 21, 46, 84, 85
Gill, Walter, 48
Gillion, K.L. 48
Gladstone, John, 23
Glenelg, Lord, 46
Gokhale, Gopal Krishna, 43, 48
Gordon, Arthur Hamilton, 32
Gottlieb, F.H., 144, 145, 151
Government of India, attitude to emigration, embargo on, 87-98; 'benevolent neutrality', 104
Governors and Administrators of Straits Settlements, 207
Gregory, Sir William, 110

Hardaker, Dr., 115-116
Hardinge, Viceroy, 49
Harris, John H., 40, 127
Hathaway, W.J., 87-88, 90, 97
Haviland, Henry A., 143
Hazareesingh, K., 51
Hewick, J.B., 144
Hill, Thomas Heslop, 84, 108, 115
Hincks, Francis, 41
Hobhouse, J.C., 86
Holland, H.E., 48
Horsman, Edward, 59
Housing on estates (the coolie lines), 186-187; rarity of good provision, 186; overcrowding, poor ventilation and lack of privacy, 187; squalor of surroundings (drainage and latrines), 187-188; prevalence of hookworm as a result, 188-189
Huttenbach, H., 203

Illegal emigration (from French port of Karikal), 133-136; French opposition to illegal trade but failure to control, 135-136

Immigration from India to the Straits Settlements (Vermont), 85

Indenture system in Straits Settlements, statistics, 210-211; reasons for: planters aversion to free and transient labour, 75; unregulated indenture (c1790-1870), evidence for, 83-86; how conducted, 84-86; ill-treatment of migrants, 85; embargo on labour emigration (1870-71), 87-98, significance of transfer of Straits Settlements from Government of India to the Colonial Office, 89; reports of kidnapping and recruitment abuses as reason for embargo, 87-88; allegations of women brought for prostitution, 92; opposition to embargo from Straits officials, 88-89; Governor Ord's enquiry disputes evidence on abuses, 90-91; planters' protest, 91-92; Madras Government Enquiry and demand for labour protection, 92-94; demand for appointments of Emigration Agent and Protector of Emigrants at expense of Straits government, 93-94; deadlock in dispute between Madras and Straits governments, 94-95; illegal recruitment, 95-97, recruitment of children, 97; diversion of illegal trade to French port of Karikal, 98-99

Indentured emigration system, evolution of, 20ff; comparative statistics, 31; conflicting interpretations of, 40-53; favourable views, 40-44; alleged benefits: savings and opportunity for enterprise, 41, 44; escape from caste and independence, 41-42; opposition from Creole populations in Caribbean, 42; abuses in early days of system, 45-48; contemporary assessments, 50-53; comparative numbers for selected countries, 209

Indentured immigration to the Straits Settlements, the balance sheet, 203-205; gap between Governmental intentions and actual conditions, 203-204

Indentured labour system in the Straits Settlement: demand for labour, 56-75; increased British demand for sugar and decline in West Indian production, 58

Indian labourers in Malaya (see Labour in Province Wellesley), 67-72; numbers, 86

Indian National Congress, opposition to indenture, 48-50; speech of Sarojini Naidu, 214-216

Indian opposition to indentured emigration, 22, 23, 42; Gokhale, Gopal Krishna, 43

Indians in Malaya: Some Aspects of their Immigration and Settlement (Sandhu), 16-17

Indians in Malaysia and Singapore (Arasatnam), 16, 17

Indigenous populations, reluctance to work on estates: Amerindians in British Guiana, 26, 63; Native Fijians in Fiji, 31-32,63; Malays in Province Wellesley, 60-63

Industrial injuries, 194-195; injuries from use of *chankol* (hoe), 194; subsequent ulceration and deaths, 195

Infirmaries on estates, 145; squalor of 151

Inspection of estates, deliberate withholding of evidence from Protector, 159; planter hostility to inspections, 160; no prosecutions of this breach of Ordinance, 160-161

Introduction of sugar planting in the Straits Settlement, 56-60; cultivation by Chinese, 56-57; in Singapore, 57; in Penang, and abandonment of, 57; unsuccessful in Malacca, 57; dominance of Province Wellesley, 58-59; alienation of land to European planters, 58; reasons for dominance: in preferential duties, 58; in favourable soil and drainage, 59; in political tranquillity, 59

Jackson, R.N., 17
Jahaji bhai relationship, 34
Javanese in Straits Settlement sugar industry, expense of importation restricts employment, 63-64;
Jenkins, Edward, 46-47

Kangany system, in Ceylon, compared to indentured recruitment, 110; preferred by emigrants, 116-118; opposition to kangany system from Province Wellesley planters, 118-119; impact of conditions in Madras on recruitment, 119-121; Tamil Immigration Fund (1907) as attempt to stimulate recruitment, 121-122; statistics for period, 208
Karikal, illegal emigration through French port of, 98-99
Kimberley, Earl (Secretary of State for Colonies), 100, 175, 195
Kingsley, Canon, 41
Kloosterboer, W., 51
Knaggs, Walter, 127, 144-145, 147
Kondapi, C., 17, 83
Krishnan, R.B., 17
Kurapen, death of, 143-144
Kynnersley, C.W.S., 68

Labour in Province Wellesley, 60-75; Malays, reluctance to work in sugar industry, 60-63; reasons for reluctance: in kerah (corvee) system, 61; in culture of leisure, 61; in successful subsistence economy and low wages offered, 62; Javanese, expense of importation restricts employment, 63-64; Chinese, 64-66; regarded as superior labourers, 64-65; independence and reluctance to accept sugar estate day rates, 65; attraction to better wages rates in tin mining, 65-66; Indian labourers in Malaya, 67-72; seen as counterpoise to Chinese, 67; seen as docile and easily managed, 67; pre-European connections between India and Malaysia, 67-68; unregulated migration and settlement, 68-69; free labour migration, 69; Tamils as main source of indentured labour, 69-70; stereotypes of Tamils as labourers in West Indies, 69-70; favourable reputations in the Straits as docile and amenable, 70; reluctance to emigrate, 70-72; patterns of transient migration, (qv. Ceylon, Burma) 71-72; desire for return and comparative statistics, 72-73; higher rates of return from Straits Settlement compared to West Indies, Fiji, Mauritius, 73
Labour shortages, 25-29
Lal, Chimman (and see McNeill, James), 43
Lamb, T., 130
Lamming, George, 52
Legal systems and inequality of indentured labourers before the law, 33, 48-49
Leith, George, 68
Light, Henry, 29
Light, Sir Francis, 68
Low, James, 56, 60, 62 64, 68
Madras Presidency, impact of local conditions on recruitment, 119-121
Mahajani, U, 17
Malacca, 15
Malakoff scandal, 148-151; trial of perpetrators of brutality to labourers, 154-156; lenient sentences for manager and *tyndals* (drivers), 154; partiality of judiciary criticised by Colonial Office, 154-155; sentences remitted, 155-156; improvement of treatments after 1884, 161
Malays, reluctance to work in Straits Settlement sugar industry, 60-63; reasons for reluctance: in kerah (corvee) system, 61; in culture of leisure, 61; in successful subsistence economy and low wages offered, 62
Master, C.G., 83, 84, 86, 92
Mauritius, indentured migration to, 15, 22
May, Henry, 43
McClosky, J.H. (Colonial Surgeon), on foul water and disease, 190, 196

McNeill, James (and see Lal, Chimman), 43
Medical facilities on estates, 195-197, variable quality, 197
Menzell, Captain, 137
Metcalfe, Charles, 29
Montgomerie, William, 57
Mortality, high rates cited as reason why indenture to Province Wellesley be ended, 198; annual figures, 198; compared to rest of population, 198-199
Mout, M.F., 40

Nanjundan, S., 17
Natal, Indian indentured migration to, 31

O' Sullivan, A.W.S., 68
Ord, Sir Harry St George, 90-91, 94, 99-100, 143, 151
Ordinance V 1884, 176

Pakiri, death of from flogging, 151
Parmer, J. Norman, 17, 67
Penang Gazette, 84, 92, 152
Penang, 15
Potable water, non-provision of in fields until 1876, 189; prevalence of contaminated supplies and endemic dysentery and diarrhoea, 190; droughts and impure water, 190-191; resulting mortality, 191
Pre-Indentured Indian emigrations schemes, 21
Premium, Barton, 24
Profits from low indentured wage levels, 176
Prohibition of indenture 1839, 23-24
Prostitution, allegation of women forced into, 92, 97; claim that migration gave recruited prostitutes second chance, 92
Protector of Immigrants (Straits Settlements), belated appointment, 156; remoteness and inaccessibility to labourers, 160-161
Province Wellesley, 15, 17
Provision of food deducted from wages, 166-168; system discontinued 1879, 167; task work and reduction of days paid, 168; estimation of earnings as inadequate to meet basic needs, 168-169; impossibility of savings until later in indentureships, 169; other deductions from wages, 169-170; fines for damage and inadequate work illegally made, 169-170; practice of some workers selling monthly rice provision for arrack, and ill-effects, 170; labourer's penury and loan-debt bondage, 170-171; introduction of daily rations, 170-171; withholding of rations and evidence of carrion and harmful eating, 171; repatriation of sickly labourers as evasion of responsibility for neglect, 171-172; deaths in India of returnees and returnees complaints, 172-173; comparative standards of diet indentured workers and penal inmates, 173; diet at hospital, 174; comparison with peasants in Madras, 174; comparison with diet of Chinese labourers in mining, 174.

Raffles, Thomas Stanford, 17
Rajkumar, N.V., 17
Ramphal, Shridath, 52
Ramsamy, death of from flogging, 150-151
Ramsden, John, 59
Recruitment (to Straits Settlements), 104-122; shortfall in labour supply, 104-106; differences in methods of organisation from other colonies, 105-106; reluctance of Government of India to allow recruiting outside Madras, 106; methods of recruitment, 106-108; recruiters' inducements and exaggerations over wages, 106-107; licensing of recruiters, 107; role of magistrates, 107-108; sample questions asked of immigrants, 212; Government of India's view of recruiters' dishonesty, 108; competition for labour, 108-113; from Ceylon 109-111, 116-117, 118; from Burma, 111-112;

from other colonies, 112-113; reasons for migrant preferences in higher wages in other colonies compared to the Straits, 111-112; advertisements for labour, 113-115; ineffectiveness as recruitment device, 115

Recruitment of labour in West Indies: Northern European labourers, 26; Madeirans, 26; from West Indian colonies, 26-27; West Africa, 27, China, 27-28

Recruitment practices, 22; abuses in system, 45-46

Redemption of contracts, 179-180; methods used by workers to escape indentureship, 179-180

Repatriation, differences between policies of colonies, 32; statistics on proportions of returnees, 32-33; reasons for decision to return, 33-34

Return passages, failure of Straits Government to pay for and impact on recruitment, 113

Returnees, poor condition of, 179

Roberts, E.L., 129

Ruhomon, Peter, on Indian experience in British Guiana, 50

Rumah kechil system, 16

Russell, Lord John, 24, 28, 30, 46

Sanderson Commission (1909), 42-43, 67

Sandhu, Kernial Singh, 16, 83

Scoble, John, 23, 45

Sea-voyages, 22

Selection of emigrants (to Straits), 115-116; stricter criteria and impact on numbers, 116

Settlement (after end of indentureship), motivations for, 34-36; inducements, 35

Sexual imbalance, 33, 191-194; failure to set minimum proportions of women in emigration to Straits Settlements, 191; actual percentages very low, 191; reasons for Indian Government reluctance to encourage women's migration, 191; evidence of prostitution of Indian women migrants, 191-192; planter reluctance to increase ratio of women, 192; low wage rates as discouragement for men to emigrate with wives, 192; lower wage rates for women as discouragement for single women to migrate, 193; reluctance of male labourers to enter exogamous marriages, 193; prevalence of Venereal disease, 194

Sexual proportions of emigrants to Penang, 97-98; difficulty of recruiting women, 98; planters failure to encourage recruitment of families, 98; Regulated Indenture resumed under Act XIV (Government of India, 1872) and Governor Ord's compliance, 99-100

Simon, Dr M.F., 131

Singapore Daily Times, 92

Singapore Free Press, 104

Singapore, 15

Slavery, abolition of, 20, 21; flight of ex-slaves from estates, 25-26; bargaining power of free villagers in British Guiana, 29

'Smart-money' (labourers borrowing to buy themselves out of indentures), 180

Smith, Clementi, criticism of low wage rates, 176-177; inadequacy of diet, 193

Stanley, Lord, 30-31, 46, 154

Stokes, H.J., 92-93

Straits Settlements of British Malaya: geographic regions, 15; contractual differences from other Indian indentured systems, 15, 16; cost of repatriation borne by labourers, 15

Straits Settlements Ordinance 1876 (regulating indentured employment), 100-101

Straits Times, 89

Sturge, Joseph, 37

Sugar industry in Straits Settlements, decline of, 204-205; sugar, increased British demand for and decline in West Indian production, 58; sugar, beginnings of cane cultivation in

Province Wellesley, 16; production levels, 24-25
Swettenham, Sir Frank, 121, 182

Tamil Immigration Fund (1907) as attempt to stimulate recruitment for Straits Settlements, 121-122
Tamils as main source of indentured labour, 69-70; compared with Telegus as migrant group, 106
Tanjore Gazette, 87
Tapioca estates in Province Wellesley, 60
Tassek incident, 143-144
Tayal. Maureen, 52
The Coolie His Rights and Wrongs (Jenkins) 46-47
The New Slavery: An Account of the Indian and Chinese Immigrants in British Guiana (Beaumont), 47-48
Thompson, J.T., 148, 151-155
Times of India, 121
Tindals, role of, 156; abuse of position, 156-157; as allocators of task work, 157-158; as administers of beatings, 157; prosecution of for illegal floggings, 158; low level of charges brought, 159
Tinker, Hugh, 17, 51-52
Trinidad, 15

Vagrancy laws (in Trinidad and British Guiana), 48
Veitch, Dr J.T., 167, 168
Venereal disease, prevalence of, 194
Vermont, J.M. (planter spokesman), 16, 85-86, 89, 159-160, 177
Voyage (to the Straits) 136-138; food provided and abuse of regulations, 136-137; overcrowding and length of voyages, 137-138; improvements with steamships, 137-138

Wage levels for indentured workers (Straits Settlements), 165-182; oppressive collective contracts (ended 1876), 165; First and second gangs and wages rates, 165-166; failure of Straits Government to protect immigrants from wage cuts, 166; Colonial Secretaries' recommendations for wage increases rejected by planters, 175-176; refusal to pay indentured same rates as unindentured, 175; dishonesty of planter claims on value of benefits in kind (provisions, medical care), 175-176; marginal improvements from new wage rates introduced 1885, 176-177; benefits undermined by rising cost of living, 176-177; planter opposition to new rates, 177; minimum wages still too low to buy recommended minimum diet, 178-179
Wage levels, immigration as a means of lowering, 29
Weld, Sir Frederick, (Governor) 66-67, 130, 166, on temptation to desert, 181, on medical facilities, 195
Wellesley, Marquess of, 17
'West Indian' (critic of Edward Jenkins), 47
Wilhelm, Captain, 133

OTHER RELATED TITLES

Surendra Bhana
Essays on Indentured Indians in Natal
ISBN:9780948833212; pp. 235; 1991; £9.99

These scholarly essays break new ground in the study of Indian indentured labour, the role of labour migration in economic development, and the history of Natal. The collection includes Daniel North-Coombes' pioneering comparison of the role of indentured labour in the sugar industries of Natal and Mauritius, Maureen Swan's study of worker accommodation and resistance, Jo Beall's investigation of the double oppression of women, and Surendra and Arvinkumar Bhana's exploration of the very high rates of suicide amongst indentured workers. Accounts of individual stories in several essays ensure that the workers are never seen as faceless victims, and Rajend Mesthrie's study of language contact and J.B. Brain's essay on religion give further reminders that these migrants brought not only their labour but their culture.

Verene Shepherd
Transients to Settlers: The Experience of Indians in Jamaica 1845-1950
ISBN: 9780948833328; pp.281; 1994; £12.99

In this valuable historical study of one of the smaller Indian communities in the Caribbean, Verene Shepherd explores the contrary tendencies towards cultural absorption and cultural autonomy which can be seen in the history of the group. The role of population size and density, the availability of economic 'niches', the activity of missionaries and educators and the attitudes of the wider society are examined as contexts within which the Indo-Jamaican community worked out its destiny. Chapters on indenture, patterns of rural and urban settlement, education, economic activity and political participation provide comparative standpoints for looking at variations within the total Indo-Caribbean experience.

Dale Arlington Bisnauth
The Settlement of Indians in Guyana 1890-1930
ISBN: 9781900715164; pp. 296; 2000; £14.99

As Guyana struggles to overcome its legacy of ethnic hostility between Indo- and Afro-Guyanese, this is a timely and unbiased study of the historical processes which led in part to these divisions.
   It focuses on the crucial period when Indian indentured labourers became a permanent part of Guyanese society. It explores both the inner processes of In-

dian settlement and the beginnings of that community's political involvement with the wider society and relationships with the Afro-Guyanese.

It charts how, in the process, Indian peasants were transformed into industrialised wage labourers on the sugar estates, rice farmers and urban professionals. In exploring how a distinctive Indo-Guyanese culture emerged, Dale Bisnauth counters the tendency amongst some sectors of the Indo-Guyanese community to deny the humble, low-caste origins of those who were its makers. His is a history that gives full weight to the efforts of the nameless and forgotten to shape their lives.

The book also looks frankly at the ethnic considerations which shaped relationships between the Indo-Guyanese and the wider Guyanese society. In looking critically at the divide and rule policies of successive colonial governments, and situating both Africans and Indians in a common history of exploitation, Dale Bisnauth's study offers a clear and insightful basis for contemporary understanding of the role of ethnicity in a plural society and a cogent discussion of the processes of settlement and cultural change.

Simon Lee writes in *Caribbean Beat*: 'Dale Bisnauth, Guyana's current Minister of Education, has provided an exhaustive study of the Indian community during the period in which it became the most significant element in Guyanese society. This vital document on the region's largest Indian settlement and culture traces the history of ethnic hostility against a background of colonial exploitation and divide-and-rule strategy, and makes an important contribution to understanding not only the South Asian diaspora but also the complexities of Caribbean society.'

Clem Seecharan
India and the Shaping of the Indo-Guyanese Imagination
ISBN: 9780948833618; pp. 98; 1993; £7.99

When the first East Indian intellectuals emerged in British Guiana at the end of the nineteenth century, most of their compatriots were still working as indentured or free labourers on the colony's sugar estates. Indians were conscious that they were looked down on as barbarous 'coolies' by other sections of the population. In response, the intellectual elite constructed a view of India, drawn from the writings of Max Muller and Tagore, which provided the Indo-Guyanese community with a sustaining sense of self-esteem and the sources of its resistance to colonialism.

Focusing on individuals such as Joseph and Peter Ruhomon, JA Luckhoo and WH Wharton, the study looks at the way the beginnings of the nationalist movement in India stimulated such individuals to start defining the nature of their presence in the New World. Seecharan argues that while the vision of 'Mother India' stimulated the community's cultural revival, it constrained the way it thought about Guyana.

'Dr. Seecharan's research is meticulous and his analysis penetrating. This is why, despite its specific Indian focus and slender look, *India* offers much insight into the broader history of Guyanese society as a whole.' – Frank Birbalsingh.

Eds. Joel Benjamin, Laxhmie Kallicharan, Ian McDonald and Lloyd Searwar
They Came in Ships: an Anthology of Indo-Guyanese Writing
ISBN: 9780948833946; pp. 304; £14.99

From 1838 until 1917, Indians arrived to work as indentured labourers in Guyana. The majority never returned to India and today over 50% of the Guyanese population is of Indian origin.

This anthology of prose and poetry shows how the Indians changed the character of Guyana and the Caribbean and how, over 150 years of settlement, Indians became Indo-Guyanese. Ranging from the earliest attempts at cultural self-definition in the 19th century (and early narrative images of the Indian presence in non-Indian writing), to the creative writing of the 1990s, this anthology provides a fascinating insight into the transformation of an ancient culture in the New World.

Extracts from novels, short stories, essays and poems explore the experience of plantation life, of relationships with other ethnic groups, issues of gender within Indo-Guyanese culture and the adjustments in cultural practices which separation from India and involvement with the new environment required.

Brief introductory essays by Jeremy Poynting set historical contexts, and there is an invaluable bibliography of Indo-Guyanese writing. This is the only anthology of its kind.

All Peepal Tree titles are available from our website:
www.peepaltreepress.com; email contact@peepaltreepress.com
Or you can contact us at Peepal Tree Press, 17 Kings Avenue, Leeds LS6 1QS, UK (Tel +44 113 245 1703)